Top Tax Issues
for 2004
Course

CCH Editorial Staff Publication

CCH INCORPORATED
Chicago
A WoltersKluwer Company

CONTRIBUTORS

Managing Editor ....George G. Jones, J.D., LL.M
Editors...George L. Yaksick, Jr., J.D.
Lisa R. Neuder, J.D., M.B.A.
Daniel L. Rinke, J.D.
Kimberly Martin Turner, J.D.
Production Coordinator... Gabriel E. Santana
Production.. Marie J. Yellen
Lynn J. Brown

This publication is designed to provide accurate and authoritative information in regard to the subject matter covered. It is sold with the understanding that the publisher is not engaged in rendering legal, accounting, or other professional service. If legal advice or other expert assistance is required, the services of a competent professional person should be sought.

ISBN 0-8080-1078-6

No claim is made to original government works; however, within this Product or Publication, the following are subject to CCH's copyright: (1) the gathering, compilation, and arrangement of such government materials; (2) the magnetic translation and digital conversion of data, if applicable; (3) the historical, statutory and other notes and references; and (4) the commentary and other materials.

Introduction

Each year, a handful of tax issues typically requires special attention by tax practitioners. The reasons vary, from a particularly complicated new provision in the Internal Revenue Code, a planning technique opened up by a new regulation or ruling, or the availability of a significant tax benefit with a short window of opportunity. Sometimes a developing business need creates a new set of tax problems, or pressure exerted by Congress or the Administration puts more heat on some taxpayers while giving others more slack. All these share in creating a unique mix that in turn creates special opportunities and pitfalls in the coming year. The past year has seen more than its share of these developments.

CCH's *Top Tax Issues for 2004 Course* identifies the events of the past year that have developed into "hot" issues. These tax issues have been selected as particularly relevant to tax practice in 2004. They have been selected not only because of their impact on return preparation during the 2004 tax season but also because of the important role they play in developing effective tax strategies for 2004. Some issues are outgrowths of several years of developments; others have burst onto the tax scene unexpectedly. Some have been emphasized in IRS publications and notices; others are too new or too controversial to be noted by the IRS either in depth or at all.

This course is designed to help reassure the tax practitioner that he or she is not missing out on advising clients about a hot, new tax opportunity or is not susceptible to being caught unaware by a brewing controversy. In short, it is designed to give the tax practitioner a closer look into the opportunities and pitfalls presented by the changes. Among the topics examined in the "Top Tax Issues for 2004 Course" are:

- Reduced Tax Rates: Impact on Income Brackets, Capital Gains, and Dividends
- Navigating the New Equipment Writeoff Rules
- Emerging Technology Issues
- Tax Shelters
- Trends in Employee Benefits
- Estate Planning Strategies
- IRS Audit Trends

Throughout the course you will find Study Questions to help you test your knowledge. To help you identify courses of action you will find two types of designations: "Observations" and "Practice Pointers". Use "Observations" to take note of certain facts that are vital to understanding a particular strategy or idea. Use "Practice Pointers" as guidance for action— positive or negative—to put suggested strategies to work.

This course is divided into two Modules. Take your time and review both course Modules. When you feel confident that you thoroughly understand the material, turn to the CPE quizzer. Complete one, or both, Module Quizzers for continuing professional education credit. Further information is provided in the Quizzer instructions on page 171.

October 2003

Course Objectives

This course was prepared to provide the participant with an overview of specific tax issues that impact 2003 tax return preparation and tax planning in 2004. More specifically, upon course completion, you will be able to:

- Understand the new tax rate structure and be able to discuss the fundamental changes that have impacted specific 2004 tax planning issues.
- Advise clients regarding the recent developments in capitalization and accelerated write-offs.
- List what transactions have been added to IRS's "hit list", what return disclosures must be made and how the IRS's focus on tax shelters has changed.
- Account for emerging technology's impact on federal tax rules.
- Enumerate the major changes made by the IRS to its audit, assessment, and collections processes and programs.
- List some of the ways that employers are packaging benefits with tax savings to hold down costs.
- Become familiar with the transitional rules and major changes on the income tax side of estate planning.
- Complete the continuing professional education exam with a grade of 70 percent or greater to earn CPE credit.

CCH's Pledge to Quality

Thank you for choosing this CCH Continuing Education product. We will continue to produce high quality products that challenge your intellect and give you the best option for your continuing education requirements. Should you have a concern about this or any other CCH CPE product, please call our Customer Service Department at 1-800-248-3248.

One complimentary copy of this course is provided with the *U.S. Master Tax Guide*. Additional copies of this course may be ordered for $20.00 each by calling 1-800-248-3248 (ask for product 0-0921-101).

Page

MODULE 1—CHAPTER 1: IMPACT OF REDUCED TAX RATES
ON INCOME BRACKETS, CAPITAL GAINS, AND DIVIDENDS

Learning Objectives. Three major tax rates changes for individuals took effect in 2003 under the *Jobs and Growth Tax Relief Reconciliation Act of 2003* (JGTRRA): (1) across-the-board reduction of income tax rates on "ordinary income," (2) the lowering of the maximum tax rate on most net capital gains to 15 percent, and (3) the new 15 percent maximum tax on qualified dividend income.

This tax year is complicated by transitional rules for the computation of capital gains tax. These rules affect not only what qualifies for the lower rate but also how gains, losses, and dividends interrelate in computing an individual's overall tax for the year. This chapter was prepared to provide an overview of the impact these changes will have on tax return preparation and tax planning. Upon completion of this chapter, you will be able to:

◆ Describe how only "eligible dividends" qualify for the new maximum 15 percent rate;

◆ Distinguish between a qualifying dividend and a dividend taxed as ordinary income subject to rates as high as 35 percent;

◆ Employ a more client-based view to examine the impact of JGTRRA tax rate changes on various taxpayer groups;

◆ Compare how higher-income individuals have benefited and how families have fared under the legislation;

◆ List which retirement savings strategies are no longer as potent, whether charitable giving programs need revision, and what factors go into deciding whether a corporation should change its dividends policy as a result of the rate changes; and

◆ Analyze the impact of the JGTRRA rates changes on choice of business because JGTRRA rates changes may tip the scales for or against operating as a partnership, regular corporation, S corporation, limited liability company, or sole proprietor.

INTRODUCTION

One of the major accomplishments of the *Jobs and Growth Tax Relief Reconciliation Act of 2003* (JGTRRA) is its across-the-board reduction of tax rates. In most instances, it is as simple as plugging the new rates—for ordinary taxable income, capital gains, and dividend income—into a taxpayer's year-end tax computation. Retroactive application of the new rates complicates matters because many transactions, business and personal, cannot be recast quickly. The reduced capital gains rates also create a new variable for investment decisions, as well as headaches for many deals that straddle the magic May 6, 2003, effective date or that involve five-year property. Finally, the temporary nature of the cuts, especially for capital gains and dividends, makes mid- and long-term financial planning more tax-driven than ever before. Choice of business entity also grows complicated for many taxpayers due to numerous factors introduced by JGTRRA.

JGTRRA ACCELERATES EGTRRA's INDIVIDUAL INCOME TAX RATE CUTS

The *Economic Growth and Tax Relief Reconciliation Act of 2001* (EGTRRA) scheduled a phased-in reduction of tax rates in excess of the 15 percent rate that are applicable to individuals, estates and trusts. Under EGTRRA, the rates were scheduled to gradually fall during eight years:

2001	27.5%	30.5%	35.5%	39.1%
2002 and 2003	27%	30%	35%	38.6%
2004 and 2005	26%	29%	34%	37.6%
2006-2010	25%	28%	33%	35%

In 2011 and after, the rates were to—and still will—revert to 26, 31, 36, and 39.6 percent.

Accelerated rate cuts

JGTRRA moves the rate cuts forward. The 25, 28, 33, and 35 percent rates, which were scheduled to take effect in 2006, jump ahead to 2003 and last through 2010:

2003-2010	25%	28%	33%	35%

Introduction of a 10 percent bracket

In addition to reducing the higher rates, EGTRRA created a new 10 percent tax bracket, effective in 2001. The 10 percent bracket applies only to individuals, not to estates and trusts. After December 31, 2007, the ceiling of the 10 percent bracket was scheduled to increase an additional $2,000 for married couples filing jointly and an additional $1,000 for single filers and married taxpayers filing separately. JGTRRA accelerates the $2,000 and $1,000 increases to tax years beginning after 2002.

> *Caution.* Expansion of the 10 percent tax bracket for 2003 and 2004 has no effect on head-of-household filers.

Marriage penalty relief

For married taxpayers filing jointly EGTRRA also gradually expanded the top end of the 15 percent tax bracket over a four-year period beginning in 2005. Upon completion of the phase-in, the amount of a joint filer's taxable income subject to the 15 percent rate would equal twice the amount of single filer's taxable income subject to the 15 percent rate.

JGTRRA also moves the married penalty relief forward. The 15 percent tax bracket of married taxpayers filing jointly is immediately increased to twice the size of a single filer's 15 percent bracket. Although the marriage penalty has been primarily an issue for couples in which both partners work, expansion of the 15 percent bracket benefits all joint filers.

> *Observation.* In 2003, a joint filer with at least $56,800 of taxable income will save $935 in taxes as a result of this provision.

Accumulated earnings and personal holding company tax rates reduced

Before JGTRRA, the accumulated earnings tax (imposed on earnings accumulated in excess of reasonable business needs, plus an exemption amount) was equal to the product of the highest rate of tax applicable to single filers and a corporation's accumulated taxable income. The personal holding company tax, which penalized closely held corporations for earnings that remained undistributed to shareholders, was computed by multiplying undistributed personal holding company income by the highest rate of tax on single filers.

JGTRRA mitigates the harshness of these taxes. The tax rate for the accumulated earnings tax and personal holding company tax is reduced to 15 percent for 2002 through 2009.

Lower capital gains rates for individuals

JGTRRA lowers the maximum tax rates that are generally applied to long-term capital gains:

♦ A new 15 percent maximum tax rate replaces the 20 percent rate;
♦ A new 5 percent rate replaces the 10 percent rate for individuals in the 10 and 15 percent brackets; and
♦ A new zero rate replaces the 5 percent rate for 2008.

> *Caution.* Because of sunset provisions, the rate reductions expire after December 31, 2008, and the old rates return.

> *Caution.* The lower rates are generally not retroactive to January 1, 2003. Therefore, special computations must be used to calculate an individual's long-term capital gains tax for a tax year that includes May 6, 2003 (see below for more details).

STUDY QUESTION

1. JGTRRA temporarily reduces the maximum tax rate generally applied to long-term capital gains from 20 percent to:

   a. 18 percent

b.   15 percent
c.   12 percent
d.   8 percent

Important exceptions. JGTRRA did *not* lower all the capital gains rates. Left unchanged is the 28 percent rate imposed on long-term gain from collectibles and net gain from small business stock. The maximum rate of unrecaptured Section 1250 gain remains at 25 percent. Property must still be held for more than 12 months to be classified as long-term and net capital losses are still subject to a limit of $3,000 per year.

Five-year holding period and its lower rates eliminated. JGTRRA has eliminated the special holding period rule pertaining to capital assets held for more than five years. Higher-income individuals who made a "deemed sale election" on their 2001 tax returns, to have the five-year property rule apply to assets they had acquired before January 1, 2001, should consider filing amended returns to reverse the election. It is likely that Congress will permit the revocation of the election in subsequent legislation.

STUDY QUESTIONS

2.   In 2008 individuals in the 10 and 15 percent tax brackets may be eligible for a maximum capital gains tax rate of:

a.   5 percent
b.   8 percent
c.   10 percent
d.   15 percent

3.   Because of sunset provisions in JGTRRA, the capital gains tax rate reductions expire after:

a.   December 31, 2005
b.   January 1, 2008
c.   December 31, 2008
d.   January 1, 2011

Transitional rule—Computing capital gains tax for 2003

A special "transitional rule" has to be followed when computing an individual's maximum capital gains tax rate for a tax year that includes May 6, 2003.

Dividend income. Qualified dividend income received in tax years starting after December 31, 2002, is eligible for a maximum capital gains rate of 15 percent. Under the transitional computation rule in effect for 2003, qualified dividend income is treated as though it were taken into account by the individual on or after May 6, 2003. This stipulation ensures that the maximum 15 percent rate will apply to all qualified dividend income for an individual's maximum capital gains tax.

Installment sale gain. The lower rates apply to installment payments received on or after May 6, 2003. In other words, the date the installment payment is received determines the capital gains rate, not the date the asset was sold under the installment contract.

Gain or loss from mutual funds. Mutual funds and other types of pass-through entities must determine when capital gain or loss is properly taken into account and distribute that information to shareholders.

Applying the transitional rule. There are two main steps and several of supplemental steps that must be followed when computing an individual's capital gains tax under the 2003 transitional rule.

> *Practice Pointer.* As a practical matter, step (1) of the transitional rule can be ignored if no portion of the individual's net long-term capital gain will be taxed at the lowest rate (for example, 5 percent). The computations under step 2 have much broader application because the 15 percent rate applies to dividend income no matter how high the individual's marginal tax rate.

1. **Applying the 5, 8, and/or 10 percent rates.** For lower-income individuals (those whose top marginal tax bracket does not exceed 15 percent), the maximum capital gains tax for 2003 is equal to the total tax determined under the following formula:

(A) 5 percent of the *lesser* of (I) the net capital gain that is determined by taking into account gain or loss realized on or after May 6, 2003 (gain from collectibles and/or small business stock is ignored for purposes of this computation) **or** (II) the net capital gain computed without regard to the transitional rule **plus**

(B) 8 percent of the *lesser* of (I) the gain from qualified five-year property that was correctly taken into account before May 6, 2003 **or** (II) the *excess* (if any) of the net capital gain computed without regard to the transitional rule **over** the amount on which the 5 percent tax rate (see A above) was computed **plus**

(C) 10 percent of the *excess* of the net capital gain computed without regard to the transitional rule **over** the total of the amounts on which the 5 and/or 8 percent tax rates were computed (see (A) and (B), above).

> *Example.* For 2003, Ellen (a single individual) has taxable income of $21,000. Included in her taxable income are the following items:

$1,000 of qualified dividend income received on February 3, 2003;

$3,000 in long-term capital gain from the sale of stock she had purchased in 1990 (five-year property); and

$2,000 in long-term capital gain from the sale of stock on June 2, 2003.

As a result of JGTRRA, Ellen's capital gains tax for 2003 is $390 [the sum of $50 ($1,000 in dividends × 5 percent), $240 ($3,000 in five-year property gain x 8 percent) and $100 ($2,000 gain from sale of stock x 5 percent)].

Ellen's total regular income tax of $1,900 is computed as follows:

10 percent on the first $7,000 of taxable income ($7,000 x 10 percent = $700) **plus**

(2) 15 percent on the amount over $7,000 that is not taxed under the capital gains rates ($21,000 taxable income – $7,000 = $14,000 excess – $6,000 in capital gains = $8,000 x 15 percent = $1,200).

Including her capital gains tax, Ellen's total tax liability for 2003 is $2,290 ($1,900 in regular income tax **plus** $390 in capital gains tax).

Note. Even though Ellen's dividend income was received before May 6, 2003, it is still subject to the new 5 percent capital gains tax rate.

2. **Applying the 10 percent and/or 15 percent rates.** For higher income individuals (those whose top marginal tax bracket exceeds 15 percent), their maximum capital gains tax for 2003 is equal to the total tax determined under the following formula:

(A) 15 percent of the *lesser* of (I) the *excess* of the amount of net capital gain determined under the transitional rule (see step 1A, above the amount to which the 5 percent rate applies) **over** the total amount on which net capital gain is determined under all three computations set forth under Step 1, above (the total amount subject to the 5, 8, and 10 percent rates) **or** (II) the net capital gain computed without regard to the transitional rule **plus**

(B) 20 percent of the *excess* of (I) the net capital gain computed under without regard to the transitional rule **over** (II) the net capital gain on which the 15 percent tax rate is used under step 2A (see above).

Example. For 2003, Harold, a single individual, has taxable income of $350,000. As a result of JGTRRA, Howard's highest marginal tax rate for the year is 35 percent. Included in his taxable income are the following items:

$5,000 in qualified dividends received throughout 2003;

$2,000 in long-term capital gain from the sale of stock on January 16, 2003; and

$3,000 in long-term capital gain from the sale of stock on May 6, 2003.

Howard's capital gains tax for 2003 would be $1,600 ($5,000 in dividends x 15 percent = $750; $2,000 in recognized long-term capital gain on January 16, 2003 x 20 percent = $400; and $3,000 in recognized long-term capital gain on May 6, 2003 x 15 percent = $450).

Practice Pointer. Keep in mind that the higher capital gains rates of 28 percent (for example, for collectibles) and 25 percent (for example, for unrecaptured Section 1250 gain) still present important tax planning issues for individuals in the higher marginal tax rates of 33 percent and 35 percent.

STUDY QUESTIONS

4. JGTRRA's lower capital gains tax rates are:

    a. Retroactive to January 1, 2003
    b. Not retroactive to January 1, 2003
    c. Scheduled to take effect in 2008
    d. Expire in 2004

5. JGTRRA did not lower all of the capital gains rates. Left unchanged are the:

    a. 28 percent rate on long-term gain from real estate and 25 percent rate for unrecaptured Section 1250 gain
    b. 39 percent rate on corporate gains and the 28 percent rate on long-term gain from collectibles
    c. 35 percent rate on dividends and the 28 percent on long-term gain from collectibles
    d. 28 percent rate on long-term gain from collectibles and the 25 percent rate on unrecaptured Section 1250 gain

DIVIDEND INCOME OF INDIVIDUALS TAXED AT CAPITAL GAIN RATES

Tax rates on dividend income reduced to 15 and 5 percent

The top federal tax rate for dividends received by an individual, estate or trust is reduced under JGTRRA to 15 percent (5 percent for individuals with incomes in the 10 or 15 percent rate bracket). These are the same rates applicable to capital gains. However, the rate reduction for dividends is retroactive. It is effective as of January 1, 2003, and continues through December 31, 2008. In addition, taxpayers in the 10 and 15 percent brackets can take advantage of a zero percent rate in 2008.

Capital losses

Although dividends now share the 15 percent rate for net capital gain, capital losses need not be offset against qualifying dividends. Thus, $3,000 of net capital losses will be applied against ordinary income; dividends will be taxed separately at capital gains rates.

Zero rate for 2008

Qualified dividends will be tax-free for taxpayers in the 10 and 15 percent bracket for one year only: 2008. The 10 and 15 percent rate brackets, as amended in 2003, include single taxpayers with taxable incomes up to $28,400 and married couples filing jointly with incomes up to $56,800. These income limits are likely to be increased for inflation before 2008. The zero rate expires on December 31, 2008.

> *Observation.* Interest earned on savings accounts, certificates of deposits, and government bonds is still subject to federal income tax at ordinary tax rates. The new lower rates apply only to qualified dividends paid on stock. Nonqualified dividends will be taxed as ordinary income.

Eligible dividends

The complexity created by the different effective and sunset dates for dividend relief and determination of exactly what is a qualifying dividend promises to create reams of regs, rules, and commentary for corporations and shareholders.

The new rates apply to dividends received from:

♦ Domestic corporations; and
♦ Some foreign corporations.

> *Practice Pointer.* Dividends passed through to investors by mutual funds, partnerships, real estate investment trusts, or held by a common trust fund are also eligible for the reduced rate if the distribution would otherwise be classified as qualified dividend income.

Ineligible dividends

The new rates do not apply to dividends paid by:

♦ Stock owned for fewer than 60 days in the 120-day period surrounding the ex-dividend date;

- Stock purchased with borrowed funds if the dividend was included in investment income in claiming an interest deduction;
- Stock to which related payments must be made with respect to substantially similar or related property; and
- Substitute payments in lieu of a dividend made with respect to stock on loan in a short sale.

In addition, dividends paid by credit unions, mutual insurance companies, farmers' cooperatives, tax-exempt cemetery companies, nonprofit voluntary employee benefit associations (VEBAs), employer securities owned by an employee stock ownership plan (ESOP), and any corporation exempt from federal tax under Code Sec. 501 or 521 are ineligible.

STUDY QUESTIONS

6. JGTRRA reduces the top tax rate for qualified dividends received by individuals, estates, and trusts to:

   a. 15 percent
   b. 10 percent
   c. 8 percent
   d. Zero

7. Qualified dividends will be tax-free for individuals in the 10 and 15 percent brackets for:

   a. 2008
   b. 2010
   c. May 6, 2003, through December 31, 2007
   d. January 1, 2003, through December 31, 2007

Preferred stock

A preferred stockholder would likely think that dividends paid on preferred stock are eligible for the lower rates. The distribution is coming from a corporation with earnings and profits to someone holding something called "preferred stock." If it is really preferred stock, the distribution would appear to be eligible for the reduced rates. However, much of what has been marketed as "preferred stock" is not preferred stock. It is debt masquerading as preferred stock, developed to enable corporations to deduct the distributions as interest expense on their returns. If the corporation is entitled to an interest expense deduction, the shares are not preferred stock, and the distributions are not dividends.

Foreign corporations

Dividends received from some foreign corporations are eligible for the reduced rates. Foreign stock that trades on an established U.S. securities market is eligible. Foreign-dividends paid on stock from a country with which the U.S. has entered into a qualified tax treaty qualifies. Any corporation incorporated in a U.S. possession is also eligible.

Foreign dividends do *not* qualify for the lower rates if the distributing corporation is a foreign investment company, a passive foreign investment company (PFIC) or a foreign personal holding company (FPHC). *However,* to be eligible, a foreign corporation that is either not incorporated in a U.S. possession or traded on a U.S. exchange must qualify for benefits under a comprehensive income tax treaty, which includes an exchange of information program.

STUDY QUESTIONS

8. The new tax rates apply to dividends received from:

   a. Domestic corporations
   b. Domestic corporations and some foreign corporations
   c. Foreign corporations owned by U.S. taxpayers
   d. Domestic corporations paying dividends for the first time

Minimum holding period

JGTRRA imposes tough restrictions on investors who purchase stock very close to the ex-dividend date (the date following the record date on which the corporation finalizes the list of shareholders receiving dividends). An investor must hold a stock for more than 60 days in the 120-day period beginning 60 days before the ex-dividend date for the lower rates to apply.

> *Example.* The ex-dividend date for ABC Co. is February 28, 2003. On January 20, 2003, Joe purchases 10,000 shares for $260,000. On March 6, 2003, having held the shares long enough to avoid the wash sale rules, Joe sells the shares for $258,000. Joe receives a dividend of $0.19 per share ($1,900). Joe's economic loss is $100. Assuming this is his only transaction, he can use the capital loss from the stock sale to offset $2,000 of other income, generating potential tax savings of $700 (35 percent x $2,000). If the 15 percent rate applies, Joe's liability on the $1,900 dividend would be $285 (at 15 percent), meaning that his economic loss of $100 produced a tax savings of $415 ($700 – $285). However, because he did not hold the shares for at least 60 days between December 30 to April 28 (60 days before and after the February 28, 2003, ex-dividend date), Joe's regular tax rate applies (35 percent). His $665 ($1,900 x 35 percent) liability on the dividend, combined with the $700 saved by the capital loss, means that his $100 economic loss produces a net savings of only $35. The holding period rule prevents Joe and other taxpayers from using price drops due to dividends to generate capital loss to offset

ordinary income while paying tax on the dividend at a lower rate.

Observation. The lower dividend rates sunset in 2009.

STUDY QUESTIONS

9. JGTRRA imposes timing restrictions on qualified dividends. A taxpayer must hold a stock for more than ____ days in the 120-day period beginning ____ days before the ex-dividend date.

    a. 30; 30
    b. 60; 20
    c. 60; 10
    d. 60; 60

10. JGTRRA's lower tax rates on dividends expire on:

    a. May 6, 2003
    b. December 31, 2008
    c. December 31, 2010
    d. January 1, 2011

IMPACT OF RATE CHANGES ON HIGHER-INCOME TAXPAYERS

Many media commentators have suggested that higher-income individuals will receive a disproportionate benefit from lower income tax rates. However, at least according to statistics released by the Treasury Department, taxpayers with incomes in excess of $100,000 will end up paying a larger share of the total income tax burden after passage of JGTRRA than before.

In any event, higher-income taxpayers will be pleased to see the top income tax rate immediately drop from 38.6 to 35 percent. High-income taxpayers will also benefit from the drop in the long-term capital gains rates and parallel treatment for stock dividends.

The rate reductions also have a positive impact on the after-tax incomes of high-level employees and entrepreneurs who derive their incomes from sole proprietorships, S corps, partnerships, and other pass-through entities.

The spread between the highest tax bracket rate and the capital gains rate before JGTRRA was 18.6 (38.6 percent less 20 percent). As a result of accelerating the cuts in the individual rates, the spread now increases to 20 percentage points (35 percent less 15 percent), making "gaming" to realize long-term capital gain, instead of either short-term gain or ordinary income, more valuable to taxpayers in the higher brackets.

> *Observation.* Excessive salaries paid to shareholders may be recharacterized by the IRS as constructive dividends. Because of the reduced rates for dividends, employee-shareholders

may actually prefer dividend treatment to receiving salaries taxed at ordinary income rates. Dividends are free from federal employment taxes. Dividends also would be preferable if the business did not need the salary deduction because its tax was fully offset by other deductions.

IMPACT OF JGTRRA ON FAMILIES

Income tax brackets

The increase in the threshold for the lowest tax rate (although by a modest amount) encourages tax planning among members of the same family. If a taxpayer has a child (or children) age 14 or older by year end, income earned by the child will first be sheltered by the child's standard deduction. Then, the first $7,000 of income (for an unmarried child) is taxed at 10 percent, which may generate substantial savings when compared to the rate of the child's parents.

> *Observation.* The "kiddie tax" (under which a child's 2003 unearned income in excess of $1,500 is taxed at his or her parent's marginal tax rate) continues to apply to children younger than age 14. Thus, transfers of assets to children under age 14 generally do not produce significant tax savings.

STUDY QUESTION

11. The "kiddie tax," under which a child's 2003 unearned income in excess of $1,500 is taxed at his or her parents' marginal tax rate is:

    a. Suspended by JGTRRA until December 31, 2008
    b. Unaffected by JGTRRA
    c. Increased by JGTRRA to $2,500 of unearned income
    d. Decreased by JGTRRA to $500 of unearned income

Capital gains shifting

The 5 percent rate on capital gains also provides a substantial opportunity for income and transfer tax planning. Taxpayers may wish to consider transferring assets to children, or other lower-income taxpayers, to cut the rate of tax on gains by two-thirds.

Taxpayers may also wish to reconsider use of other tax-favored savings vehicles, such as 529 plans and Coverdell Education Savings Accounts. The potential tax-free benefit of these vehicles may be outweighed by the low 5 percent rate, or zero rate for 2008, that a child would pay if he or she held the assets directly.

POTENTIAL NEGATIVE IMPACT OF JGTRRA

What are the potentially negative aspects of JGTRRA on investors? First, the lower capital gain rates are not applicable to all assets. Profits on sales of collectibles and unrecaptured Code Sec. 1250 gain is are subject to a 25 percent rate. In addition, although the increased spread between the rates applicable to long- and short-term capital gains should discourage short-term trading, it would seem to encourage schemes for taxpayers to "game" the system by converting short-term gain or ordinary income into long-term gain.

Qualified plans, IRAs, nonqualified plans, and equity compensation

The benefit of the lower capital gains rates will not apply to gains generated in qualified plans, such as 401(k) plans and IRAs. Distributions from these accounts will still be taxed as ordinary income. Taxpayers may wish to revisit their asset allocation between taxable accounts and tax-favored accounts, taking into account the sunset of the lower rates in 2009.

Charitable giving

The lower capital gains rates may have a dampening effect on the use of appreciated property for charitable purposes, both directly and through split interest vehicles, such as charitable remainder trusts. Taxpayers will have less of an incentive if their tax rate would be 15 percent or less.

Probable change in dividend policies

Will corporations respond by paying more dividends? It would appear likely that corporations will at least initiate or increase dividend payments in the hope of attracting capital, raising their stock price, and, therefore, making it easier to raise equity capital. Whether growth-oriented companies will feel that dividend payments still taint their growth-focused image remains to be seen. The six-year sunset may encourage corporations to proceed cautiously and respond to market pressures rather than taking bold action at the outset.

CHOICE OF ENTITY

Tax factors play an important role in the business owner's choice of business entity. Choice of entity generates different federal tax treatment at both the enterprise and the individual owner levels. Although tax rates should not be the only factor in choosing a business structure, tax factors do figure importantly as ongoing expenses. Moreover, the *Jobs and Growth Tax Relief Reconciliation Act of 2003* (JGTRRA) may change choice of entity dynamics. The predominant forms of business enterprise are the C corporation, S corp, partnership, limited liability company (LLC), and sole proprietorships. JGTRRA's lower rates for dividends, capital gains, and individual income will have a great impact on business planning as well as selection of business form.

JGTRRA and the C corporation

Some practitioners have suggested that JGTRRA's dividend tax rate reductions will make C corps more attractive entities because of the benefits C corps offer: a separate tax-rate structure, financing advantages, and limited liability. Other practitioners believe that even with a reduced tax rate on dividends, a pass-through structure, such as an S corp, LLC, partnership, or sole proprietorship, is more advantageous.

Dividends. The new dividends tax rate mitigates the impact of double-tax on corporate earnings at the shareholder level.

Capital gains. A shareholder of a C corp has capital gain upon selling stock in the corporation. Now that gain will be taxable at 5 or 15 percent, the tax blow is softer when a shareholder sells shares held for a year or more.

Individual tax rates. Shareholders/employees who perform services for the corporation can enjoy lower individual income tax rates.

JGTRRA and pass-through entities

Although JGTRRA reduced the dividend tax rates, it did not eliminate the "double" taxation of a regular corporation's profits. For that reason, pass-through entities have not lost their luster. S corps, partnerships, and limited liability companies (LLCs) are pass-through entities. Profits and losses "pass through" to the business interest owners, generally without being taxed at the enterprise level. Pass-through entities are popular because they offer the benefit of a single level of tax.

JGTRRA and the S corp

A Subchapter S corporation is a pass-through entity that enables owners of closely held corporations to eliminate double taxation by passing income, losses, and credits to the shareholders without an intervening corporate tax. Income is not taxed at the corporate level but is passed through and taxed to the shareholders. Corporate losses are deductible at the shareholder level, to the extent of the shareholder's basis.

Owners of S corp closely held businesses may choose between the corporate and partnership forms of conducting their business. By electing S corp status, shareholders enjoy the benefits of the corporate form while being taxed as though they were partners. To qualify as an S corp, the business must meet certain requirements. The S corp:

♦ Must be a domestic corporation;
♦ Have no more than 75 shareholders;
♦ Include only eligible shareholders; and

♦ Have only one class of stock.

Only individuals, certain types of estates and trusts, and exempt organizations can own stock in an S corp. Like C corp shareholders, S corp shareholders enjoy limited liability. Although an S corp has an unlimited life span, revocation of the S election can affect the continuity of a business.

JGTRRA may make S corps less attractive. Although S corps avoid double taxation, they are viewed as less flexible than are partnerships and LLCs. With the relative advantage of pass-through treatment somewhat reduced by JGTRRA because it lowered tax rates on dividends, the S election might be made more cautiously.

Dividends. Before JGTRRA, the higher dividend tax rates prevented many corporations from declaring dividends. Instead, corporations retained their earnings to avoid the additional shareholder-level tax. However, even with JGTRRA's reduced tax rates on dividends (which brightens the prospects of choosing the C corp as a business form), the S corp is attractive to owners who don't mind foregoing distributions. An S corp that retains its earnings forces shareholders to pay tax on earnings. Shareholders, however, receive a basis adjustment in the amount of the undistributed earnings.

Individual tax rates. The JGTRRA-accelerated cuts in the individual income tax rates are another incentive to taxpayers opting for pass-through treatment. Partners and shareholders of S corps pay tax at the rates applicable to ordinary income. Even after JGTRRA, the top individual tax rate is 35 percent. The top corporate rate is also currently 35 percent.

JGTRRA and partnerships and LLCs

A partnership is a business owned by two or more persons. Partnerships are an attractive business form because they are relatively easy to create. There are few formal requirements. Other than the sole proprietorship, the partnership is probably the most common business entity. However, partnerships do not offer the same type of limited liability as corporations. A limited partner's liability is usually limited to the amount of capital the limited partner contributed. A general partner, however, is usually individually liable for all debts of the partnership.

A limited liability company (LLC) offers its owners protection from liability and the avoidance of double taxation. An LLC with two or more members is treated as a partnership, unless it elects to be treated as a corporation. For income tax purposes, there is essentially no difference between a partnership and an LLC. The LLC, however, typically offers liability protection. LLCs have greater flexibility of ownership and have an advantage over the S corp in that they are not subject to limitations on the number or type of shareholders. An individual, a corporation, a partnership, or any other entity can be a member of an LLC and an LLC can have any number of members.

Partnerships and LLCs taxed as partnerships are treated as tax conduits. They are not subject to taxation at the enterprise level. Income, gains and losses flow through to the individual partners and are reported on personal income tax returns. Partnerships and LLCs taxed as partnerships are subject to one level of tax imposed on the member or partner's distributive share of the LLC or partnership income, whether the share is actually distributed or not. Partnerships and LLCs also pass through losses to active members, subject to limitations.

As with C and S corps, JGTRRA's provisions should be a consideration in choosing the partnership or LLC business form.

Dividends. Partnerships and LLCs are not taxed on dividend income; instead, the income passes through to the partner or the LLC member.

Capital Gains. When a partner or member of an LLC taxed as a partnership, sells an interest in the entity, some of the gain may be taxable as ordinary income rather than as capital gain. If so, the partner or member will be unable to take advantage of the new lower capital gains rates on that portion.

Individual tax rates. The reduction in individual income tax rates, while corporate rates remain the same, may make partnerships and LLCs more attractive.

Tax issues differentiate business forms and are a dominant consideration in choosing one business entity over another. Taxpayers and business planners must consider all factors when selecting the proper business form.

STUDY QUESTIONS

12. The new dividends tax rate affects choice of entity by:

    a. Reducing the impact of double taxation
    b. Increasing the impact of double taxation
    c. Avoiding double taxation
    d. Distributing double taxation

13. Reduced tax rates on dividend income:

    a. Increase shareholder tax liability
    b. Make the C corporation entity form more attractive
    c. Do not affect the business entity selection dynamic
    d. Will increase the number of partnerships

CONCLUSION

The broad rate reduction accomplished by the *Jobs and Growth Tax Relief Reconciliation Act of 2003* has a specific impact on many different "types" of taxpayers. The across-the-board rate reduction helped everyone keep more than had been allowed previously. Wages, short-term capital gains, "ordinary income," retirement savings distributions—even the form of unincorporated business selected from the get-go of an enterprise—are all suddenly subject to these new lower tax rates.

Congress, however, did not stop there. The maximum tax on capital gains was lowered by 25 percent—reduced from 20 percent to 15 percent. As a percentage, reducing capital gains rates for the otherwise 15-percent bracket taxpayer – from 10 percent, to 5 percent (or zero in a few years)—brings even more of a dramatic savings, and incentive for family tax planning in which lower-rate members realize more of the family's income.

Congress did not stop at capital gains, either. Dividends are now given as much of a tax break as long-term capital gain—a maximum rate of 15 percent. For that preferred rate to stick, however, the dividends must be "qualified," bringing in a host of special rules— especially so for foreign dividends.

Rate reduction, in short, creates an entirely new set of variables against which business and investment decisions must be weighed. Although far preferable to deciding how to manage a multi-rate *crease*, rate reductions in ordinary income, capital gains and qualified dividend income presents its challenges ...and rewards.

CHAPTER 2: NAVIGATING THE NEW WRITEOFF RULES FOR BUSINESS ASSETS

Learning Objectives. This chapter was prepared to give you information about three important developments that affect significantly the amount that a business may deduct for the cost of a business asset in its year of purchase. These developments include (1) recent IRS guidance and case law on the capitalization of business assets; (2) a quadruple increase in the amount of "Section 179 expensing" allowed for some assets that must be capitalized; and (3) an increase in the amount of bonus first-year depreciation allowed on other capitalized assets, from 30 percent to 50 percent. Upon completion of this chapter, you will be able to:

♦ Describe the key factors used by the IRS and the courts to determine when a business must capitalize an asset purchase and when it is entitled to an immediate business expense deduction;

- ◆ Determine what environmental-related business costs are immediately deductible and what expenses must be capitalized;
- ◆ Understand the sweeping impact that new IRS regulations will have on how a business writes off its intangible property;
- ◆ Discern what assets and businesses qualify for the new $100,000 expensing election introduced by 2003 tax legislation;
- ◆ Compute all the variables that go into the final amount that may be expensed each year, and what gets left over;
- ◆ Identify situations in which not taking the expensing election makes better sense;
- ◆ Account for what assets and businesses qualify for the 50 percent bonus first year deprecation enhanced by 2003 tax legislation;
- ◆ Compute bonus depreciation using the correct assumptions and computational sequence required under the new law; and
- ◆ Identify the impact that electing bonus depreciation has on the use of other tax breaks, now and in the future.

INTRODUCTION

2003 has seen three important changes that directly affect the amount that a business may recover, in the form of tax deductions, on the cost of purchasing business assets. These changes include:

- ◆ Stepped-up guidance on whether a cost can be deducted immediately or must be capitalized;
- ◆ A quadruple increase--to $100,000 annually--in the amount of capitalized costs that a business may expense in the year an asset is purchased; and
- ◆ A significant increase--from 30 percent to 50 percent—in the amount of "bonus" first-year depreciation that a business can deduct in the year business assets are purchased.

The adage "time is money" is especially appropriate here: The sooner a business can write off the cost of an asset, the sooner the business can realize the cash-in-hand saved by reducing its tax liabilities. Put concretely, a dollar written off in 2003 or 2004 is usually a lot more valuable to a business now than a dollar that will be written off years hence.

Successfully arguing that a business expense may be deducted all in the year in which it is incurred, as an "ordinary and necessary" business expense deduction rather than as a capitalized cost, is the first line of attack in getting costs written off as soon as possible. If the expense must be capitalized, however, the next best thing to an ordinary and necessary business expense deduction is to be able to deduct as much of the cost as possible in the year of purchase under other tax provisions. The two most helpful provisions in accelerating the deduction of capitalized costs are now:

♦ The $100,000 Section 179 expensing deduction, and
♦ The 50 percent bonus first year depreciation, both made effective in 2003 by the *Jobs and Growth Tax Relief Reconciliation Act of 2003*.

Skillful use of these provisions, either in tandem and otherwise, can help a business maximize its writeoff of a substantial portion of its capitalized assets in the year of purchase.

The debate over what must be capitalized or expensed will continue. Use of enhanced Section 179 expensing and bonus depreciation, however, carry a definite deadline, so businesses should consider swift action to take advantage of these temporary tax breaks—before they are gone:

♦ After December 31, 2005, Section 179 expensing returns to its relatively low pre-2003 law level of $25,000; and
♦ After December 31, 2004, bonus first-year depreciation is eliminated entirely.

CAPITALIZATION OF EXPENDITURES

The IRS, as well as the courts, continues to wrestle with the ongoing issues of capitalization versus expensing. A fundamental purpose of the relevant Tax Code provision—Code Sec. 263(a)—is the prevention of the distortion of taxable income through the current deduction of expenditures that relates to the production of income in future taxable years. The U.S. Supreme Court has therefore held that expenditures creating or enhancing separate and distinct assets, or producing certain other future benefits of a significant nature, need to be capitalized under Code Sec. 263(a). That ruling 10 years ago in *INDOPCO, Inc. v. Commr*, 503 U.S. 79 (1992) continues to fuel the capitalization versus expensing controversy.

For many years the courts have recognized the difficulty of translating general capitalization principles into standards that are clear, consistent, and easily administered. Courts generally focus on the specific facts that are presented to them, so that the results they reach are often difficult to reconcile. Also, especially in recent years, the varying results reached by the courts have contributed to much uncertainty and controversy.

The IRS has noted that the level of uncertainty and controversy is unfair to taxpayers in that it hinders sound and effective tax administration. During the past year, the IRS has issued key guidance—both general and on an industry-by-industry basis—that has resolved some issues (while stirring up others). Meanwhile, the courts have been relatively, although not completely, silent on the issue (perhaps more a reflection of the IRS's willingness to settle many more issues than any reluctance on the part of the judiciary to join the debate).

Basic rules of capitalization

Taxpayers generally may deduct ordinary and necessary business expenses only for the tax year in which they are paid or incurred under the taxpayer's method of accounting. In contrast, capitalized expenditures are added to basis and recovered through depreciation, amortization, or when the property is sold or otherwise transferred. In addition, taxpayers subject to uniform capitalization rules must capitalize the costs associated with production of property or property acquired for resale in accordance with the uniform rules.

Many Code provisions provide specific deductions for capital expenditures. Costs of construction usually must be capitalized. Costs of acquiring, disposing of, and protecting rights in property and costs of organizing, reorganizing, or liquidating businesses are capital expenditures. Tax straddles and short sales generate costs that must be capitalized.

STUDY QUESTION

1.   Which of the following would be capitalized?

   a.   Current business expenses
   b.   Replacements
   c.   Personal expenses
   d.   Costs of organizing and reorganizing a business

Uniform capitalization. Uniform capitalization rules require capitalization of direct and indirect costs of property produced by a taxpayer and property acquired for resale. There is a gross receipts exception for taxpayers acquiring property for resale. Costs are allocated using various allocation methods. For interest, capitalization is only required during the production period of designated real and tangible property produced by the taxpayer.

Under the uniform capitalization rules for costs other than interest, taxpayers must capitalize direct costs, and a properly allocable share of specified indirect costs. Taxpayers must allocate or apportion the direct and indirect costs to various activities, including production or resale activities. After costs are allocated to the appropriate production or resale activities, they are generally allocated to the items of property produced or property acquired for resale during the tax year and capitalized to the items that remain on hand at the end of the tax year.

Nonuniform capitalization assets. Whether expenditures are capital in nature under nonuniform rules usually depends on whether benefits extend beyond the tax year, whether separate and distinct assets are created, whether expenditures are recurring, and whether the taxpayer's method of accounting for expenditures clearly reflects income. Some expenditures are specifically provided a current expense deduction or a ratable deduction, such as amortization, over a period of time, even if the expenditure would otherwise be considered capitalizable.

One common issue is whether a particular expense is in fact connected with the purchase or disposition of a capital asset so that it must be capitalized. In making this determination, courts apply the origin of the claim test, which looks to the fundamental nature of a transaction, rather than the reasons the transaction is conducted, in determining the appropriate tax treatment. If the origin of the claim is in a capital transaction, such as the process of acquisition (or disposition) itself, the expenditure must be capitalized. Under the origin of the claim test, the taxpayer's subjective purpose in making the expenditure is irrelevant.

Generally, costs of ordinary and necessary repairs are currently deductible. Costs of repairs and improvements must be capitalized if they relate to production or resale activities subject to the uniform capitalization rules, if they add to the value of an asset or prolong its useful life, or if they adapt an asset to a different use. Costs of repairs must be capitalized when they are made as part of a general plan of rehabilitation.

STUDY QUESTIONS

2. Improvements may include:

    a.   Replacing a part
    b.   Maintenance checks
    c.   Repairs
    d.   Installing a new roof

3. A taxpayer can take a current deduction for:

    a.   A capital expense
    b.   A repair to maintain the operating condition of the property
    c.   An improvement
    d.   Expenses to get a business started

ENVIRONMENTAL CLEANUP COSTS

Environmental cleanup costs may qualify as ordinary and necessary business expenses. (See the discussion of *Cinergy Corp.*, FedCl March 10, 2003, on the following page) However, expenditures to acquire or increase the value of property, prolong the life of property, or adapt it to a different use are capital expenditures. In addition, the uniform capitalization rules may require allocation and capitalization of cleanup costs.

Taxpayers may elect current expensing for capital expenditures to abate or control hazardous substances at designated contaminated sites under Code Sec. 198. As in the case of other trade or business expenses, a cleanup expense is not deductible prior to the tax year for which it is paid or incurred. These provisions are intended to match expenses with revenue of the tax year to which the expenses are properly attributable, thereby resulting in a more accurate calculation of net income for tax purposes.

Cinergy Corp. The U.S. Court of Claims recently approved of the immediate deduction of the costs of asbestos abatement. The court stressed that the abatement work was necessary to keep the taxpayer's property in ordinary operating condition as an office building. The court also made an important distinction between the taxpayer's abatement activities and environmental remediation expenses, which frequently must be capitalized.

In 1972, the taxpayer constructed an addition to one of its office buildings. Fireproofing material used in the new building contained asbestos. Over time, the fireproofing became friable and the taxpayer decided to encapsulate or remove the asbestos. The abatement work took about six months and included a mix of removal and encapsulation of the asbestos. The ultimate cost to the taxpayer was more than $800,000.

The taxpayer viewed the abatement costs as ordinary and necessary business expenses, deductible under Code Sec. 162. The IRS countered that the expenses were capital and nondeductible.

The court began its analysis by indicating that there is not, and probably cannot be, an exact definition of the term "ordinary and necessary" and each case must be determined on the basis of its own facts and circumstances, the court observed.

In this case, the court departed from a strict interpretation of remediation case law. Rather, it emphasized that the property defect was not present at the time the taxpayer acquired the building. Indeed, the health risks were neither known nor anticipated at the time of the construction of the addition. Contamination developed over the course of 18 years as the asbestos became friable.

The court further concluded that the asbestos abatement did not increase the value and original service life of the building. Likewise, the building was not adapted to a new or different use. The purpose of the abatement work was to arrest and correct a condition of deterioration that threatened the premature end of the building's useful life.

4.   Code Sec. 198 addresses which of the following?

    a.   Capitalization of costs
    b.   Trade or business expenses
    c.   A cleanup expense
    d.   Acquisition of intangibles

WHAT'S NEXT FOR THE CAPITALIZATION OF INTANGIBLES?

In much-anticipated relief that is being called "historic" and "ground-breaking" in its concessions to taxpayers, the IRS has issued proposed regs (REG-125638-01) concerning applying capitalization rules to amounts paid to acquire, create, or enhance intangible assets.

Why the regs?

The driving force behind the issuance of the proposed regs stems from a long line of inconsistent and seemingly contradictory court cases dealing with the issue of capitalization. Part of the problem in this area is the fact-intensive nature of these types of cases. The issuance of the proposed regs was an acknowledgement by the government that litigation in general is much too expensive, time-consuming and unpredictable to be of any real use in creating guidelines for taxpayers in this area. The proposed regs contain a series of bright-line tests that may rid this area of the subjective nature of such cases and provide certainty for taxpayers and practitioners.

Exclusive list. The new proposed regs interpret *INDOPCO* as a mandate to capitalize costs generating a significant future benefit "flavored by practicality and common sense." Rather than embodying such a vague mandate as the rule, the IRS stated that it used the significant benefits test as a measuring rod for creating an exclusive list of categories in which to capitalize costs. Items not on the list simply are no longer required to be capitalized, but with one safety-net caveat for the IRS: if a non-listed expenditure is found to produce future benefits, the IRS may identify it in published guidance as significant enough to warrant capitalization.

Safe harbors/administrative assumptions. The IRS and Treasury also created safe harbors and administrative exceptions to significantly reduce taxpayer recordkeeping burdens and IRS costs:

♦   *12-month rule.* Amounts paid to create or enhance intangible rights or benefits for the taxpayer that do not extend beyond the period of 12 months will be treated as not having a useful life extending substantially beyond the close of the tax year and therefore need not be capitalized;

♦   *De minimis rules.* If transaction costs, other than compensation and overhead, and measured on a transaction-by-transaction basis, do not exceed $5,000, the costs are considered de minimis and are not required to be capitalized;

♦ *Employee compensation rule.* Employee compensation and overhead costs, whether paid in the form of salary, bonus or commission, will not be considered as facilitating the acquisition, creation or enhancement of an intangible asset, regardless of the percentage of the employee's time allocable to capital transactions; and

♦ *15-year safe harbor.* A 15-year safe harbor amortization period applies for certain created or enhanced intangibles that do not have readily ascertainable useful lives (for example, memberships of indefinite duration).

Highly contentious items remain

Although the acquisition of intangibles is already a fairly well-settled area of the tax law as governed by Code Sec. 197, the capitalization of self-created intangibles and transaction costs is highly contentious.

Self-created intangibles. The proposed regs provide that expenses that fall into one of eight categories must be capitalized. The categories include: (1) financial interests; (2) prepaid expenses; (3) certain types of membership rights; (4) rights obtained from the government; (5 and 6) certain types of contractual rights or contractual terminations; (7) benefits arising from real property improvements; and (8) expenses incurred in connection with the defense or perfection of title. The business process reengineering costs, inducements paid to create long-term relationships with clients and amounts paid to protect a taxpayer's business reputation do not need to be capitalized and may be immediately expensed.

The listed categories are not intended to be exclusive and the IRS may add more categories as the need arises in order to address changes in the marketplace. The category approach will most likely remain in the final regs and that, if the IRS was to add more categories, such additions would only be effective prospectively.

Transaction costs. This is also a highly contentious issue, particularly with regard to mergers and acquisitions. The transaction costs can be broken down into two categories: (1) those that facilitate an acquisition and (2) those that facilitate a business restructuring such as a stock issuance or bankruptcy reorganization. In either case, the expenses at issue concern those that facilitate the transactions, which is determined under the facts and circumstances of each particular case. Facilitative expenses typically include fees paid to attorneys or brokers who aid in negotiating the deal. In-house expenses attributable to the transaction, such as employee and overhead expenses, do not need to be capitalized, primarily because allocating these expenses among the transaction and normal business operations would prove too difficult. In addition, there is a *de minimis* exemption for transactional expenses that do not exceed $5,000.

The primary issue in the mergers and acquisitions context concerns the point at which investigatory costs should be capitalized. The proposed regs state that transaction costs should be capitalized on the earliest of the issuance of a letter of intent or upon approval of the transaction by the board of directors. However, because most sellers will not allow prospective purchasers to entertain a transaction or begin due diligence until a letter of intent is received, it is possible that a purchaser may be incurring expenses that must be capitalized before a final decision to proceed with the purchase has been made.

Effective date. A public hearing was held in April to discuss comments received about the proposed regs. The IRS expects the regs to be issued in final form sometime before the end of the calendar year. Most of the provisions in the proposed regs are expected to be adopted and apply retroactively to all open tax years when in favor of a taxpayer's position. When the regs as proposed favor a position that the taxpayer protests, their effective date will depend upon whether the rule as ultimately adopted by final regs arises out of a general principle that favors retroactive application, or out of a more arbitrary desire to create "bright line," in which case the final regs themselves are expected to be more explicit on the effective date.

WRITING OFF CAPITALIZED ASSET EXPENSES

Upfront deductions are generally preferred over depreciation deductions taken gradually over the life of an asset that must be capitalized. Not only does an upfront deduction permit the business taxpayer to recoup an asset's cost before inflation devalues part of that writeoff, but it also contributes to immediate cash flow by lowering estimated tax payments, thereby helping to directly defray the asset's purchase price. An immediate deduction also provides more certainty to the business that the deduction will be used against otherwise current taxable income rather than more uncertain future earnings.

Two "upfront" business deductions that have been enhanced tremendously by the *Jobs and Growth Tax Relief Reconciliation Act of 2003* (JGTRRA) are the Section 179 expensing deduction and the first-year bonus depreciation deduction.

Both deductions are intended to encourage capital spending. For smaller businesses, the Section 179 expense limit is increased from $25,000 to $100,000, while the phaseout based on total capital expenditures for the year now starts at $400,000 rather than $200,000. For all businesses, the first-year bonus depreciation enacted in the Act is expanded from 30 percent to 50 percent. In any case, the tax benefits attributed to these deductions—which are temporary in nature— should not be overlooked.

5. Which of the following is *untrue?* Under the *Jobs and Growth Tax Relief Reconciliation Act of 2003* (JGTRRA), the "upfront" business deductions (Section 179 and first-year bonus depreciation):

    a. Have been enhanced to encourage current deductions
    b. Have been enhanced to encourage capital spending
    c. Are permanent in nature
    d. Have been enhanced to encourage depreciation

SECTION 179 EXPENSING DEDUCTION

Business taxpayers are generally entitled to elect an expense deduction, in place of depreciation, for the first year that tangible personal property is placed in service in a trade or business. The dollar amount of the expense that the taxpayer may elect is limited on an annual basis. This choice to take the deduction is usually referred to as "the expensing election" or "Section 179 expensing" after the Internal Revenue Code section that permits it.

Amount of the expensing deduction

Dollar limitation increased to $100,000. JGTRRA has increased the maximum dollar amount that may be deducted under Section 179 from $25,000 to $100,000 for qualifying property placed in service in tax years beginning after 2002 and before 2006; the amount will be adjusted for inflation each year. The maximum allowable deduction for qualifying property placed in service after 2005 is scheduled to return to the 2003 level: $25,000.

The allowable amount of a direct expense deduction is based on the cost of qualifying property purchased and placed in service during the tax year. The cost does not include any portion of the basis in the property placed in service that is determined by reference to basis in other property held by the taxpayer. For example, a taxpayer's cost does not include the value of previously owned property traded in on new property in a like-kind exchange

> *Example.* Smith purchases a new drill press for $8,000. Smith pays $6,000 cash and trades in an old machine. Smith's old drill press had an adjusted basis of $2,000. Smith's direct expense deduction for the new machine is limited to $6,000.

> *Caution.* Since the effective date for the $100,000 limit is written in terms of "tax years beginning after 2002," fiscal (non-calendar) year taxpayers will not qualify in fiscal years ending anytime in 2003 (except December 31st).

Phaseout limitation is raised, too. The $100,000 amount is reduced dollar-for-dollar (but not below zero) by the amount by which the cost of all qualifying property placed in service during the tax year exceeds

$400,000, the phaseout threshold that has doubled from its 2002 level of $200,000.

> *Example.* In 2003, Acme Co., a manufacturing company, purchases a machine for business use. The cost of the machine is $410,000. Because the cost of the qualified property (in addition to any other qualifying property purchased in 2003) exceeds $400,000, the $100,000 deduction limitation must be reduced dollar-for-dollar by the amount that the cost of the machine and other qualifying property exceeds $400,000. Thus, Acme Co. is entitled to deduct $90,000 ($100,000 - $10,000) of the cost of the machine.

> *Caution.* Taxpayers should also keep in mind that the $400,000 phaseout threshold will return to the previous $200,000 threshold in 2006 unless Congress passes new legislation. In addition, the $100,000 maximum amount that can be deducted for qualifying property will revert to $25,000 in 2006 without the enactment of new legislation.

Taxable income limitation remains. The expensing deduction is further limited by the amount of taxable income derived by the taxpayer from the active conduct of any trade or business. The deduction disallowed under this limitation may be carried forward, which can especially help a new business still establishing itself during its startup phase. The basis of qualifying property, however, must be reduced by the elected expense amount even if all or a portion of it must be carried forward. To the extent that some basis remains in a particular property after expensing has been taken, depreciation may be taken for that first year and thereafter over the life of the asset.

Qualifying property

Section 179 qualifying property is "tangible Code Sec. 1245 property, depreciable under Code Sec. 168, and acquired by purchase for use in the active conduct of a trade or business." Generally, this includes:

- Personal property;
- Other tangible property used as an integral part of manufacturing, production, or extraction; or of furnishing electricity, gas, water, or sewage disposal services; or used in a research facility for these activities; and
- Part of any real property that has an adjusted basis reflecting amortization deductions set forth in Code Sec. 1245(a)(3)(C); single-purpose agricultural or horticultural structures; storage facilities (other than buildings and their structural components) that are used in connection with the distribution of petroleum or

primary products of petroleum; and any railroad grating or tunnel bore.

Off-the-shelf computer software. Off-the-shelf (as opposed to custom) computer software to which Code Sec. 167 applies and that is placed in service in tax years beginning after 2002 and before 2006 is now included as qualifying property that may be expensed under Code Sec. 179. Computer software is defined as software that is readily available for purchase by the general public, is subject to a nonexclusive license, and has not been substantially modified. In addition, computer software does not include any database or similar item unless it is in the public domain and is incidental to the operation of otherwise qualifying computer software (Code Sec. 197(e)(3)(A)(i) and (B)).

Automobiles and SUVs. JGTRRA has one quirk that is not detailed in Code Sec. 179. Taxpayers who purchase "large" SUVs in 2003 for business purposes can have Uncle Sam pay as much as $35,000 of the cost the first year the SUV is placed in service (with a maximum $100,000 deduction taken in the 35 percent rate bracket). To qualify for this tax break, the SUV must be placed in service after December 31, 2002, and have a loaded gross vehicle weight rating of more than 6,000 pounds. Automobiles can also qualify, provided that the curb weight exceeds 6,000 pounds. Otherwise, the maximum depreciation writeoff for cars for the first year commencing under the revised Code Sec. 168(k) is $10,710.

> *Caution.* States that have been decoupling their tax treatment of depreciation from the federal tax treatment of bonus depreciation may be less generous to taxpayers in the state tax treatment of acquisitions of heavy SUVs.

Who may expense?

Estates, trusts, and specified noncorporate lessors are the only business taxpayers officially excluded from using Section 179. However, in practice because all asset purchases of Section 179-type property cannot exceed $499,000 for any one property to qualify, Section 179 expensing is limited to small businesses.

Married couples. Married taxpayers filing a joint return are treated as one taxpayer for purposes of the annual dollar limit and the $400,000 phaseout reduction. Married persons filing separately are also treated as one person and may allocate the expenses election deduction among themselves as they wish. However, the taxable income limitation applies to married individuals filing joint returns as one taxpayer, and as two separate taxpayers if they file separately.

Pass-through entities. The annual dollar limitation on the expense election applies separately to a partnership and each of its partners, as well as to an S corp and each of its shareholders. The taxable income limitation applies at both the partnership and partner level, as well as to the S corp and each of its shareholders. Partnerships and S corps may carry forward the disallowed portion (as a result of the taxable income limit) at the entity level.

Partnerships and S corps must reduce the basis of their qualifying property to reflect the amount of the direct expense deduction elected by the partnership or S corp and passed through to the partners or shareholders. This reduction must be made even if the annual dollar limitation prevents a partner or shareholder from deducting all or a portion of the direct expense deduction passed through.

STUDY QUESTIONS

6. Under Section 179, married taxpayers filing a joint return:

   a. Are treated as separate taxpayers for all purposes
   b. Qualify for the annual dollars limit and the $200,000 phase-out reduction
   c. Are treated as one taxpayer
   d. Are not affected by the annual dollar limit and the phase-out reduction

7. The annual dollar limitation on the expense election under Section 179 for pass-through entities:

   a. Applies in a combined amount to the partnership and to each of the partners
   b. Applies only at the partnership level
   c. Applied only at the partner's level
   d. May be carried forward at the entity level, if there is a disallowed portion

Making the election

The taxpayer usually elects to expense these items on his or her original return for the tax year to which the election relates. In order to revoke the election, the taxpayer must obtain the consent of the IRS.

Revocation of election. The taxpayer may revoke any election to expense property under Code Sec. 179 with respect to tax years beginning after 2002 and before 2006 for any property. However, once the revocation is made, it is irrevocable.

Additional strategies

Before a taxpayer decides to elect the Section 179 deduction, he or she should consider some long-range tax issues. For example, if the taxpayer is in a tax bracket of 15 percent or less, it may be better not to take the deduction if he or she expects to be in a higher income bracket in later years. Depreciation may provide a more valuable tax benefit to reduce taxable income in higher-income years.

If assets purchased in a tax year have different useful lives for depreciation purposes and the taxpayer elects to take the Section 179 deduction, it is usually better to take the deduction on the longest-lived assets first.

Small businesses should evaluate how to time the purchases of equipment, and how elections should be taken, in light of the new law. The interactions among the capitalization-versus-expensing rules, the Section 179 expensing limitations, bonus first-year depreciation restrictions, and the regular accelerated depreciation rules create the need for spreadsheet precision. (Timing purchases toward the end of 2004 involves another, entirely separate set of considerations because bonus depreciation is scheduled to end after 2004, whereas enhanced Section 179 expensing continues for another year.) For now, however, a small business's timing and treatment of purchases should take into account several primary considerations:

1.   The cost of the asset may be immediately and fully deductible as a business expense under Code Sec. 162, thus avoiding any requirement to capitalize and depreciation it altogether. There is some risk, however, in being too aggressive on the side of claiming an immediate deduction. If, on audit, the IRS concludes that the asset must be capitalized, the IRS could deny a late election at that time to use either Section 179 expensing or bonus depreciation advantageously. Nevertheless, if a purchase can safely fit under the section 162 business expense rules, that deduction generally should be taken without hesitation since it does not count against the Section 179 expensing limitation at all.

2.   Once a business decides that an asset must be capitalized, it must decide whether it qualifies for either Section 179 expensing or bonus depreciation on that asset and, if so, which one to take first. Fortunately, the final decision does not need to be made until after year-end when the return for the tax year is filed. Nevertheless, knowing what immediate first-year writeoff will be available is critical to many small businesses' upfront purchasing decisions.

   If the asset is used property, the decision to expense or take bonus depreciation is easier to make because, as used property, the asset automatically cannot qualify for bonus depreciation. The decision then comes down to which qualifying Section 179 assets should be designated to count toward the new $100,000 annual expensing limit. Initially, the taxpayer can compute whether all qualifying Section 179 property for the tax year comes within the new $400,000 limit on purchases; otherwise, the deduction will be phased out quickly, dollar for dollar, on the excess. Assuming that limit is not reached, however, the Section 179 $100,000 deduction generally should be taken on assets in reverse order of useful life, because property with a shorter useful life will be subject to faster depreciation.

3.   If qualifying Section 179 property is also new, the alternative option of taking the 50 percent bonus depreciation must be factored into the decision. If a single asset is involved, it is generally more advantageous to take a full first-year deduction than one for 50 percent. If multiple assets are under consideration, first using up the Section 179 expensing limitation on the assets with the longest depreciation period generally makes the most sense.

4.   An asset may be able to support both an expensing deduction and bonus depreciation. For example, a new asset purchased for $330,000 could be entitled to $100,000 expensing, $115,000 bonus depreciation on the remaining $230,000 basis, and regular first-year depreciation on the reduced $115,000 basis.

STUDY QUESTIONS

8.   Qualifying property under Code Sec. 179 does *not* include:

   a.   Off-the-shelf computer software
   b.   Personal property
   c.   Tangible property used in manufacturing
   d.   An unlimited writeoff amount for cars

9.   Who may expense under Code Sec. 179?

   a.   Small businesses
   b.   Estates
   c.   Noncorporate lessors
   d.   Trusts

BONUS DEPRECIATION DEDUCTION

Bonus depreciation is a tax break that no business owner should leave to chance. Bonus depreciation has become so generous that it has become incumbent on any business tax advisor to suggest that capital purchases that are being planned for some date in the future be made now or at least before 2005. It is also important to remind business owners that business expansions that have not been considered previously be given a second look.

To encourage capital investment immediately after the 9-11 tragedies, the *Job Creation and Worker Assistance Act of 2002* (JCWAA) created a 30 percent additional first-year depreciation allowance for qualifying depreciable property. To obtain the "bonus," qualifying property had to be acquired after September 10, 2001, but before September 11,

2004, and placed in service before January 1, 2005 (January 1, 2006, for certain longer-term property).

To stimulate the economy further, the *Jobs and Growth Tax Relief Reconciliation Act of 2003* (JGTRRA) increased the additional first-year depreciation allowance percentage from 30 percent to 50 percent. To qualify for the higher percentage, the qualifying property must be acquired after May 5, 2003, and placed in service before January 1, 2005 (January 1, 2006, for property with a longer production period). The 50 percent rate does not apply if a binding written contract for acquisition of the property was in effect before May 6, 2003.

> **Example.** Jones purchases property for $100,000 that is depreciable over 10 years. Jones is now able to claim a bonus depreciation of $50,000 in the year he purchases the asset for his business. He also can take regular depreciation starting in the year of purchase on the remaining tax basis in the property (now $50,000 depreciated over the 10-year period).

Treasury Department regulations define a "binding contract" as any contract enforceable under state law that does not limit damages to a specified amount. However, the regs allow one important exception: a contractual provision that limits damages to at least 5 percent of the total contract price will not be treated as limiting damages at all for purposes of determining a "binding contract." In addition, an option to either acquire or sell property is not treated as a binding contract.

Except for the qualifying acquisition and placed-in-service dates, property of the type that qualifies for the 50 percent bonus depreciation is the same as property that had qualified for the 30 percent bonus depreciation. Taxpayers also may elect to continue to use the 30 percent rate instead. Proposed IRS regulations released in September make it clear, however, that this election must be made on a class-by-class basis, applicable to all property with each depreciable class of property.

STUDY QUESTION

10. A bonus depreciation:

    a. Encourages business expansion
    b. Is not considered a tax break
    c. Is not so generous under the Jobs and Growth Tax Relief Reconciliation Act of 2003 (JGTRRA)
    d. Under the *Jobs and Growth Tax Relief Reconciliation Act of 2003* (JGTRRA), created a 10 percent additional first-year depreciation allowance for qualifying depreciable property

Bonus depreciation on New York Liberty Zone property

The increased 50 percent rate does not apply to bonus depreciation that is claimed on "qualified New York Liberty Zone property" under Code Sec. 1400L(b). The 30 percent rate continues to apply to New York Liberty Zone property even if it is acquired after May 5, 2003.

Qualifying property

For purposes of a bonus depreciation deduction, qualified property is:

♦ New MACRS property with a recovery period of 20 years or less (MACRS is the cost recovery system used to determine the amount of the depreciation deduction for tangible personal property);
♦ Computer software that is depreciable under Code Sec. 167 (as opposed to software subject to a 15-year amortization under IRC Code Sec. 197);
♦ Qualified leasehold improvement property; and
♦ Water utility property.

> *Observation.* The special depreciation bonus is not available to property that must be depreciated under the alternative depreciation system (ADS) of MACRS.

Original use. The original use of qualified property must commence with the taxpayer on or after September 11, 2001, for 30 percent bonus depreciation; and on or after May 6, 2003, but before January 1, 2006, for 50 percent bonus depreciation. Original use means the first use to which the property is put, whether or not such use corresponds to the taxpayer's use of the property.

For purposes of this rule, additional capital expenditures incurred to recondition or rebuild property acquired or owned by the taxpayer would satisfy the original use requirement. However, the cost of reconditioned or rebuilt property acquired by the taxpayer would not satisfy the original use requirement because its first use is not by the taxpayer.

> *Example.* Taxpayer purchases a used machine before September 11, 2001, for $50,000. He then pays $20,000 to recondition it. The $50,000 purchase price does not qualify for the depreciation bonus. However, the $20,000 qualifies for the bonus, assuming that it is capitalized.

Whether property is reconditioned or rebuilt is a question of fact. Treasury regulations provide a safe harbor that property containing used parts will not be treated as reconditioned or rebuilt if the cost of the used parts is not more than 20 percent of the total cost of the property.

Treasury regulations also help define self-constructed property for purposes of qualifying for bonus depreciation. The property acquisition requirement is meet if a taxpayer manufactures, constructs, or produces the property (or contracts to have it produced) for its own use if such manufacturing, construction, or production began after September 10, 2001 (for 30 percent property), or May 5, 2003 (for 50 percent property), and before January 1, 2005. Construction is deemed to begin when "physical work of a significant nature begins." Preliminary planning and design work doesn't count for this purpose. However, in a safe-harbor break, the IRS will concede that physical work of a significant nature has begun when the taxpayer incurs or pays more than 10 percent of the total cost of the property (excluding land and preliminary activities costs).

Placed in service. Qualified property must be placed in service by January 1, 2005. The date the property is acquired is not necessarily the same as the date the property is placed in service. An extension of the deadline date until January 1, 2006, is available for certain property with a recovery period of 10 years or longer and certain transportation property. Transportation property is defined as tangible personal property used in the trade or business of transporting persons or property.

Computing the deduction

The bonus depreciation deduction is claimed on the cost of the property after reduction by any Code Sec. 179 (or Section 179) expensing allowance claimed. Regular MACRS deductions are claimed as a cost, and reduced by any Code Sec. 179 allowance and bonus depreciation.

> *Example.* On July 1, 2003, John Jones purchases qualifying five-year MACRS property subject to the half-year convention for $1,500 and claims a $500 Code Sec. 179 allowance. The bonus depreciation is $500 (($1,500 – $500) x 50%). Regular MACRS depreciation deductions are computed on $500 ($1,500 – $500 – $500). The regular first-year MACRS allowance is $100 ($500 x 20 percent (first-year table percentage)).

When Code Sec. 179 expensing is not elected for an asset that qualifies for 30 percent bonus depreciation, the bonus depreciation is taken off the top first, followed by regular MACRS depreciation.

> *Example.* Jane Smith purchases $100,000 of new machinery on January 17, 2003. Assume that the machinery is MACRS 5-year property, that the half-year convention applies, and that no amount is expensed under Code Sec. 179. Smith is entitled to deduct a $30,000 ($100,000 x 30 percent) special depreciation allowance. The depreciable basis of the property

is reduced to $70,000 ($100,000 – $30,000). Regular MACRS depreciation (using the table percentages for five-year property) would also allow a $14,000 MACRS deduction in 2003 ($70,000 x 20 percent). Thus, total bonus depreciation and regular MACRS depreciation taken in 2003 would be $34,000.

Raising bonus depreciation to 50 percent allows for heavier, "front loaded" deductions. While taking a deduction sooner rather than later is usually preferable, the taxpayer should realize that MACRS depreciation will be smaller as a result as the asset ages, creating less of an offset against income in future years.

Example. Assume in the above example that Smith purchases the machinery on May 15, 2003, instead. Smith's 2003 bonus depreciation deduction is $50,000 ($100,000 cost x 50 percent). Her MACRS depreciation would be recovered as follows:

Year	Deduction	
2003	Bonus depreciation	$ 50,000
2003	$50,000 x 20% =	10,000
2004	$50,000 x 32% =	16,000
2005	$50,000 x 19.20% =	9,600
2006	$50,000 x 11.52% =	5,760
2007	$50,000 x 11.52% =	5,760
2008	$50,000 x 5.76% =	2,880
		$ 100,000

The shorter the depreciable life of an asset, the faster the depreciation not only in the first year, but also in the second year when that year is compared to later years. This "rule of thumb" is made even more dramatic when an asset qualifies for 50 percent rather than 30 percent bonus depreciation.

Example. Three-year property costing $100,000 and subject to the half-year convention is purchased on May 1, 2003. The taxpayer claims 30 percent bonus depreciation. The combined first-year depreciation deduction and 30 percent bonus depreciation allowance is $53,331 ($100,000 x 53.331 percent). The second-year depreciation deduction is $31,115 ($100,000 x 31.115 percent). The third-year depreciation deduction is $10,367 ($100,000 x 10.367 percent). The fourth-year deduction is $5,187 ($100,000 x 5.187 percent).

Example. Three-year property costing $100,000 and subject to the half-year convention is purchased on May 7, 2003. The taxpayer claims the 50 percent bonus depreciation deduction. The combined first-year depreciation deduction and 50 percent bonus depreciation allowance is $66,665 ($100,000 x 66.665 percent). The second-year depreciation deduction is

$22,225 ($100,000 x 22.225 percent). The third-year depreciation deduction is $7,405 ($100,000 x 7.405 percent). The fourth-year deduction is $3,705 ($100,000 x 3.705 percent).

Practice Pointer. There is one last useful planning tip to consider. Assume a taxpayer purchases seven-year property early in the year and three-year property later in the year. Unless there is a business need to make the purchases in this order, the taxpayer should consider making the purchases in reverse order, especially if there is a chance that the mid-quarter convention might apply. By reversing the order of the purchases, the taxpayer will get the full benefit of the short recovery period of the three-year property, the full Section 179 expensing election on the seven-year property and avoid application of the mid-quarter convention.

STUDY QUESTIONS

11. For purposes of the bonus depreciation, qualifying property does not include:

    a. Computer software subject to a 15-year amortization under Code Sec. 197
    b. New MACRS property with a recovery period of 20 years or less
    c. Computer software that is depreciable under Code Sec. 167
    d. Qualified leasehold improvement property

12. On July 1, 2003, John Jones purchases qualifying 5-year MACRS property subject to the half-year convention for $1,500 and claims a $500 Section 179 allowance. The bonus depreciation is:

    a. $500
    b. $300
    c. $100
    d. $50

Coordination of Section 179 expensing and bonus depreciation

In planning the purchase of property to maximize tax savings, the following differences between Section 179 expensing and bonus depreciation should be remembered:

♦ The Section 179 expensing deduction, if taken, must reduce the asset's tax basis before the bonus depreciation percentage is applied;
♦ Section 179 expensing property may be used or new property, whereas qualified property for bonus depreciation purposes must be new;

- Unlike Section 179 expensing, there is no taxable income limitation or investment limitation on the bonus allowance; and
- The Section 179 expensing limit of $400,000 in total qualifying property before phaseout begins can be triggered by purchasing property that qualifies for bonus depreciation, regardless of whether part of the $100,000 expensing deduction is elected for the bonus property.

Special rule for "luxury" autos

In connection with the depreciation bonus, JCWAA increased the first-year cap under Code Sec. 280F for allowable depreciation on a business-use automobile by $4,600 for passenger vehicles that qualify for the bonus, raising the overall depreciation and expensing limit in 2002 to $7,650. JGTRRA again increased the first-year depreciation cap, to $10,710, in order to reflect the higher 50 percent bonus depreciation.

Impact on AMT

The depreciation bonus may be claimed for purposes of the alternative minimum tax (AMT) for the tax year in which the property is placed in service. Although the basis of the property and the depreciation allowances in the year of purchase and in later years need to be adjusted to reflect the additional first-year depreciation for regular tax purposes, these adjustments are not made for purposes of computing AMT.

Bonus depreciation is allowed in full for AMT purposes. If bonus depreciation is claimed, no AMT adjustment is required on the regular MACRS deductions (i.e., the deductions are allowed in full for AMT purposes).

Election out

The bonus depreciation must be claimed unless a taxpayer makes an election out. The election out is made at the property class level. This decision applies to all property in the class or classes for which the election out is made that is placed in service for the tax year of the election.

Form 4562 is generally used to claim the depreciation or amortization deduction and is attached to the taxpayer's tax return. A corporation (other than an S corp) claiming depreciation or amortization on any asset, regardless of when it was placed in service must file this form. Form 4562 indicates that the election out of bonus depreciation is made by attaching to the taxpayer's return a statement indicating the class of property for which the election not to claim bonus depreciation is made.

Practice Pointer. Taxpayers who anticipate being in a higher tax bracket in future years may want to consider making the election out of bonus depreciation or making the election to use the 30 percent rate rather than the 50 percent rate. This situation may occur, for example, if the taxpayer is using net operating loss (NOL) carryforwards to reduce taxable income in the year that bonus depreciation could be claimed.

The election out of bonus depreciation is made separately for each class of property that qualifies for the 30 percent rate and for each class of property that qualifies for the 50 percent rate. Thus, for example, a taxpayer may elect out of bonus depreciation with respect to one class of property that qualifies for 30 percent bonus depreciation but decide not to elect out of bonus depreciation for property in the same class that qualifies for bonus depreciation at the 50 percent rate.

Example. A calendar-year taxpayer places 10 machines in service in 2003 before May 6, 2003, and 5 cars in service in 2003 after May 5, 2003. The machines and cars are five-year property (same MACRS property class). The taxpayer may: (1) claim bonus depreciation on the machines (30 percent rate applies) and bonus depreciation on the cars (a 50 percent rate applies unless a 30 percent rate is elected); (2) elect not to claim bonus depreciation the machines and elect not to claim bonus depreciation on the cars; (3) claim bonus depreciation on the cars (at the 50 percent rate unless a 30 percent rate is elected) and elect not to claim bonus depreciation on the machines; or (4) elect not to claim bonus depreciation on the cars and claim bonus depreciation on the machines (30 percent rate applies).

STUDY QUESTIONS

13. The new bonus depreciation:

    a. Is not required to be claimed
    b. Does not apply to most businesses
    c. Will not further stimulate the economy
    d. Must be claimed

14. Who is required to file Form 4562?

    a. Corporate taxpayers
    b. Noncorporate taxpayers (including S corps)
    c. Corporate taxpayers and individual filers
    d. Partnerships

CONCLUSION

The decision whether to purchase a particular business asset, and when to time that purchase, has been compounded as never before by the tax law. Fortunately, the end result of these tax-driven factors, however, is largely positive. Tax savings that may be realized in working through these tax considerations may be able to "finance" a significant part of the asset's purchase price.

♦ If you can treat the purchase as an ordinary business expense under Code Sec. 162, it may be written off all in the year of purchase. If you are in the 35 percent tax bracket, for example, that is equivalent to getting back 35 percent of your purchase price immediately.

♦ If you must capitalize the asset, you still might be able to deduct its entire purchase price, up to $100,000, immediately through Section 179 expensing.

♦ If you can not use, or do not chose to use, Code Section 179 expensing for your capitalized purchase, you might be able to write off well over half of its purchase price in the first year anyway, through "bonus" depreciation, taken on top of, rather than in lieu of, regular first year depreciation.

Within each opportunity to write off all or part of the purchase price of a business asset "up front" rather than gradually over its life, is a decision tree. Sometimes foregoing a particular deduction makes better sense in the long run. Sometimes it does not, in whole or in part, or in combination with other benefits. In no circumstance, however, should a business do nothing unintentionally and let the IRS put its default rules into motion. The tax benefits from these temporary tax breaks are too rich to leave to chance.

CHAPTER 3: TECHNOLOGY AND TAXES—AN EVOLVING FRONTIER

Learning Objectives. This chapter was prepared to provide an overview of taxes associated with computer technology. More specifically, upon course completion, the taxpayer will be able to:

♦ Comprehend the basic differences between deductible expenses and capital expenditures as each relates to technology-related assets;

♦ Apply certain tax rules to determine the tax treatment of computer software, computer hardware, and web site development;

♦ Correctly account for technology-based deductions;

- ♦ Describe the changes in the law under the *Jobs and Growth Tax Relief Reconciliation Act of 2003* that specifically affect the tax treatment of computer technology;
- ♦ Understand how leased software is accounted for use in the taxpayer's trade or business;
- ♦ Become familiar with the treatment of software in Rev. Proc. 2000-50;
- ♦ List requirements for deducting donations of computer equipment and;
- ♦ Answer questions regarding tax issues for the telecommuting employee.

INTRODUCTION

Computer systems are virtually indispensable in a wide variety of businesses, from large businesses in the media spotlight to small businesses, including start-ups. Taxpayers who have expenditures associated with computers, software, and web site development need to be familiar with the tax ramifications of these expenditures. Such issues should be considered by executives and business owners as they decide to adopt more high-tech strategies.

Although technology here is examined as a unit, the tax treatment of technology-driven transactions is all over the board. A variety of Code sections may affect a single issue; technology issues as a unit span more than seven major Code provisions.

The 2003 Technology and Taxes chapter is intended for anyone who wishes to better comprehend the treatment of expenditures associated with computers, software, and web site development.

The chapter will review such areas as the basics of deductible expenses and capital expenditures, the methods to account for deductions, changes under the new tax law, the tax treatment of computer software, and the basic tax issues facing the telecommuting employee.

As for the business expenditures related to intangibles under the recently proposed regs, the Treasury Department and the IRS are just undertaking the process of modifying and refining the issues. Additional time will be needed in order for the government to determine the appropriate tax treatment of these expenditures.

WHY IS SOFTWARE UNIQUE?

Until recently, the IRS had a difficult time providing guidelines on the treatment of software costs. This issue has generally been settled in Rev. Proc. 2000-50. However, other key issues, for example, those associated with web site development, remain open for debate and are being considered by the Treasury Department and the IRS. There are also now some big changes to consider because of the *Jobs and Growth Tax Relief Reconciliation Act of 2003* (JGTRRA '03).

To capitalize or to expense

The decision involving when to capitalize or when to expense costs is also key for many businesses' high-tech budgets.

Forming part of this important equation are specific costs such as:

♦ Software development;
♦ Purchased software;
♦ Web site design and maintenance; and
♦ Research and experimentation.

These expenses should be considered right down to the details involved in completing IRS Form 4562, Depreciation and Amortization, which must provide the supporting documentation attached to the return.

Form 4562

Form 4562 is generally used to claim the depreciation or amortization deduction and is attached to the taxpayer's tax return. The form can be considered the "point of sale" in the sense that the business "sells" its position to the IRS on how its technology is written off largely through the data on Form 4562. A corporation (other than an S corp) claiming depreciation or amortization on any asset, regardless of when it was placed in service, must file this form.

Noncorporate taxpayers (including S corps) are not required to file Form 4562 for a current tax year unless they claim any of the following deductions: a depreciation or amortization deduction on an asset placed in service in the current tax year; a Code Sec. 179 expense deduction (including a carryover from a previous year); a depreciation deduction on any vehicle or other listed property (regardless of when the listed property was placed in service); or a deduction based on the standard mileage rate (which reflects an allowance for depreciation expense). With technology expenses becoming integral to most businesses, Form 4562 has become a necessary form to file annually by most noncorporate taxpayers as well.

> *Practice Pointer.* For an amortization deduction on property placed in service in the current tax year, required information includes the following: a description of the costs amortized, the date that the amortization period begins, the amortizable amount, the Code section under which amortization is claimed, the amortization period or percentage, and the amortization deduction for the year.

Companies also can use Form 4562 to reclassify costs associated with computers, software, and other technology on their tax returns. These costs are prepared in two different parts of the form.

> *Practice Pointer.* The election to expense long-term property is made on Part 1 of the form. Property placed in service during the year is set out in its proper depreciation category, and depreciation for property placed in service in prior tax years, which appears as one sum on the proper line. Items that are amortized appear at the bottom of the form, and questions regarding restricted property appear on Part 2 of this form.

STUDY QUESTION

1. Who is required to file Form 4562?

   a. Corporate taxpayers
   b. Noncorporate taxpayers (including S corps)
   c. Corporate taxpayers and individual filers
   d. Partnerships

Donation of equipment and software

At times a company's particular equipment and software are no longer needed or become obsolete. The business manager should consider making a charitable contribution as a "win-win" strategy that can benefit both the charity and the company's after-tax position. For corporations, this deduction is limited to 10 percent of taxable income. Some entities may not qualify for the deduction, such as social welfare organizations or agricultural organizations.

KEY POINTS OF LAW

The tax treatment of technology-related assets and costs in many ways has been driven by existing concepts developed years before personal computers, software and "the web" ever became indispensable business tools. Like the response to most innovation, existing principles have been applied in new circumstances. Only when these applications have not worked, or have needed adaptation to accommodate the specific nature of new technologies, has the tax law carved out special rules or exceptions.

The general tax law concepts described here are especially important in determining the tax treatment of computers, software, and similar business assets and expenses.

Deductible business expenses

A taxpayer — whether a corporation, an individual, or a partnership — generally may deduct from gross income the ordinary and necessary expenses of carrying on a trade or business that are paid or incurred in the tax year. This is the so-called "section 162 deduction," or "regular business expense deduction," named after its allowance in Code Sec. 162 of the IRC.

What is an ordinary expense? An ordinary expense is one that is common and accepted in a taxpayer's trade or business. In high-tech purchases, there is often considerable leeway on what is considered "ordinary" as far as price range is concerned. For example, a high-end laptop computer model ordinarily won't be questioned by the IRS as a reasonable expense as long as the business has a use for a computer of some sort and business profits (or expected profits) can justify purchasing a computer. In this situation the IRS concerns are where the taxpayer can substantiate the claim by a receipt and that the computer's use is not personal.

What is a necessary expense? A necessary expense is one that is helpful and appropriate for a taxpayer's trade or business. However, an immediate expense deduction is not permitted for any expenditure that is a capital expense. If it is a capital asset, it generally must be depreciated over the anticipated life of the asset.

> *Practice Pointer.* Generally, an individual cannot deduct personal, living, or family expenses. However, if an expense is for something used partly for business and partly for personal purposes, the taxpayer may divide the total costs between the business and personal parts. An individual usually can deduct as a business expense the business part. However, see below, for special rules for certain "listed" property (which includes personal computers) when personal use is the primary use (i.e., more than 50 percent).

Small business expensing. In lieu of depreciation (which will be discussed below), business taxpayers (pre-JGTRRA '03) could elect to immediately deduct under Code Sec. 179, rather than depreciate, up to $25,000 in qualified property placed in service for the year.

JGTRRA '03 boosts expensing to $100,000 and raises the phaseout threshold for all section 179-type purchases for the year from $200,000 to $400,000. Property placed in service in 2003, 2004, and 2005 will be eligible for the special treatment. For 2004 and 2005, the amounts are indexed for inflation.

> *Practice Pointer.* The increase in expensing for new investment should encourage small business owners to purchase technology, machinery, and other equipment for company expansion. The increase from $25,000 to $100,000 should boost compliance and ease recordkeeping burdens. Many small businesses thus will be able to avoid the inherent complexity of depreciation provisions.

How much can a taxpayer deduct? The taxpayer cannot deduct more for a business expense than the amount actually spent. There is usually no other limit on how much can eventually be deducted (either immediately, or over time as depreciation) if the amount is reasonable. However, if a taxpayer's deductions are large enough to produce a net business loss for the year, the tax loss may be limited.

STUDY QUESTIONS

2. An ordinary expense is defined as:

    a.   An expense that is helpful and appropriate for a trade or business
    b.   A capital expenditure
    c.   An expense that is common and accepted in a trade or business
    d.   A reasonable allowance of the exhaustion, wear and tear, and obsolescence on certain types of property used in a trade or business

3. A taxpayer ____ deduct more for a business expense than the amount you actually spend.

    a.   Cannot
    b.   May
    c.   Can always
    d.   Can usually

Capital expenditures

A company must capitalize an expense if it does not, or is not permitted to, deduct it. Those costs are a part of the investment in the business and are called "capital expenses." In general, there are three types of costs capitalized:

♦   Going into business;
♦   Business assets; and
♦   Improvements.

Going into business. These costs may include expenses for advertising, travel, or wages for training employees. If a taxpayer goes into business, all costs to get the business started are treated as capital expenses. The costs can be recovered through depreciation.

Business assets. The cost of any asset in a business is a capital expense. Business assets include machinery, furniture, trucks, and franchise rights. The full costs of the assets are capitalized, including freight and installation charges.

> *Practice Pointer:* Capital expenditures are those assets of a more or less permanent nature—those with useful lives of more than one year. Such expenditures may not be deducted

all at once in the year in which they are incurred, even though connected with a trade or business (the one exception is that if it qualifies for the section 179 expensing election discussed above. Capital expenditures, however, are usually subject to depreciation.

Improvements. The costs of making improvements to a business asset are classified as capital expenses if the improvements add to the value of the asset, appreciably lengthen the time it can be used, or adapt it to a different use. Repairs that keep property in a normal, efficient operating condition are treated as business expenses. That is, expenses that keep property in an ordinarily efficient operating condition and do not add to its value or appreciably prolong its useful life are generally deductible as repairs.

> ***Examples.*** Improvements include upgrading computer memory or keyboards. Repairs include virus elimination, fixing a fan or disk drive on a CPU, or maintaining a service contract.

STUDY QUESTIONS

4. Which of the following would be capitalized?

    a. Going into business costs
    b. Current business expenses
    c. Replacement costs
    d. Personal expenses

5. A taxpayer can take a current deduction for a:

    a. Capital expense
    b. A repair to maintain the operating condition of the property
    c. An improvement
    d. Expenses to get a business started

6. When a taxpayer goes into business, all costs incurred to get a business started are:

    a. Expensed
    b. Not amortized
    c. Capitalized
    d. Ignored

7. Capital expenditures are:

    a. Those with a useful life of more than one year
    b. Those with a useful life of less than one year
    c. Ignored when a taxpayer goes into business
    d. Associated with repairs

8. The cost of any business assets is:

a. A depreciable expense
b. A capital expense
c. Immediately expensed
d. Amortized

9. Improvements may include:

   a. Replacing a part
   b. Maintenance checks
   c. Repairs
   d. Installing a new roof

Deductions: Depreciation or amortization

Although a taxpayer cannot generally take a current deduction for a capital expense, he or she may be able to take deductions for the amount spent through depreciation (Code Sec. 167(a)) or amortization (Code Sec. 197). These rules allow a taxpayer to deduct part of his or her costs each year over a number of years and "recover" these capital expenses.

Depreciation. Depreciation is a reasonable allowance for the exhaustion, wear and tear, and obsolescence of certain types of property used in a trade or business or for the production of income. Depreciation may not be claimed until the property is placed in service for either the production of income or use in a trade or business.

Property is depreciable if it:

♦ Is used for business or held for the production of income;
♦ Has a determinable useful life exceeding one year; and
♦ Wears out, decays, becomes obsolete, or loses value from natural causes.

Assets with useful lives that do not exceed one year may be currently deducted as expenses (rather than depreciated) for the year in which their costs are incurred. Although assets with longer useful lives must be depreciated throughout those lives, depreciation deductions in the early years of use can often be much higher than in the later years, due to both accelerated depreciation and "bonus" first-year depreciation. Accelerated depreciation of most assets is governed under the "modified accelerated cost recovery system" ("MACRS").

Amortization. Amortization is the recovery of certain capital expenditures that are not ordinarily deductible, in a manner that is similar to straight-line depreciation. That portion of the basis of property that is recovered through amortization may not also be depreciated. The capitalization of most other intangibles is ratably amortized over a 15-year period (Code Sec. 197). Intangibles amortizable under this provision are referred to as "section 197 intangibles."

Summary List of General Internal Revenue Code Provisions Relevant to Technology-Driven Costs	
Code Sec. 162	Trade or business expenses
Code Sec. 167	Depreciation
Code Sec. 174	Research and experimentation expenditures
Code Sec. 179	Election to expense certain depreciable business assets
Code Sec. 195	Current deduction of investigatory, startup, preopening expenses
Code Sec. 195	Amortization of goodwill and certain other intangibles
Code Sec. 263	Capitalization of costs

STUDY QUESTIONS

10. Property is depreciable if it:

 a. Is used for business or held for the production of income
 b. Does not have a determinable useful life exceeding one year
 c. Does not wear out, decay, become obsolete, or lose value from natural causes
 d. Is currently deducted as an expense for the year in which its costs are incurred

11. Capital expenditures:

 a. Are usually currently deducted
 b. Are never currently deducted
 c. May be currently deducted
 d. Are associated with repairs

12. Code Sec. 162 addresses which of the following?

 a. Research and experimentation expenditures
 b. Capitalization of costs
 c. Trade or business expenses
 d. Treatment of costs of computer software

COMPUTERS AS LISTED PROPERTY

"List property" is subject to certain limitations. The Internal Revenue Code defines "listed property" to include any passenger automobile, any other property used as a means of transportation, any property of a type generally used for purposes of entertainment, recreation, or amusement, *any computer or peripheral equipment*, and any other property of a type specified by the IRS. From their association with the other items on the list, it is clear that "computers or peripheral equipment" are viewed as more susceptible than other business property to unwarranted deductions for personal use.

Fortunately, the listed property label only becomes an issue for computers if they are not used exclusively in business. Under Treasury regulations, neither listed entertainment property nor computer or peripheral equipment are considered listed property if used exclusively at the taxpayer's regular business establishment or in the taxpayer's principal trade or business.

Qualified business use generally requires that an asset be used in a trade or business by a taxpayer. The use of listed property in an investment or other activity conducted for the production of income does not constitute a qualified business use. Notwithstanding the general rule, there are several exceptions under which the use of listed property in a trade or business by 5-percent owners (owners of 5 percent or more of a business) or related parties does not constitute a qualified business use of the property. Qualified business use does not include:

- Leasing property to a 5-percent owner or related person;
- Use of property allowed as compensation for the performance of services by a 5-percent owner or related person; or
- Use of property allowed as compensation for the performance of services by any other person unless an amount is included in that person's gross income for that use and, where required, is subject to withholding.

LIST-PROPERTY RESTRICTIONS

If a computer or peripheral equipment falls into the category of "listed property," more rigorous substantiation rules are imposed and certain tax-benefit limitations may follow.

Substantiation. Treasury regulations require that a taxpayer must prove each of the following elements to substantiate a deduction for an expense relating to any item of listed property:

- The amount of the expenditure;
- The amount of use; and the amount of time the property was used for business purposes and in total;
- The date of the expenditure or use; and
- The business purpose of the expenditure or use of the listed property.

Depreciation limitations. Any listed property subject to depreciation under MACRS (the modified accelerated cost recovery system) that is not used more than 50 percent for business use must be depreciated under ADS (the alternative depreciation system, which is much slower), both for that year and for all subsequent years. ADS must continue to be used even if more than 50-percent business use of the property is resumed in a later year.

If the more than 50-percent business use test is not met in the year in which the property is placed in service, the taxpayer also cannot elect to expense any portion of the property under the Code Section 179 expensing rules that allow up to $100,000 of the cost of selected property to be written off in its first year of use.

Finally, the first-year bonus depreciation allowance (either 30-percent or 50-percent bonus depreciation) may not be claimed on a listed property that is used 50 percent or less for business purposes in the first tax year that it is placed in service. Mandatory ADS property is not eligible for bonus depreciation.

TREATMENT OF SPECIFIC TECHNOLOGY-BASED COSTS

Guidance on deduction and capitalization of expenditures

The IRS tinkers regularly with the rules on the issue of capitalization versus expensing. In part, this tweaking is a response to complaints by businesses and their tax advisors that the rules are too vague for taxpayers to discern which assets may be expensed or must be capitalized. At press time, proposed regs (Reg-125638-01) under Code Sec. 263(a) set forth the general principle that requires capitalization of amounts paid to acquire, create, or enhance intangible assets, which include computer software.

These proposed regulations also provide rules for determining the extent to which taxpayers must capitalize transaction costs that facilitate the acquisition, creation, or enhancement of intangible assets or that facilitate certain restructuring, reorganizations, and transactions involving the acquisition of capital. Final regulations are expected by the end of 2003 or early 2004.

Tax treatment of computers: Hardware

Hardware refers to physical equipment, which includes the computer itself and related peripheral equipment designed to be placed under the control of the computer's central processing unit. Currently, there is a distinction between stand-alone computers and computers used as an integral part of technology.

For tax purposes, expenditures associated with stand-alone computers (the purchase of computers and related hardware) are depreciated over five years under MACRS. In contrast, computers used as an integral part of other equipment (or a system) are depreciated on a composite basis as part of the underlying asset. Their costs generally are recovered over 5, 7, 10, or more years.

Practice Pointer. Each item of property depreciated under MACRS is assigned to a property class, which establishes the number of years during which the basis of an asset is recovered (the recovery period). Recovery years are 12-month periods. The 12-month period begins on the date that the property is considered placed in service under the applicable convention.

Example: If a computer with a five-year recovery period is placed in service in the 2001 calendar tax year and the half-year convention applies, the recovery period begins on July 1, 2001 and ends on June 30, 2006. Depreciation is claimed in each of six tax years (2001, 2002, 2003, 2004, 2005, and 2006).

Payments to rent a computer. Payments to rent a computer or to lease Internet server space from an Internet service provider should be currently deductible if they constitute ordinary and necessary business expenses.

Tax treatment of computers: Software

Computer software is defined broadly to include:

♦ Any program designed to cause a computer to perform a desired function;
♦ All programs or routines used to cause a computer to perform a desired task or set of tasks; and
♦ The documentation required to describe and maintain those programs.

Software also includes all forms and media in which the software is contained, whether written, magnetic, or other. Included is computer software of all classes, for example, operating systems, executive systems, monitors, compilers, and translators. It does not include procedures that are external to computer operations.

Depreciable property. Generally, real property, personal property, and intangible property (not subject to a 15-year amortization) are depreciable only if the property: (1) is used in a trade or business or held for the production of income, and (2) is not inventory or stock in trade.

Computer software that is not an amortizable Code Sec. 197 intangible is depreciated using the straight-line method over a three-year period beginning on the first day of the month that the software is placed in service.

Practice Pointer. Computer software is considered a Code Sec. 197 intangible only if acquired in a transaction involving the acquisition of assets constituting a trade or business. Therefore, computer software acquired, developed, leased, or licensed in connection with the acquisition of assets that constitute a trade or business or a substantial portion of a trade or business may be a Code Sec. 197 intangible and required to be amortized over 15 years.

Practice Pointer. Computer software that is readily available for purchase by the general public, is subject to a nonexclusive license, and has not been substantially modified is not a Code Sec. 197 intangible even if acquired in connection with the acquisition of a trade or business.

If a depreciation deduction is allowable under Code Sec. 167(a) for computer software, the deduction is computed by using the straight-line method and a useful life of 36 months. A 30 percent additional first-year depreciation bonus (see the discussion below about application of the 50 percent bonus under JGTRRA '03) is available for depreciable software that is "qualified property."

If the costs for developing computer software that the taxpayer has elected to treat as deferred expenses under Code Sec. 174(b) result in the development of property subject to the allowance for depreciation, the 36-month amortization rule applies to the unrecovered costs. The 36-month amortization rule also applies to the costs of separately acquired software when the costs are separately stated and the costs must be capitalized. If computer software costs are included, without being separately stated, in the cost of the hardware or other tangible property, it is treated as part of the cost of the hardware or other tangible property.

Practice Pointer. A program loaded onto a computer and included in the price of the computer without being separately itemized, is depreciated as part of the cost of the computer.

Additional first-year depreciation allowance. For property acquired between September 11, 2002, and May 5, 2003, a taxpayer may claim an additional first-year depreciation allowance. The additional allowance is equal to 30 percent of the adjusted basis of the property.

Now under JGTRRA '03, the bonus depreciation jumps to 50 percent for property acquired after May 5, 2003, and before January 1, 2005. Property does not qualify for 50 percent bonus depreciation if a binding written sales contract was in effect before May 6, 2003. The bonus continues to apply in addition to the regular depreciation (as has been the case with the 30 percent bonus depreciation). Taxpayers may elect out of the additional first-year depreciation.

Practice Pointer. The 50-percent bonus is automatic unless the taxpayer opts out. In addition, the 50-percent first-year bonus is not on top of the 30-percent bonus.

Development costs. Depreciable programs developed by a taxpayer are treated in a manner similar to that of research and development expenses under Code Sec. 174.

They may be either:

♦ Deducted as a current expense; or
♦ Capitalized and amortized using the straight-line method over a period of three years beginning in the month the software is placed in service if a Code Sec. 174(b) election is made.

> *Practice Pointer.* Code Sec. 174 allows a taxpayer to currently deduct qualifying research or experimental expenses (R&D expenses) incurred during the year in connection with a trade or business. The Supreme Court has expanded the "trade or business" requirement so that it applies not only to on-going or established businesses but also to new businesses despite the fact that no trade or business is being conducted at the time the R&D expenses were incurred. This rule is tempered by a requirement that there be a realistic prospect that the taxpayer will later enter into a trade or business using the technology developed.

For development costs that are not treated as current expenses under Code Sec. 174(a), the amortization period can be 60 months from the date of completion of the development or 36 months from the date the software is placed in service. These rules apply to developed computer software even it is patented or copyrighted and regardless of whether it is used by the taxpayer or held for sale or lease to others.

Deductible expenses include telephone, promotion, and transportation expenses incurred in developing a computer-monitoring program. Alternatively, the taxpayer may treat these costs as capital expenditures that are recoverable through ratable amortization under rules similar to those relating to the amortization of research and experimental expenses under Code Sec. 174. (See the discussion under Rev. Proc. 2000-50.)

> *Observation.* Computer software with a useful life of less than one year is currently deductible as a business expense. A deduction is also allowed for rental payments made for software leased for use in a trade or business.

Purchased software. The treatment of purchased computer software depends on whether its costs are separately stated. If the costs are included in the cost of computer hardware without being separately itemized, the costs are treated as part of the cost of the computer hardware and are depreciated over the useful life of the computer hardware.

Regulations provide that the capitalized cost of separately acquired computer software is depreciated on a straight-line basis over 36 months if the costs are separately stated from the hardware. Under guidelines issued before the enactment of Code Sec. 167(f)(1), if the costs of the computer software are separately itemized, the costs are amortized ratably over a five-year period or any shorter period that the taxpayer can establish as the software's useful life.

Computer software is considered purchased if the software is custom made for a taxpayer and the developing party is responsible for its operation. However, computer software is considered to be self-developed if the taxpayer bears the risk of the functional utility of the software.

> **Observation.** Computer software includes all programs or routines used to cause a computer to perform a desired task or set of tasks, and the documentation required to describe and maintain those programs. It includes all forms and media in which the software is contained, whether written, magnetic, or other. It does not include procedures that are external to computer operations.

Leased software. When a taxpayer leases or licenses computer software for use in the taxpayer's trade or business, rental payments for leased software are generally deductible as business expenses throughout the term of the lease in the same manner as any other rental payments.

STUDY QUESTIONS

13. Which of the following statements is correct?

    a. Payments to rent a computer should be capitalized if they constitute ordinary and necessary business expenses.

    b. Payments to rent a computer should be depreciated if they constitute ordinary and necessary business expenses.

    c. Payments to rent a computer should be currently deductible if they constitute ordinary and necessary business expenses.

    d. Payments to rent a computer should never be depreciated if they constitute ordinary and necessary business expenses.

14. For costs associated with software that is developed that are *not* treated as current expenses, the amortization can be:

    a. 30 months from the date of completion of the development

    b. 60 months from the date of completion of the development

    c. 30 months from the date the software is placed in service *d.*   5 months from the date the software is placed in service

Acquired versus developed software issues pending under proposed regulation

On January 24, 2002, the IRS and Treasury Department published an advance notice of proposed rulemaking (ANPRM) announcing the department's intention to provide guidance without addressing software costs. The ANPRM requested public comment on the rules and principles that should apply to distinguish *acquired* software from *developed* software. As mentioned above, under existing law, costs to *acquire* software are capitalized and may be amortized over 36 months or in some cases 15 years. On the other hand, costs to *develop* software may be deducted in accordance with Rev. Proc. 2000-50.

The determination of whether software is developed or acquired is a factual inquiry that depends on an analysis of the activities performed by the various parties to the software transaction. Although a few commentators identified factors that help to distinguish acquired software from developed software, they suggested that this issue should be addressed in separate guidance and not in the proposed regs.

Many experts suggested that the proposed regs should provide guidance concerning the treatment of costs to implement *acquired* software. For example, they noted that issues often arise regarding the extent to which Code Sec. 263(a) requires capitalization of costs to implement Enterprise Resource Planning (ERP) software. ERP software is an enterprise-wide database software system that integrates business functions such as financial accounting, sales and distribution, materials management, and production planning. Implementation of an ERP system may take several years and usually involves various categories of costs.

WEB SITE DESIGN AND MAINTENANCE

When a business is purchased, created, or expanded, many intangible assets are acquired or enhanced. Intangible assets may arise:

- By a purchase from an unrelated person;
- From the creation of a new business (brick-and-mortar expansion into e-commerce via a web site);
- Out of a project, such as software development; or
- As a by-product of ordinary business operations.

The IRS has not issued formal guidance on the treatment of web site development costs. However, informal internal IRS guidance suggests that an appropriate approach is to treat these costs like ones for software and depreciate them over three years.

Treatment of software: Rev. Proc. 2000-50

In Rev. Proc. 2000-50, the IRS allows taxpayers to treat software development costs in a manner similar to that of Code Sec. 174. The guidance, which covers the costs of developing, acquiring, leasing or licensing computer software, is consistent with the final regs issued January 25, 2000, and supersedes Rev. Proc. 69-21.

> *Practice Pointer.* The revenue procedure does not apply to any computer software that is subject to amortization as an "amortizable Code Sec. 197 intangible" as defined in Code Sec. 197 and the regs thereunder, or to costs that a taxpayer has treated as a research and experimentation expenditure under Code Sec. 174. However, under the exclusion from Code Sec. 197 for self-created property, the costs of developing software generally won't be subject to Code Sec. 197 unless the software is developed for the taxpayer in connection with the taxpayer's acquisition of a trade or business.

> *Practice Pointer.* Rev. Proc. 2000-50 is a safe harbor, not a set of limitations on how taxpayers can treat computer software costs.

Research and experimentation expenditure costs are reasonable costs incurred in a trade or business for activities intended to provide information that would eliminate uncertainty about the development or improvement of a product. Uncertainty exists if the information available does not establish how to develop or improve a product or the appropriate design of a product.

Whether costs qualify as research and experimental costs depends on the nature of the activity to which the costs relate rather than on the nature of the product or improvement being developed or the level of technological advancement.

The term "product" includes any of the following:

♦ Formula;
♦ Invention;
♦ Patent;
♦ Pilot model;
♦ Process;
♦ Technique; or
♦ Property similar to the previous items.

It also includes products used in trade or business or held for sale, lease, or license.

Costs not included. Research and experimental costs do not include expenses for any of the following activities:

- Advertising and promotions;
- Consumer surveys;
- Management studies;
- Quality control testing;
- Research in connection with literary, historical, or similar projects; or
- The acquisition of another's patent, model, production, or process.

When and how to choose. A taxpayer makes the choice to deduct research and experimental costs on the tax return for the year in which he or she first paid or incurred research and experimental costs. If the election to deduct is not in the first year, the costs can be deducted in a later year only with approval from the IRS.

The distinction between software development costs qualifying as Code Sec. 174 expenses or ones being handled under the rules that are "similar to" those of Code Sec. 174 is significant. This is because only software development costs that actually meet the requirements of Code Sec. 174 can be considered for the R&E credit under Code Sec. 41 (research credits). Moreover, Code Sec. 174 costs incurred during a company's startup period are usually deductible and not subject to Code Sec. 195. Code Sec. 174 costs do not cover expenditures for the acquisition or improvement of depreciable property. These costs must be capitalized.

> *Practice Pointer:* The cost of acquiring a computer must be capitalized, even if it if is intended for use in software development. The cost of acquisition can be expensed under the rules for cost recovery.

Costs of web site software development are ordinarily capitalized under Code Sec. 263. Capitalized software costs are amortized over 36 months, starting in the year in which the software was placed in service. Notwithstanding this rule, taxpayers can elect to currently deduct these costs. As mentioned, development costs that are R&E expenditures under Code Sec. 174 are deductible currently. Even if software development costs do not meet the requirements of Code Sec. 174, Rev. Proc. 2000-50 says that they can be accounted for under rules similar to those of Code Sec. 174 (deducted or capitalized).

CHARITABLE CONTRIBUTIONS: COMPUTER EQUIPMENT DEDUCTION FOR CORPORATIONS

Generally, corporations are entitled to deductions for qualified contributions of inventory and property. Code Sec. 170(e)(6) allows a special enhanced corporate deduction for charitable contributions of qualified computer technology or equipment to elementary or secondary schools, to a Code Sec. 501(c)(3) organization devoted primarily to supporting elementary and/or secondary education, and to public libraries.

> *Note.* The term "computer technology and equipment" is defined as computer software, computers and peripherals, and fiber optic cable for computer use.

For the donation to qualify for the deduction, it must be donated for one of the uses just listed and must consist of new or used (original use by donee or donor) computers or computer technology that is not more than three years old and that fits into the donee's education plan.

The donee must furnish the donor a statement that substantially all of the property's use will be for K–12 education within the United States and that the property is not transferred for anything beyond costs of shipment and installation.

> *Example.* ABC, Inc., donates 20 new computers (fair market value = $50,000, basis = $32,000) to Lincoln High School for use in its curriculum. ABC's charitable contribution is $41,000 ($50,000 less $9,000 (18,000 × 50 percent)).

> *Observation.* Charitable contributions not allowed in the current tax year may be carried forward for five years and applied, after the current year's contributions, in time order (oldest first). Carryback of charitable contributions is not allowed.

TAX ISSUES FOR THE TELECOMMUTING EMPLOYEE

Cost savings, safety (since the 9/11 terrorist attacks), and convenience are just some of the reasons that more employees are telecommuting full- or part-time out of their homes. The phenomenon raises a number of tax considerations for employees and employers alike.

Home-office issues

One primary question is whether the employee may deduct the direct and indirect expenses of his or her home office (the space he or she uses for employment-related work).

> *Observation.* Direct expenses relate only to the home office, such as the cost of painting the room where the home office is located. Indirect expenses relate both to the personal portion of the home and the business-use portion (the home office). These expenses include items such as utilities, real estate taxes, home mortgage interest, and rent or depreciation.

Direct expenses and the business-use part of the indirect expenses relating to a home office within a residence are deductible only if part of the home is used regularly and exclusively as (1) a principal place of business, or (2) as a place to meet or deal with customers or clients in the ordinary course of business.

> *Practice Pointer.* For the home to be considered the principal place of business, the following criteria must be met: (1) the office must be used exclusively and regularly for administrative or management activities of the trade or business; (2) there must be no other fixed location where substantial administrative or management activities of the trade or business can be conducted.

If these qualifications are met, and gross income from the business use of a taxpayer's home equals or exceeds total business expenses (including depreciation), all expenses for the business use of the home can be deducted by the employee on Schedule A as a miscellaneous itemized deduction subject to the 2-percent-of AGI limit. If the taxpayer's gross income is less than total business expenses, then home office deductions are limited to the excess of the gross income derived from business use of the home over the sum of:

- The deductions allocable to business use that are allowable whether or not the dwelling unit was so used; and
- The deduction allocable to the business activity in which business use of the home occurs, but which is not allocable to business use of the home.

Taxpayers/employees must meet an additional test. Use of the home office must be for the convenience of the employer. This "convenience of the employer test" is met if the employer asks the employee to work out of the home, or if he or she is not in the office on a regular basis because of the nature of the job. Generally, if the employee asks the employer to telecommute instead of working at the office, this test probably won't be met.

Deductions qualify under Code Sec. 280A only if the home office is used regularly and exclusively as the employee's principal place of business. This test is met where the employee telecommutes full-time.

Transportation expenses

If a taxpayer's principal place of business, as defined under Code Sec. 280A, is in his or her residence, daily transportation expenses between the office in the taxpayer's residence and other work locations related to the same business are deductible. Thus, a telecommuting employee whose home office is his or her principal place of business may deduct the costs of round-trip travel from home to the employer's offices (such as to attend meetings).

Computer and related equipment

An employer that supplies a telecommuting employee with a computer used 100 percent for business will deduct it just as if the machine were located in the company's office. That rule also applies for related equipment, such as a printer or copier.

If the telecommuting employee buys a computer for employment-related use, he or she can depreciate it (or expense it under Code Sec. 179) only if it is required as a condition of employment and is used for the convenience of the employer.

Employment-related business telephone calls

A taxpayer can't deduct any charge (including taxes) for basic local telephone service with respect to the first telephone line provided to any of the taxpayer's residences.

However, long distance business phone calls on the first or second telephone line, as well as the cost of a second line used exclusively for business, are deductible business expenses even if the taxpayer doesn't qualify for the home-office deduction. For employees, the deduction is a miscellaneous itemized deduction subject to the 2-percent-of-AGI floor.

Reimbursed expenses related to telecommuting

An employer may supply a telecommuting employee with office supplies and equipment or it may reimburse him or her for these expenses as well as for some or all of the utilities and maintenance expenses allocable to the home office. Employer-provided property and services qualify as tax-free working condition fringe benefits only if the employee would be entitled to a business expense deduction under Code Sec. 162 or Code Sec. 167 for the items that the employee had paid for.

CONCLUSION

There are myriad expenditures associated with computers, software, and web site development. The treatment of these costs remains a bit murky, as the rules continue to develop. Until recently, the IRS had a difficult time providing guidelines on the treatment of software costs. Some of these issues have been settled in Rev. Proc. 2000-50. However, costs associated with web site development still remain open for debate, and revised rules are being considered by the Treasury Department and the IRS. In fact, it is precisely because of the unsettled aspects under which "old" tax code provisions, enacted before the technological revolution, are applied to new technologies that the concepts presented in this discussion have become so critical.

An understanding of the specific nature of tax issues for software development costs, purchased software, web site design and maintenance expenses, and research and experimentation costs has become important to almost any business in which computers, software, and the web have become essential. Also critical to maximizing tax benefits—and minimizing tax mistakes on which hefty penalties may be assessed—is how expenses are applied on IRS Form 4562, the destination at which most planning and positions taken on technology-based costs eventually must arrive.

CHAPTER 4: TAX SHELTERS—ENFORCEMENT A PRIORITY

Learning Objectives. This chapter was prepared to provide guidance for practitioners about current objectives and activities of the IRS in combating tax shelter abuses. Upon completion of this chapter, you will be able to:

♦ Discuss current tax shelter enforcement strategies embraced by the IRS and Treasury Department;

♦ Identify the various tax shelter transactions as described in the recent final tax shelter regulations and note their exceptions;

♦ Generally understand that there are disclosure, registration, and list maintenance requirements imposed on tax shelter promoters and advisors for tax shelters;

♦ Be familiar with the types of IRS programs and initiatives aimed at aiding taxpayers as they return to compliance;

♦ Understand that the IRS has the power to obtain information on tax shelter transactions and participation and that the use of this power has significant consequences for the tax practitioner privilege;

♦ Prepare for the IRS plans to continually add additional types to its list of abusive transactions by issuing public guidance;

♦ Identify listed transactions as discussed under current published guidance;

♦ List the garden variety tax shelter scams aimed at less sophisticated taxpayers; and

♦ Realize that tax shelter abuses are a high governmental priority and that lawmakers are planning to implement additional legislation to shore up compliance.

INTRODUCTION

Although 2002 proved to be a turning point in the government's pursuit of tax shelter abuses due to shifts in policy, 2003 revealed that the IRS's battle has just begun and that there are many challenges that need to be faced and shrinking resources with which to accomplish them. The IRS appears to be besieged on all sides. Lawmakers are crying out for enhanced enforcement and compliance and swifter modernization efforts. Taxpayers are demanding better service, more guidance, and simpler tax rules. And the administration is faced with record budget deficits and a poor economic recovery.

Combating tax shelter abuses, from the government's perspective, represents a means by which many of the foregoing can be addressed, so pursuing such abuses has been deemed a high priority by Congress, the IRS, and the administration. Cracking down on tax shelters boosts tax revenue, improves compliance, shores up confidence and belief that the tax system works and is fair, and may ultimately free up resources. To accomplish these goals, the IRS and Treasury Department announced a strategic approach early in the spring of 2003. It has three broad foundations, outlined here.

Flushing out investors and promoters

The first foundation involves taking actions to reduce taxpayers' willingness to invest in abusive tax shelters by reducing the incentive to "play the audit lottery." Such actions involve increasing the disclosure requirements for taxpayers and promoters and opening up the doors to access and identify tax shelter participants from various sources. These resources include an examination of promoter compliance with tax shelter registration and investor list maintenance requirements, disclosures made by taxpayers under disclosure initiatives, and taxpayer returns.

Early interdiction

The second foundation concerns the identification and analysis of tax shelter transactions as they are marketed to taxpayers early in the process and issue public guidance expressing the Service's view of the transaction. In the IRS's view, the issuance of published guidance early in the process puts taxpayers and promoters on notice and should discourage potential investors from participating in the scheme. By deterring participants, the IRS hopes it will be able to free up resources to focus on those taxpayers and promoters who are already engaged in the transaction. The IRS has warned that the failure to put forth a position does not indicate that a particular type of deal is legitimate, but that such failure may only indicate that the Service is either not yet aware of the arrangement or is still gathering information to conduct an analysis.

Vigorous enforcement efforts

The final foundation hinges on enforcement efforts, such as the issuance of summonses to gather information or initiating targeted litigation aimed at stripping a transaction of its tax benefits. To aid in this endeavor, the Service is using information garnered from promoter audits, taxpayer returns, voluntary disclosures, and other sources to further identify taxpayers and issues for audit purposes.

These issues are then resolved through settlement, litigation or concession.

NEW REGULATIONS

The true key to the IRS's efforts to combat abusive tax shelters lies in its ability to persuade and/or force taxpayers to disclose their participation in such schemes without resorting to costly litigation. Former rules regarding disclosure were subjective and ill-defined, often leaving it to the taxpayer's discretion whether disclosure would be appropriate. Without meaningful guidance, previous enforcement and disclosure efforts proved only mildly successful. Now, the Treasury Department and the IRS have taken serious aim at ensuring that taxpayers and their advisors have a meaningful framework in order to properly address tax shelter issues.

The new tax shelter regulations, proposed in late 2002, were finalized in March of 2003. Yet although they will undoubtedly prove an effective set of rules to aid in providing guidance, the IRS and Treasury have made it quite well known that there will be additional guidance issued to taxpayers as novel issues arise. Taxpayers and their advisors had complained that the old rules were complex and unnecessarily broad. The new tax shelter regulations address those complaints—with mixed success.

Categories of reportable transactions

A complex "projected tax effect" test for reportable transactions has been removed and in its place are six new inclusive categories of reportable transactions. Although reportable transactions are more narrowly defined, the new regs also cast a wider net by providing that indirect participants, as well as direct participants in abusive shelters, now must comply with the disclosure rules.

Reportable transactions, now defined under Reg. 1.6011-4(b), comprise six categories:

1. Listed transactions (identified by the IRS as tax avoidance transactions);

2. Transactions marketed under conditions of confidentiality;

3. Transactions with contractual protection;

4. Transactions generating a tax loss (under Code Sec. 165) exceeding specified amounts (and those from assets with a qualifying basis);

5. Transactions resulting in a book–tax difference exceeding $10 million (this only applies to corporations); and

6. Transactions generating a tax credit when the underlying asset is held for a brief period of time (45 days).

Any such transaction must be reported on Form 8886, "Reportable Transaction Disclosure Statement," for each taxable year that the taxpayer's federal income tax liability is affected by the transaction.

In addition, taxpayers who have participated in a transaction subject to disclosure are required to retain all marketing, tax advice, or analysis documents, including correspondence for three years (six years for gross income understatements) commencing from the final year the disclosure was required.

Listed transaction. A listed transaction is the "same or substantially similar to one of the transactions" that the IRS has determined to be a tax avoidance transaction and identified by notice, reg, or other form of published guidance. A transaction that is "substantially similar" is one that is expected to obtain the same or similar type of tax benefit and is based on the same or similar type of tax strategy.

STUDY QUESTION

1. A "listed transaction" is defined as:

    a. A transaction that is identical to a list of transactions published quarterly along with the IRS guidance plan

    b. A transaction in which the taxpayer confesses to his/her participation in an abusive tax shelter transaction

    c. Any transaction in which a taxpayer receives a tax benefit greater than $2,500 that cannot be substantiated

    d. Any transaction that is the same or similar to any transaction that the IRS determines to be a tax avoidance transaction as identified by notice, regulation or any other form of published guidance

Confidential transaction. A confidential transaction is a transaction offered under conditions of confidentiality. All the facts and circumstances relating to the transaction will be considered when the IRS determines whether a transaction is offered under conditions of confidentiality, including the prior conduct of the parties. Generally, if disclosure of the transaction is limited in any way, by an express or implied understanding between the taxpayer and the tax advisor, the transaction is considered confidential.

Exceptions include

♦ Security law disclosure restrictions, which are generally not a condition of confidentiality; and

♦ Certain tax free acquisitions, which are not confidential if a taxpayer is permitted to disclose the tax treatment and structure at the earliest of the time the transaction or acquisition discussions are made public or the agreement is executed

A transaction is presumed nonconfidential if the tax advisor provides unlimited written authorization to the taxpayer permitting disclosure to any person of the tax structure and aspects of the transaction, including all

Transactions with contractual protections. Transactions with contractual protections include those for which a taxpayer was given a contractual protection against the possibility that part or all of the intended tax consequences will not be sustained. Contractual protections are generally found when there was a contingent fee arrangement or rights to a full or partial refund of fees.

Loss transaction. A loss transaction is any transaction resulting in, or that is reasonably expected to result in, a loss under Code Sec. 165 of at least:

- ♦ $10 million in any single taxable year or $20 million in any combination of taxable years for corporations;
- ♦ $5 million in any single taxable year or $10 million in any combination of taxable years for partnerships or S corps, whether or not any losses flow through to one or more partners or shareholders;
- ♦ $2 million in any single taxable year or $4 million in any combination of taxable years for individuals or trusts, whether or not any losses flow through to one or more beneficiaries; and
- ♦ $50,000 in any single taxable year for individuals or trusts, whether or not the loss flows through from an S corporation or partnership, if the loss arises with respect to a Code Sec. 988 transaction.

Simultaneous to issuing the regs, the IRS issued Rev. Proc. 2003-24 to further explain the loss transaction exception as it related to specific transactions. In that procedure, the IRS determined that both losses from the sale or exchange of an asset with a "qualifying basis" (as defined in the procedure) or various "other losses" will not be taken into account in determining whether a transaction is a loss transaction. "Other losses" for this purpose includes those generated from situations not likely to be planned as tax shelters, such as casualty losses, involuntary conversions, mark-to-market losses, basis increases, losses resulting from hedging transactions, or abandonment losses.

STUDY QUESTIONS

2. A reportable loss transaction includes a transaction that generates a:

    a. $10 million loss in any single taxable year for General Electric *b.* $3 million loss in any combination of taxable years for George Bush

    c. $4 million loss in a single taxable year for a limited partnership

    d. $25,000 loss in a single taxable year for an individual if the loss arises with respect to a Code Sec. 988 transaction.

3.   All of the following are losses that are not to be taken into account under Rev. Proc. 2003-24 *except:*

    a.   Losses attributable to basis increases

    b.   Losses resulting from compulsory or involuntary conversions

    c.   Losses resulting from the sale of an asset that lacks a qualifying basis

    d.   Losses arising from any mark-to-market treatment of an item

Book–tax difference. A transaction with significant book-tax difference is one in which the treatment for federal income tax purposes of any item or items from the transaction differs, or is expected to differ, by more than $10 million on a gross basis from the treatment of the item or items for book purposes in any taxable year. When the taxpayer makes this calculation, offsetting items are not netted for either tax or book purposes. This provision generally only applies to reporting companies under the Securities and Exchange Act, related businesses, or businesses with $250 million or more of gross assets. There are a few special rules worth noting:

♦   Transactions between members of an affiliated group are disregarded;

♦   Only U.S. assets shall be taken into account for purposes of the gross asset test; and

♦   Items arising from transactions between an entity and its owner shall be disregarded.

A transaction with a significant book-tax difference is one in which the amount for tax purposes of any item of income, gain, expense, or loss from the transaction differs by more than $10 million on a gross basis from the amount of the item for book-tax purposes in any taxable year.

Supplementing this rule as set forth in the regs, Rev. Proc. 2003-25 listed more than a dozen book-tax differences that were not to be taken into account in determining whether a transaction is a reportable transaction for purposes of the disclosure rules. These differences include, for example:

- Depreciation, depletion, and amortization relating solely to differences in methods, lives or conventions as well as differences, including Code Sec 481 adjustments;
- Percentage depletion and intangible drilling costs deductible;
- Capitalization and amortization;
- Bad debts or cancellation of indebtedness income;
- Federal, state, local, and foreign taxes;
- Compensation of employees and independent contractors, including stock options and pensions; and
- Charitable contributions of cash or tangible property.

STUDY QUESTION

4. All of the following are book–tax differences that are not to be taken into account under Rev. Proc. 2003-25 *except:*

    a. Code Sec. 481 adjustments
    b. Capitalization and amortization
    c. Sales generating losses from hedging transactions
    d. Charitable contributions of cash or tangible property

Transaction having brief asset holding period. A transaction involving a brief asset holding period is one resulting in, or that is expected to result in, a tax credit exceeding $250,000 if the underlying asset, giving rise to the credit, is held by the taxpayer for fewer than 45 days.

> *Observation.* Regulated investment companies (RICs) or investment vehicles owned 95 percent by RICs and leasing transactions exempt from the registration requirements under Code Sec 6111(d) and the list maintenance requirements under Code Sec. 6112 are both excluded from reporting confidential transactions, contractual protections, loss transactions, book-tax differences, and brief-asset holding period transactions.

STUDY QUESTIONS

5. Which of the following is *not* a reportable transaction?

    a. A transaction with contractual protections
    b. A transaction marketed under conditions of confidentiality
    c. A transaction involving a producer owned reinsurance company
    d. A transaction that generated a Code Sec 165 loss of $1.5 million in a single taxable year for a trust

6. A transaction is reportable if it generates a _____ tax credit where the underlying asset has been held for _____ or fewer days.

a. $250,000; 60
b. $250,000; 45
c. $100,000; 30
d. $250,000; 180

Registration

Code Sec. 6111 requires that all tax shelters be registered with the IRS by the tax promoter on or before offering them for sale. The definition of tax shelter has been expanded to include "confidential corporate tax shelters." These are tax shelter transactions for which:

♦ A significant purpose of the transaction is to avoid or evade tax. Two types of transactions are considered to have as their purpose tax avoidance: listed transactions and tax-structured transactions;

♦ The transactions were offered under conditions of confidentiality; and

♦ An aggregate minimum fee of $100,000 for the transactions and all substantially similar transactions was received by the promoter.

The registration requirements apply to tax shelter promoters. A promoter is any party who was principally responsible for or participated in the organization, management, or sale of a tax shelter, and any related parties under Code Sec. 267 or 707.

Promoters register tax shelters by using Form 8264, "Application for Registration of a Tax Shelter." Failing to register the transaction may result in the imposition of civil and/or criminal penalties.

List maintenance

Under Code Sec. 6112, each organizer and seller of a potentially abusive tax shelter transaction must prepare and maintain a list of participants, which must be turned over the IRS upon request. Organizers and sellers fall under the category of "material advisors" which is discussed in more detail below.

CURRENT ENFORCEMENT PROGRAMS

The IRS has tried to leave little to chance in its enforcement efforts against abusive tax shelters. The Service uses the carrot, the stick, and methods in-between. Even critics admit that the IRS's multipronged tax shelter programs have been intelligently developed.

> *Observation.* One major shortcoming is that the IRS continues to operate under limited resources—not enough trained personnel and not enough dollars to fully develop each program to its potential.

Voluntary offshore compliance initiative

In mid-January of 2003 the IRS announced an amnesty program aimed at encouraging participants in abusive tax shelters to come forward and disclose their participation. The Offshore Voluntary Compliance Initiative (OVCI) allowed taxpayers involved in offshore financial or payment card arrangements to disclose participation on or by April 15 in exchange for amnesty from criminal prosecution and the imposition of the civil fraud penalty, though participants were still subject to back taxes, interest, and certain accuracy- and delinquency-related penalties. However, solicitors and promoters of such arrangements were ineligible for OVCI participation. In addition, taxpayers would lose eligibility if they failed to disclose participation before the IRS discovered it. The Service hoped that this type of arrangement would encourage taxpayers to rush into the protection of the IRS before the amnesty was lost.

Tax shelter toolkits

To aid taxpayers in getting back into compliance with the tax laws, the IRS offers two types of tax shelter toolkits. The first toolkit addresses abusive tax evasion trust schemes and the other concerns scheme involving transactions that take place offshore avoidance. Both kits provide detailed outlines describing suspect transactions and the procedures that are to be followed in order to correct them and can be accessed on the IRS website.

Abusive trust toolkits. Abusive trusts fall into two categories: foreign and domestic. Once initial foreign or domestic trusts are formed, the taxpayer and scheme promoter set up a series of vertically layered trusts that distribute income down to each layer to reduce taxable income. Essentially, the personal expenses generated by the taxpayers are transformed into deductible business items or the true ownership of the income is ignored. However, well-established tax law principles treat these trusts as sham transactions because, apart from the tax savings, they lack economic substance. The IRS warned that once it determines the existence of an abusive trust, it may impose a series of civil or criminal penalties.

Offshore toolkit. Offshore tax-avoidance schemes do not appear to be as numerous as abusive trusts, but the concept behind offshore tax schemes is similar to the goal underlying abusive trusts. A scheme is usually undertaken with the purpose of shifting assets and/or income into offshore accounts or entities, making it appear as though the taxpayer has given up control of the assets while, in reality, that has not happened. Because U.S. taxpayers are taxed on their worldwide income, taxpayers participating in such transactions claim that the income is not attributable to them because they do not control or own it.

7.   The IRS offers two types of tax shelter "toolkits" to aid taxpayers in getting back into compliance with the tax law. These kits concern:

    a.   Abusive trust and offshore transactions
    b.   Abusive corporate and individual transactions
    c.   Abusive accounting procedures and aggressive characterization
    d.   Abusive foreign trusts and domestic trusts

John Doe summonses

The government's use of summonses in its war against tax shelters began in earnest in mid-2002.

> *Observation:* IRS Commissioner Mark Everson said, "The IRS is committed to enforcing the law, particularly in the corporate arena and in pursuing high-income individuals who enter into abusive tax shelters. Attorneys and accountants should be pillars of our system of voluntary tax compliance, not the architects of its circumvention."

Tax practitioner and identity privileges. Two contrasting Tax Code provisions govern the realm of taxpayer confidentiality:

♦   *Code Sec. 7525* extends the same type of common law attorney–client protections of confidentiality to communications between a taxpayer and a federally authorized tax practitioner. Courts recognize the existence of a tax practitioner–client privilege when: (1) tax advice of any kind is sought, (2) from a federally authorized practitioner in his capacity as such, (3) the communication is made in confidence, (4) that relates to that purpose, and (5) is made or received by the client. However, in tax matters, the privilege is considered waived where the communication is used to prepare the taxpayer's nonconfidential tax return. The waiver only applies to information intended to assist in the return preparation.

♦   *Code Sec. 6112* and regulations, by contrast, require organizers and sellers (known under the regulations as material advisors) of tax shelters, to maintain (and disclose to the IRS upon request) lists of persons participating in a transaction. The 6112 regulations recognize the right of a tax practitioner to assert the privilege, provided the practitioner states, under penalties of perjury, the nature of each document not produced so the IRS can determine the applicability of the privilege, along with a representation that the communication is confidential and that it has not been disclosed to any other person that might result in a waiver.

Caution. The definition and scope of material advisors are quite broad. The Code Sec. 6112 regulations generally define a material advisor as any party that is required to register the shelter under Code Sec. 6111 as a promoter (a party that receives or expects to receive a minimum fee and provides a tax statement to a taxpayer relating to a reportable transaction or tax shelter). The minimum fee is generally $250,000 for advice rendered to corporations and $50,000 for advice given to pass-through entities.

IRS view. Using the rationale underpinning Code Secs. 7525 and 6112, the IRS propagated the general rule that the mere identification of taxpayers involved in tax shelter transactions is not considered a communication to which the privilege applies. The mere identification of a taxpayer does generally not relate to rendering tax advice, nor is there the general expectation that giving one's name is a confidential communication.

The IRS also takes the position that a taxpayer's name, address, and social security number are not privileged because this information would need to be provided to the tax practitioner for purposes of preparing a return. However, courts have carved out an exception where the disclosure of the taxpayer's identity would ultimately led to a disclosure of the client's motive for seeking the advice, as such motivation has been found by courts to evidence a confidential communication.

Courts' position. In carving out the exception making this determination, courts generally have focused on four factors: (1) whether the purpose of the representation was to provide tax advice; (2) whether revealing the taxpayer's identity would reveal his or her motives for seeking such advice; (3) whether the client waived the privilege; and (4) whether the documents at issue communicated or generated for the purpose of preparing the client's tax return. Although any one of these factors would prove crucial to the outcome of a given case, the second factor is most telling.

STUDY QUESTIONS

8. A practitioner is considered to be a material advisor if he or she receives a minimum fee of _____ for rendering tax shelter advice to a corporation.

    a. $50,000
    b. $250,000
    c. $100,000
    d. $25,000

9. Which of the following is *not* necessary to create a tax payer–practitioner relationship under Code Sec. 7525?

   a. The rendering of tax advice
   b. By a federally authorized tax practitioner
   c. After the receipt of payment
   d. With the expectation of confidentiality

10. Which of the following is most likely a privileged communication under Code Sec. 7525?

    a. The submission of a client's W-2 form to a return preparer
    b. A letter between the client and practitioner regarding the client's investment in an offshore account
    c. A letter between the client and the practitioner regarding a prior year's tax return
    d. The client's name, social security number, phone number, and address

Settlement initiatives

The Fast Track Dispute Resolution Program is a joint effort between LMSB and the Appeals Office to resolve cases at the lowest and earliest points available in the process, with an overriding goal of reaching resolution within a 120-day period. The initial fast track pilot program began in late 2001 but was so successful that, early in 2003, the Internal Revenue Service issued guidance to make permanent two programs that facilitate agreement between taxpayers and the IRS on tax disputes more quickly. These have relevance for taxpayers caught in abusive tax shelter schemes:

♦ *Fast Track Mediation:* This program gives small businesses, self-employed taxpayers, and the IRS the opportunity to mediate disputes through an IRS appeals officer, who acts as a neutral party. The mediator does not exercise settlement authority and will not render a decision; and

♦ *Fast Track Settlement:* This program enables the IRS to resolve tax disputes with large and mid-size businesses at an earlier stage—often within a much shorter time than through the normal audit and Appeals processes. Under this option, the parties reach a resolution using Appeals' delegated settlement authority, enabling the parties to consider the hazards of litigation. Neither the Service nor the taxpayer is required to accept a settlement, and either may withdraw from the process at any time. However, if an agreement is reached, the parties will enter into a closing agreement.

The Office of Tax Shelter Analysis (OTSA) will turn four years old in January 2004. The recent accounting scandals brought the abuses of tax shelters into the public limelight and with them the IRS's plans for how it will proceed from here. This concern has been expressed not only by those who wish to pursue aggressive tax opportunities in the future but also by taxpayers and practitioners who now have second thoughts about the appropriateness of past tax-sheltered arrangements that have been reflected on recently filed returns.

OTSA serves as a clearinghouse for information that comes to the attention of the IRS relating to potentially improper tax shelter activity.

New Chief Counsel officer to work with OTSA

The IRS announced on February 12, 2003 (IR-2003-16), the creation of a new senior executive position within the Office of Chief Counsel to focus on potentially abusive tax avoidance transactions. Washington attorney Nicholas J. DeNovio was selected to fill this post. He works with IRS personnel on early identification and interdiction of abusive tax avoidance transactions through various sources, including review of disclosure statements, tax shelter registrations, and information from taxpayer and promoter examinations. As the new Senior Counsel, DeNovio supervises a staff of attorneys and leads task force initiatives to expedite the published guidance process addressing questionable transactions. In addition to leading efforts within Chief Counsel, this group works closely with the IRS's operating divisions and the Treasury Department to craft timely administrative responses to abusive transactions.

Listed transactions

Once the IRS "lists" a transaction, tax benefits claimed on a return as the result of that transaction, as well as transactions substantially similar to it, must carry with them a disclosure that they arose from a listed transaction. Not only does this mandatory disclosure raise a red flag in helping the IRS audit that particular taxpayer's return, but it also allows the IRS to gather general information on the particular tax shelter being marketed. That information can help the IRS track down the names of other participants, which has been a key to the IRS's growing success in this area.

Listed in 2000. Following is a synopsis of the types of listed transactions that the IRS prepared in 2000:

◆ Transactions generating deductions for contributions to a qualified cash or deferred arrangement or matching contributions to a defined contribution plan when contributions are attributable to compensation earned by plan participants after the end of the taxable year (Rev. Rul. 90-105);

♦ Trust arrangements purported to qualify as multiple employer welfare benefit funds exempt from the limits of Code Sec. 419 or 419A (Notice 95-34);

♦ Multiple-party transactions intended to allow one party to realize rental or other income from property or service contracts to allow another party to report deductions related to that income ("lease strips") (Notice 95-53);

♦ Transactions in which the reasonably expected economic profit is insubstantial compared to the value of foreign tax credits described in Part II of Notice 98-5;

♦ Contingent installment sales of securities by partnerships to accelerate and allocate income to a tax-indifferent partner (*ACM v. Commr*, CA-3, 1998; *ASA v. Commr*, CA-DC, 2000);

♦ Transactions involving distributions described in proposed Treas. Reg. § 1.643(a)-8 from charitable remainder trusts;

♦ Immediate sublease of property back to lessor after initial lease (Rev. Rul. 99-14); claims an artificially high tax basis in partnership interests in an attempt to create deductible losses on the sale of these partnership interests (Notice 2000-44);

♦ Transactions using employee stock compensation arrangements in a series of transactions between a parent corporation and its subsidiary to create artificial losses for the parent (Notice 2000-60); and

♦ Certain trusts purportedly qualifying for special income-exclusion treatment under the laws of Guam (Notice 2000-61).

Listed in 2001. In 2001, the IRS identified three more tax shelters as abusive listed transactions:

♦ *Abusive intermediary transactions,* in which a seller purports to sell the stock of a target corporation to an intermediary. The target corporation then purports to sell some or all of its assets to a buyer. The buyer subsequently claims a basis in the assets of the target corporation that equals its purchase price. For tax avoidance, the target corporation is included as a member of the intermediary's affiliated group, which files a consolidated tax return. The group reports losses or credits that offset the gain or tax from the target's sale of assets (Notice 2001-16).

♦ *Contingent liability shelters,* in which an asset with a high basis is exchanged for stock. The transferee assumes a liability that the transferor has not yet taken into account for tax purposes and for which it remains obligated. The basis and the fair market value of the asset usually are only marginally greater than the value of the assumed liability. The transferor subsequently sells the shares for their fair market value and claims a loss for value of the liability assumed by the transferee (Notice 2001-17).

♦ *"Basis-shifting" shelters,* in which a U.S. taxpayer uses options or other vehicles to treat a redeemed shareholder as owning stock in the redeeming corporation, which is owned or treated as being owned by the taxpayer under the attribution rules of Code Sec. 318. The U.S. taxpayer subsequently claims that attribution of ownership causes the redemption to be treated as a dividend. The basis of the redeemed stock is added to the basis of stock in the redeeming corporation. The U.S. taxpayer sells the stock and claims a loss or experiences a reduction in income (Notice 2001-45).

Listed in 2002. These transactions were listed in 2002:

♦ *Loan-assumption/up-basis transaction,* in which a loan assumption agreement is used to claim an inflated basis in assets acquired from another party. A third party (transferor) borrows money from a lender, then uses the proceeds to purchase the assets. Part of the assets is then sold by the transferor to a U.S. taxpayer in consideration of the taxpayer agreeing to assume the whole loan as a liability (2002-21).

♦ *Notional Principal Contract (NPC) transactions,* under which a stream of payments is exchanged with another party. The payments are divided into three categories: periodic, nonperiodic, and termination. Periodic and nonperiodic payments are recognized at different points in time during the term of the contract. The abusive use of NPCs fails to recognize nonperiodic payments throughout the term of the contract (Notice 2002-35).

♦ *Tax straddle using tiered partnerships,* for which the IRS claims that the use of "layered" transactions taking place in multiple steps tries to hide the true nature of the arrangements, which include partnerships that fail to make the Code Sec. 754 election (Notice 2002-50).

♦ *Pass-through entity straddle,* which uses a straddle, one or more transitory shareholders, and the rules of subchapter S, to "allow" a shareholder to claim an immediate loss while deferring an offsetting gain in an S corporation investment (Notice 2002-65).

Listed in 2003. Finally, the following were listed this year:

♦ *Lease strips* that improperly separate income from related deductions and generally should not produce the tax consequences desired by the participants. Lease strips are transactions in which one participant claims to realize rental or other income from property and another participant claims the deductions related to that income, such as depreciation or rental expenses. Depending on the facts of a particular case, the IRS may apply Code Sec. 165, 269, 382, 446(b), 701 or 704 to challenge a lease strip. The Service also may challenge certain assignments or accelerations of future payments as financings.

- *Common trust fund straddle,* a tax shelter" generally involving the use of a common trust fund that invests in economically offsetting gain and loss positions in foreign currencies and allocates the gains to one or more tax indifferent parties and the losses to another taxpayer (Notice 2003-54).

- *Compensatory stock options,* involving transfers of compensatory stock options by executives to related parties attempt to avoid or evade federal income and employment taxes. The steps involve employees who are granted a nonstatutory compensatory stock option and transfer that option to a related party, a family member, or family partnership in exchange for a long-term balloon note that is equal to the value of the option. Promoters of these arrangements contend that the options should be treated as sold or otherwise disposed of in an arm's-length transaction for purposes of Reg. 1.83-7; thus, the individual will not recognize compensation income when the related person exercises the option. Moreover, if the related party pays for the option with a note or other deferred payment obligation, promoters take the position that the individual does not recognize compensation income for the purchase price until the related person pays the amounts due (Notice 2003-47).

- *Welfare benefit funds,* which are set up through sham labor negotiations to exploit a special tax rule that allows deductions for contributions made to welfare benefit funds set up through good-faith bargaining by labor unions legitimately representing their members' interests (Notice 2003-24).

- *Offshore deferred compensation,* involving certain domestic and foreign employee leasing companies Notice 2003-22).

- *ESOP arrangements,* under which certain employee stock ownership plans (ESOPs) hold employer securities in an S corporation from which the initial employees of the entity forming the ESOP do not receive more than insubstantial benefits or insubstantial ownership interests. These ESOPs are being used primarily for the purpose of claiming eligibility for the delayed effective date of Code Sec. 409(p) (Rev Rul 2003-6).

- *Producer-owned reinsurance companies (PORCs),* which are set up to shift income from taxpayers to related companies purported to be insurance companies that are subject to little or no U.S. federal income tax. The transaction usually involves a taxpayer (typically a service provider, automobile dealer, lender, or retailer) that offers its customers the opportunity to purchase an insurance contract through the taxpayer in connection with the products or services being sold. The taxpayer forms a wholly owned corporation, typically in a foreign country, to reinsure the policies under the tax-exempt protection of Code Sec. 501(c)(15) (Notice 2002-70).

STUDY QUESTIONS

11. A lease-stripping transaction generally occurs when:

    a.   One party claims rental income and another party claims the deductions related to that income

    b.   The owner gifts away leases under an implied agreement that the lessees will gift back goods or services of equal value, avoiding income

    c.   The landlord overcharges for rent and deposits the overpayments in an offshore account and does not report the income

    d.   A party matches income and deductions on rental property held by its wholly owned corporation, but "strips" the income by failing to report it

12. A "PORC" transaction involves which type of arrangement?

    a.   A producer who buys insurance on its own goods

    b.   A passive offshore real estate holding company

    c.   A type of reinsurance arrangement between a taxpayer agent/producer and an offshore reinsurance company

    d.   A type of straddle transaction involving foreign currencies

SETTLEMENT PROGRAMS

As of publication date of this chapter, the IRS has no outstanding settlement programs. The likelihood, however, is that future settlement programs regarding certain tax shelters will be offered in situations in which the IRS cannot otherwise easily discover participants. As in past settlement programs, the IRS likely will also use the information obtained from the tax shelter participants to discover the promoters and the other shelter participants who do not choose to come forward.

Settlement offers in the past have covered the following three abusive transactions:

◆ Section 302/318 basis-shifting shelters;
◆ Section 351 contingent liability shelters; and
◆ Corporate-owned life insurance (COLI) plans.

Although settlement offers relating to these transactions were extended, all the programs officially expired by mid-2003.

ROUTINE REQUESTS FOR WORKPAPERS

Taxpayers should expect to receive requests for tax accrual workpapers during audits of suspected tax avoidance transactions. Although the IRS has had the power to summon tax accrual workpapers since 1984, this tactic has not been a standard examination technique—until recently.

The IRS has indicated that requesting tax accrual workpapers is critical to curbing tax shelters and such requests will be standard practice when examiners are confronted with abusive tax avoidance transactions. Taxpayers filing returns after July 1, 2002, have been subject to the new policy. The IRS also will request workpapers for returns filed before July 1, 2002, but only if the taxpayer failed to disclose the shelter.

> *Note.* Tax reconciliation workpapers are not subject to this request.

STUDY QUESTION

13. Which of the following types of workpapers are not subject to inspection for taxpayers suspected of participating in tax shelters?

    a. Tax reconciliation workpapers
    b. Tax accrual workpapers from disclosed transactions
    c. All Tax accrual workpapers where undisclosed transactions are involved
    d. Tax accrual workpapers relating to multiple investments in listed transactions

Chief Counsel's notice

This notice sets out procedures to use with the Service's policy regarding requests for tax accrual and other financial audit workpapers relating to the tax reserve for deferred tax liabilities. The procedures also apply to footnotes disclosing contingent tax liabilities appearing on audited financial statements. It modifies existing procedures for requests for audit and tax accrual workpapers that are not affected by Announcement 2002-63.

Announcement 2002-63 provides that the IRS may request tax accrual workpapers in the course of examining any return filed on or after July 1, 2002, that claims any tax benefit arising out of a transaction that the Service has determined to be a listed transaction at the time of the request within the meaning of Treas. Reg. § 1.6011-4(b)(2). If the listed transaction was disclosed under Treas. Reg. § 1.6011-4, the Service will routinely request the tax accrual workpapers pertaining only to the listed transaction. If the listed transaction was not disclosed, the Service will routinely request all tax accrual workpapers.

In addition, if the IRS determines that tax benefits from multiple investments in listed transactions are claimed on a return, regardless of whether the listed transactions were disclosed, the Service, as a discretionary matter, will request all tax accrual workpapers. Similarly, in connection with the examination of a return claiming tax benefits from a disclosed listed transaction, if there are reported financial accounting irregularities (such as those requiring restatement of earnings), the Service, as a discretionary matter, will request all tax accrual workpapers. In general, these requests will be limited to the tax accrual workpapers for the years under examination but may extend to other years if directly relevant to the years under examination.

COMMON TAX SCAMS IDENTIFIED

Relatively sophisticated tax shelter arrangements relying on a web of transactions and "clever" interpretation of the Code are not the only tax shelters on the IRS's hit list. A different variety of tax shelters have gone mainstream and Main Street. These are pitched to the unsophisticated individual taxpayer who believes that certain tax positions, when combined with the limited risk of audit based upon current audit statistics, make participation in these shelters sensible.

The IRS has listed a group of transactions, described here, that it found currently typifies the common tax shelters being marketed to individual taxpayers:

Offshore transactions

Some people use offshore transactions to avoid paying U.S. income tax. Use of an offshore credit card, trust, or other arrangement to hide or underreport income or to claim false deductions on a federal tax return is illegal. Through April 15, 2003, the IRS offered individuals with improper offshore financial arrangements the chance to step forward and avoid facing civil fraud and information return penalties.

Improper home-based business

This scheme purports to offer tax "relief" but actually is illegal tax avoidance. The promoters of this scheme claim that individual taxpayers can deduct most, or all, of their personal expenses as business expenses by setting up a bogus home-based business.

Armed Forces

The IRS has seen isolated instances of the scam that targets the families of those serving in the Armed Forces. The IRS warns consumers to beware of any variation of a scenario in which a telephone caller posing as an IRS employee tells a family member that he is entitled to a $4,000 refund because his relative is in the Armed Forces. Then the caller requests a credit card number to cover a $42 fee for postage. The con artist provides an actual IRS toll-free number as the call back number in order to make the call seem legitimate.

Medical professionals as targets

Scam artists and scheme promoters often prey on busy professionals who don't have a lot of time to focus on their finances. As a result, the IRS has seen an increase in tax fraud in the professional community, including individuals in healthcare/medical professions.

PRIORITY GUIDANCE

As noted earlier, the IRS has identified the issuance of published guidance as a high priority means by which the Service can handle the proliferating number of tax scams quickly, without sapping scarce resources. By identifying potential abusive transactions early and subsequently issuing guidance to taxpayers and practitioners to give a timely indication of how the IRS is thinking about a particular transaction, the Service hopes to stem the flow of abuses, reducing workloads in order to focus on the most egregious cases.

To aid in its endeavor, the IRS publishes an annual priority guidance plan under which it outlines several hundred items the Service will try to address within its fiscal year. The plan has been surprisingly effective in keeping the IRS on track. The guidance plan is updated quarterly in order to keep pace with the ever-changing marketplace. For FY 2003–2004, the IRS has indicated that it will continue to add to the compilation of "listed transactions" and that it intends to issue final regulations under Code Secs. 6662 and 6664 regarding tax shelter penalties.

CURRENT TAX SHELTER LEGISLATION

U.S. House Ways and Means Committee Chairman William M. Thomas (R-Calif.) unveiled a number of tax-related legislative proposals in late July 2003 under the American Jobs Creation Act of 2003 (H.R. 2896), a large portion of which contains specific legislative recommendations concerning tax shelters. The bill largely adopts current administration thinking on tax shelters by enhancing the disclosure and penalty provisions applicable to such abuses and by restricting the application of the tax practitioner privilege. However, the legislation does not attempt, as previous legislative proposals have done, to codify the economic substance doctrine.

The legislation would create several new penalty-related code sections. Many feel that stiffening tax shelter penalties is necessary to add teeth to existing tax shelter rules. One such provision would impose a penalty on any person whose tax return fails to include information regarding a reportable transaction under Code Sec. 6011. The penalties for such an infringement range from $10,000 to $50,000 for standard reportable transaction infractions, but rise from $100,000 to $200,000 for information reporting failures regarding listed transactions. The bill also creates a section that imposes an accuracy-related penalty on understatements with respect to a reportable transaction. Other penalty provisions encompass failures to maintain investor lists, failures to report interests in foreign financial accounts, and harsher promoter penalties.

Several of the bill's provisions also provide guidance that might resolve the current court battles over whether the Code Sec. 7525 tax practitioner privilege applies to taxpayer–advisor communications and list disclosures. The bill contains a provision that specifically states that the Code Sec. 7525 privilege shall not apply to tax shelter communications. Another provision would require material advisors to file returns identifying and describing any tax shelter transaction with which they were involved. The bill also includes a provision that would make it unequivocal that the disclosure of tax shelter investor lists is not subject to claims of confidentiality.

STUDY QUESTION

14. Under the proposed tax shelter legislation, persons failing to provide information along with a return as required under Code Sec. 6011, face a penalty of:

    a. $10,000 to $50,000 for failures relating to listed transactions
    b. $100,000 to $200,000 for failures relating to listed transactions
    c. $100,000 to $200,000 for failures relating to reportable transactions
    d. $50,000 to $250,000 for failures relating to reportable transactions

CONCLUSION

Virtually every agency and legislative body that has jurisdiction over the tax system has indicated that tax shelter abuses and transactions are a serious matter because they cost billions in lost revenue annually and threaten to undermine confidence in the system. As such, the IRS and Treasury Department have made clear their commitment to catching and, where appropriate, punishing promoters and participants in such schemes. Toward that end, both agencies, the administration, and Congress have expressed the need and will to commit resources and funding to battle such abuses and will continue to do so for the foreseeable future.

It is, therefore, in the interest of practitioners and taxpayers to tread carefully in developing and participating in tax shelter transactions. Attention must focus on the new tax shelter regulations and published guidance. The broad approach embodied in the regulations leaves the

IRS an avenue to not only develop and implement a position with regard to new shelter transactions quickly but also to disrespect transactions that are merely roughly similar to those transactions that are "listed." Clearly, the IRS is not interested in routine legal transactions, but taxpayers and practitioners who prefer to skate close to the edge will likely notice that the ice beneath them is thinning.

MODULE 2—CHAPTER 5: TRENDS IN EMPLOYEE BENEFITS

Learning Objectives. This chapter was prepared to give you information on trends in employee benefits: Health Reimbursement Arrangements (HRAs), Voluntary Employee Benefit Associations (VEBAs); benefits for domestic partners, and a look at developments in Congress. Upon completion of this chapter, you will be able to:

♦ List the key attributes of HRAs, VEBAs, and domestic partnership arrangements;
♦ Comprehend how HRAs, and VEBAs operate;
♦ Become familiar with trends in the usage of HRAs and VEBAs;
♦ Identify trends and policies connected with benefits for domestic partners;
♦ Describe future health care savings incentives;
♦ Be able to explain the tax significance of HRAs, VEBAs, and domestic partnerships

INTRODUCTION

It is no secret that the recent economic slowdown has not only put the squeeze on job creation but also on salaries and employee benefits. Simultaneously, rising health care costs have made it difficult to maintain medical fringe benefits at the level that employees have grown to expect. Additionally, as a significant overlay on these developments, the growth of domestic partner benefits (which not that long ago were unknown, but which have revolutionized people's expectations for health care coverage) cannot be ignored.

This chapter explores some trends that have developed recently in the area of employee fringe benefits. The following are the focal points of this chapter:

1. *HRAs:* The development of a Health Reimbursement Arrangements (HRA) plan placed a cap on employer responsibility for medical expenses while providing (in practice) the same medical benefits as a full-blown medical plan to a large majority of workers;
2. *VEBAs:* The resurgence of Voluntary Employee Beneficiary Associations (VEBAs) as a good solution for many small and mid-size businesses allowing them to self-fund benefits to

employees and their dependents through a tax-favored vehicle; and

3. *Domestic Partner Benefits:* Domestic partners are increasingly included as participants in many employee fringe benefit programs.

HEALTH REIMBURSEMENT ARRANGEMENTS

Health reimbursement arrangements (HRAs) are employer-funded accounts used by employees to pay for medical expenses and/or health insurance premiums. HRAs are increasingly popular with employers because they give employers greater control over the cost of employee health care benefits while shifting cost-cutting incentives to employees. Employees also favor HRAs because employer contributions to, and reimbursements from, HRAs are excluded from employees' gross incomes. Unused funds may be rolled over from year to year.

> *Observation.* The temptation to convert taxable income to tax-friendly HRA benefits is negated by rules against cash-outs and funding an HRA through salary reduction.

Characteristics

A health reimbursement arrangement (HRA) has the following characteristics:

♦ It is funded solely by the employer and not provided under a salary reduction election or a cafeteria plan;

♦ It reimburses the employee for medical care expenses incurred by the employee, his or her spouse, and dependents; and

♦ It provides reimbursements up to a maximum dollar amount for a coverage period.

Generally, employers have wide latitude to determine which employees are eligible to participate in an HRA. Employers may also open HRAs to inactive employees, such as retirees. The timing rules for enrollment are also flexible. However, HRAs may not be linked to a deferred compensation or salary reduction plan. An HRA will fail if it interacts with a cafeteria plan in such a way as to permit employees to use salary reductions to fund it.

> *Example.* ABC Co. offers a reimbursement plan plus other health coverage. The annual cost for family coverage is $4,500. Employees can elect to reduce their salaries by $2,500 or $3,500 to fund the coverage. An employee who selects family coverage and $2,500 salary reduction receives a $1,000 maximum reimbursement. An employee who selects family coverage and $3,500 salary reduction receives a $2,000 maximum reimbursement. Under these examples, a portion

of the salary reduction is attributable to the reimbursement arrangement. Consequently, the reimbursement arrangement does *not* qualify as an HRA.

HRAs are not portable; they remain with the employer. However, they may be part of COBRA postemployment coverage. An HRA may continue to reimburse former or retired employees for medical care expenses after termination of employment or retirement even if the employee does not elect COBRA coverage. Generally, employers must increase the maximum amounts for COBRA-covered participants if they increase the maximum amounts for active employees.

> *Practice Pointer.* HRA dollars can be rolled over. Any unused portion of the maximum dollar amount at the end of the coverage period carries forward to increase the maximum reimbursement amount in subsequent coverage periods.

An HRA can be set up in conjunction with other plans or as a stand-alone plan. Several other plans can complement an HRA or vice versa. For example, in conjunction with a group health plan, an HRA can be a payment source for the employee share of the premium as well as medical expenses outside the scope of the insurance plan. HRAs are also valuable when used with a flexible spending account (FSA). The employee uses the funds in the FSA first, which reduces the risk of losing FSA funds.

> *Observation.* Unlike FSAs, there is no "use it or lose it" feature in an HRA resulting in forfeiture of unused funds at the end of the coverage period.

STUDY QUESTION

1. Unused funds in an HRA at the end of the coverage period may:

    a. Not be rolled over to the next coverage period
    b. Be subject to a penalty
    c. Roll over to the next coverage period
    d. Be forfeited

Benefits

Each medical care expense submitted for reimbursement to an HRA must be substantiated. An HRA may not reimburse a health care expense from a prior tax year. In addition, an HRA may not reimburse an expense that is incurred before the date the HRA is established nor one occurring before the date the employee becomes enrolled.

If an employee can receive cash or any other taxable or nontaxable benefit other than reimbursement of medical expenses, all distributions are included in the employee's gross income. This harsh rule applies even if some of the distributions are reimbursements for medical expenses and/or health insurance premiums.

> *Example.* Allison retires from ABC Co. and receives a bonus that is related to her maximum reimbursement amount remaining in her HRA. No amounts paid under the HRA are reimbursements of medical expenses, so they must be included in Allison's gross income.

STUDY QUESTION

2. All distributions from an HRA will be included in an employee's gross income if:

    a.   The employee is age 55 or older
    b.   The HRA is part of COBRA health plan coverage
    c.   The HRA contains unused funds at the end of the coverage period
    d.   The employee receives cash or any other taxable or nontaxable benefit other than reimbursement of medical expenses and/or health insurance premiums

Eligible participants

Current and retired employees may participate in an HRA along with their spouses and dependents. Reimbursements for medical expenses are excludible from income if they are made to:

♦   Current employees;
♦   Retired employees;
♦   Spouses of current and retired employees;
♦   Dependents of current and retired employees; or
♦   Spouses and dependents of deceased employees.

STUDY QUESTION

3. Eligible participants in an HRA include:

    a.   Current employees and their spouses
    b.   Current employees, their spouses, and their dependants
    c.   Current and retired employees, their spouses and dependants, and spouses and dependants of deceased employees
    d.   Retired employees, their spouses and dependants, and spouses and dependants of deceased employees

DEBIT CARDS AND INSTANT REIMBURSEMENTS

In May 2003, the IRS authorized HRA reimbursements to be made by debit or credit cards. The government cautioned that adequate controls must be in place to guarantee that only medical costs are reimbursed.

The green light for debit and credit card reimbursements came in a revenue ruling (Rev. Rul. 2003-43). The IRS examined two uses for HRAs:

1. Employees are issued a debit or credit card to use for eligible medical expenses at employer-authorized service providers, such as physicians, dentists, pharmacists, and hospitals. If the employee attempts to use the card at nonauthorized providers, it is rejected.

2. Credit cards are issued to employees with limits equal to the coverage available under the health plan. The cards can be used only at employer-authorized service providers. The employer agrees to be responsible to the sponsor bank for any service charges. Generally, all expenses other than copayments, recurring expenses and real-time substantiation are treated as conditional, pending confirmation of the charge.

Employees agreed that the cards will be used only for eligible medical care expenses for themselves and their spouses and dependents. Expenses paid with the card cannot be eligible for reimbursement under any other arrangements. The terms were printed on the backs of the cards and were reaffirmed every time the cards were used.

In both scenarios, the IRS said that it would treat the charges on the debit or credit cards as fully substantiated medical expenses and excludable from employees' gross incomes.

Generally, permissible debit-credit card arrangements must have the following attributes:

♦ Employees keep receipts for expenses paid with the card;
♦ The transaction dollar limit equals the copayment for the service (for example, an employee is enrolled in a medical plan with a $20 copayment for visits to his or her physician. When the employee uses the card to pay for the copayment, the transaction is no more, or less, than $20);
♦ Recurring expenses match previously approved expenses as to amount, provider, and time period (for example, a prescription drug refill);
♦ Service providers or independent third parties verify that the charge is made for a medical expense (verification may be by telephone or e-mail). When verification is made in real time, the charge is substantiated.
♦ Additional charges for treatment at a physician's office are subject to preauthorization.

Example. Julia, an employee of ABC Co., uses her employer-provided HRA debit card to fill a prescription at an employer-authorized pharmacy. The pharmacy benefits manager (under Laura's major medical coverage) verifies that $35 of the cost of the prescription is a medical expense that is *not* covered by Laura's coverage. Because the information about the medical expense matches the amount of the transaction, the IRS would treat the transaction as substantiated. The transaction would also be substantiated if treatment at a physician's office results in charges exceeding the copayment and, after securing authorization for the card, the provider is prompted to enter treatment codes and charges. This additional third-party information about the type of care, date of service, and amount of charge substantiates the expense.

In addition, employers must have adequate procedures in place to identify improper payments. Employees must repay any improper charges. The employer could: (1) require the employee to pay back the amount of the improper payment; (2) withhold the amount from the employee's wages; or (3) handle the improper charge with a claims offset; that is, no future reimbursement would be made for a substantiated claim until the improper claim is paid back. If none of these methods works, employers could treat the improper payments as it would any business debt and take legal action against the employee to recover costs.

> *Practice Pointer.* Use of debit and credit cards in HRAs will help make payments seamless and are just as easy as using a health insurance card.

Sampling impermissible

The IRS also examined a scenario in which the employer used sampling techniques based on transaction amounts to determine the validity of charges. Because the employer did not substantiate all reimbursements, the IRS ruled it would treat none of the charges as excludable from income.

> *Example.* ABC Co. reviews 20 percent of dental office transactions that have not otherwise been substantiated. It also only reviews charges above $100 because it assumes that no dental procedures are available for less than $100. In addition, ABC Co. also reviews five percent of physician office transactions that have not been otherwise substantiated. It only reviews charges that are less than $150 because it assumes that almost all of these charges are for eligible medical care. ABC Co. does not review any transaction below $25 on the assumption that these amounts are copayments. In the IRS's view, because ABC Co. does not substantiate every reimbursement, none of the charges would be excludable from income.

4. A permissible debit-credit card arrangement in an HRA has which one of the following attributes?

   a. The transaction dollar amount equals the copayment for the service.

   b. Service providers and third parties verify that the charge is for a medical expense.

   c. In emergency situations, the participant or a family member notifies the employer within 24 hours of an emergency admission to a hospital.

   d. Copayments must be less than $20.

CONGRESS DEBATES HEALTH SAVINGS ACCOUNTS

If proponents are correct, 40 million Americans could benefit from having Health Savings Accounts (HSAs). The new savings vehicle was recommended by President Bush and is being debated in Congress. HSAs share some important characteristics with Archer Medical Savings Accounts, Flexible Spending Accounts, and HRAs. They also operate similarly to IRAs: Contributions would be tax-free and distributions would be tax free when used for qualifying medical expenses.

Tax-free contributions. Employer contributions to an HSA would be excluded from an employee's gross income. They would also be free from federal employment taxes. Individuals could also make deductible contributions to an HSA. Family members could contribute to an individual's HSA, but their contributions would not be tax-deductible.

Distributions. When money saved in an HSA is used for qualified medical expenses, it would not be included in income. Distributions could be used for the benefit of the owner of the HSA or his or her spouse and/or dependents. Distributions not used for medical expenses would be treated as income to the taxpayer.

VOLUNTARY EMPLOYEE BENEFICIARY ASSOCIATIONS

VEBAs are special tax-exempt entities that employers use to self-fund benefits to employees, their dependents, and others. In essence, they are welfare associations of employees and are independent of the employer. In today's expensive benefits environment, VEBAs are important vehicles to help employers reduce costs of benefits.

VEBAs are flexible and can be tailored to fit the particular needs of small businesses, family-owned businesses, partnerships, and other business entities at particular stages in their life cycles. A new business may want to create a VEBA to help attract top talent. A business that is nearing the end of its life cycle can use a VEBA to provide valuable life insurance benefits to its employees.

VEBAs are attractive because they fund current benefits, and participants can secure distributions at any age without risk of a penalty (which typically would occur when an individual removes money from an IRA prematurely).

VEBAs also help businesses by pooling employer and employee contributions. Rather than creating a new VEBA, a business frequently will join an existing VEBA with similar participants.

Characteristics

Governing statute. VEBAs are governed by Code Sec. 501(c)(9). The IRS determines whether a VEBA qualifies under Code Sec. 501(c)(9) for tax-free status. If it does, the IRS sends the VEBA a favorable determination letter.

Voluntary association of employees. Participation in a VEBA must be voluntary. If membership is designated because of employment status, it is not voluntary. If an employee has to take an affirmative step to join; that is an indication that participation is voluntary.

> *Observation.* The rules change when employees are unionized. If participation in a VEBA is required by a collective bargaining agreement, it does not automatically make membership involuntary. Rather, it is still treated as voluntary.

Independent entity. A VEBA must be managed independently of the employer. It can operate as a nonprofit corporation or a trust. If participants opt to organize the VEBA as a trust, the trustees must be independent of the employer. Frequently, a bank or other financial institution serves as trustee. The employer cannot exercise any control over the direction of the VEBA or its investments.

> *Example.* Employees of ABC Co. organize a VEBA and name First National Bank as trustee. The terms of the VEBA provide that ABC Co. may direct the investments of the VEBA. The VEBA is not an independent entity because the employer has power over investments.

Member control. Members direct the activities of the VEBA through trustees or officers whom employees select. Trustees or officers must conduct regular meetings and direct the daily affairs of the VEBA. Employees may elect or appoint the trustees or officers.

If a collective bargaining agreement is in place, trustees or officers may be designated by the contract. Trustees or officers may be selected by management and labor.

Example. ABC Co. and the Allied Workers Union negotiate a contract for ABC's hourly paid employees. Under the terms of the contract, ABC agrees to establish and contribute to a VEBA. Trustees are selected by ABC and the union. The trustees hold and invest the assets of the VEBA. In this scenario, the employees are deemed to possess the requisite control over the VEBA through their trustees.

Employee status. Membership in a VEBA is restricted to individuals who qualify based on their employee status. An individual's status may be as an active employee or as a retired employee.

> *Observation.* It is important to distinguish membership in a VEBA from participation in its benefits. Only active and retired employees may be members of a VEBA. However, other individuals, such as spouses and dependents of active and retired employees, may participate in the VEBA's benefit plans.

Three types of employees and retirees are generally eligible for VEBA membership:

1. Active and retired employees of a common employer or of affiliated employers;
2. Employees covered under a collective bargaining agreement; and
3. Individuals belonging to a labor union or to a local branch of a national union.

STUDY QUESTIONS

5. A voluntary employee benefit association must be _____ of the employer.

    a. Independent
    b. A fully controlled subsidiary entity
    c. Under the control of the employer
    d. Quasi-independent

6. Members direct the activities of a VEBA through trustees or officers:

    a. Selected by their employer
    b. Selected by a joint labor–management committee
    c. Appointed by an international union
    d. Appointed or elected by the members

> *Observation.* Employees of a local union may participate in a VEBA covering members of the local union. The union employees are deemed to share a common bond with members of the local union. Similarly, a proprietor of a business may participate in a VEBA covering his or her

employees. Generally, nonmembers cannot account for more than 10 percent of total membership. Under the IRS's safe harbor, a VEBA will be treated as being composed of employees if 90 percent of the total membership on one day of each quarter of the VEBA's tax year consists of employees.

Caution. The IRS strictly enforces its 90 percent rule and is quick to disqualify VEBAs that exceed the threshold.

Groups of similar employees. Often a group of similarly situated employees, especially in different labor organizations in the same industry or profession, will join together to establish a VEBA. For example, separate unions of teachers, administrators, and principals in a state may jointly create a VEBA for all of their members. Each labor organization may designate members to act as trustees.

Location of employees. Sometimes, VEBA members are not employed by a common employer. The IRS has determined that geography can create an employment bond so long as membership is limited to individuals engaged in the same line of business in the same locality. This exercise of rule making by the IRS is not without its critics, including the courts. In 1986, the Seventh Circuit Court of Appeals, in *Water Quality Association Employees' Benefit Corp. v. U.S.*, 795 F.2d 1303, decided that the geographical limit imposed by the IRS was not authorized by statute. To date, only the Seventh Circuit has adopted this rule.

The IRS has created a safe harbor for determining whether an area is a single geographical locale. Generally, if an area does not exceed the boundaries of three contiguous states, it will be treated as a single geographical locale. If an area fails the safe harbor, the IRS may deem it a single geographical locale if two or more VEBAs would not be economically feasible and employment characteristics support the particular states included.

Contributions

Generally, employer contributions to a VEBA are deductible as ordinary and necessary business expenses. If the contributions benefit the employer or revert to the employer, either directly or indirectly, they lose their tax-favored status. Contributions must be used to pay benefits. Otherwise, they are not deductible.

Employee contributions generally are not deductible. However, an employee's contributions to a VEBA that provides medical care are deductible.

Retiree medical expenses. In February 2003, the Tax Court in *Wells Fargo & Co v. Commr.*, 120 T.C. No. 5, allowed an employer to deduct its contributions for retiree medical benefits.

The employer contributed to a VEBA from 1991 to 1994. It engaged the services of an actuarial firm, which calculated that the present value of future benefits for active employees was $14 million for active employees and $27 million for current retirees.

The actuarial firm divided the $14 million for active employees by the present value of future service and calculated a 1991 funding amount of $3 million for active employees. The firm also recommended that the full amount needed to fund current retirees be funded in 1991. The employer followed the recommendations of the actuarial firm and contributed 30 million to the VEBA for 1991. The employer deducted the $30 million contribution.

The IRS challenged the deduction. It determined that the amount of benefits contributed for retirees in 1991 exceeded the authorized reserve limit. The Tax Court disagreed. According to the court, for an employee who retired when the reserve was created, the present value of the employee's projected benefit would be allocable to the year the reserve was created. Therefore, the employer was entitled to the deduction.

> *Observation.* The deduction in this case was taken just after the Financial Accounting Standards Board (FASB) changed the suggested financial and tax accounting treatment for retiree medical benefits. Until 1990, employers generally accounted for retiree medical benefits on a pay as you go basis. Under the new rule, employers must accrue over the course of the employee's employment the projected cost of future health care benefits to be paid after retirement.

Benefits

Types of benefits. Although a VEBA may provide benefits in cash or noncash form, its range of benefits is limited to life, sickness, accident, and similar benefits. A VEBA *cannot* provide any benefit that is similar to a pension; otherwise, the VEBA fails. VEBAs must provide current as opposed to future benefits.

Permissible benefits include:

- ◆ *Life benefits.* These may be direct benefits or payable through life insurance. Burial benefits are also included under this category.
- ◆ *Sickness and accident benefits.* These are amounts paid to the participant or on behalf of a participant for expenses arising from physical and mental illness and injury.
- ◆ *Similar benefits.* This is a broad category covering child care, education, supplemental unemployment compensation, and other current benefits.

Practice Pointer. Disability benefits also qualify as sickness and accident benefits.

Impermissible benefits include:

♦ Any benefit similar to a pension or annuity;
♦ Malpractice insurance;
♦ Commuting expenses/reimbursements;
♦ Loans to members in times of economic hardship; and
♦ Severance pay that is contingent on retirement.

Example. The Anytown Firefighters Union paid a dividend to members who retired from the fire department with 25 years of service. Severance pay is generally a permissible "similar" benefit. However, in this case the benefit is not current. It is contingent on a future event: retirement.

If an impermissible benefit is extremely small, it may be permissible. The IRS calls these benefits *de minimis.* In one case, an impermissible benefit—authorization of a nonqualifying cash surrender payment—was used by only one percent of members and accounted for less than one percent of the total benefits.

STUDY QUESTION

7. Permissible VEBA benefits are restricted in scope to:

   a. Pension benefits
   b. Malpractice insurance
   c. Loans to members in times of hardship
   d. Life, sickness, accident, and similar benefits

Domestic partner benefits. In 2000, the IRS determined that a VEBA could provide health coverage to a domestic partner who is a dependent of the member and the coverage would not be included in the employee's gross income or be deemed wages for employment tax purposes (*Private Letter Ruling 200108010*).

In this scenario, the VEBA was funded by multiple employers having collective bargaining agreements with a union. The collective bargaining agreements required the employers to make contributions. The amount of an employer's contributions was the same for single or family coverage.

The VEBA made payments to health care providers for the costs of medical, dental, and hospital care for participants. It also paid for coverage for dependents and domestic partners. Payments generally followed a schedule of benefits contracted with the providers.

The VEBA also reimbursed participants, dependents, and domestic partners for out-of-pocket expenses. Benefits were paid from the general assets of the VEBA.

Unless the member showed otherwise, the VEBA assumed that the domestic partner was not a dependent. Members could establish that an individual was a domestic partner by showing that the individual had been claimed as a dependent on his or her federal income tax return.

Alternatively, the member could execute a written certification that the individual qualified as a domestic partner under the IRS's support test.

> *Observation.* The relationship between the member and the domestic partner cannot violate local law.

VEBA checklist

Following are descriptions of the key attributes of VEBAs and important rules to remember:

- A VEBA is an association of employees that must be independent of the member employees and their employer. A VEBA trustee must be independent.
- Employee participation in a VEBA must be voluntary.
- Employees must control the VEBA and elect or designate the membership.
- Membership is generally limited to employees but may be open to retirees.
- Nonemployees may participate if they share an employment-related bond with employee members.
- Membership may be restricted to employees working for employers in the same geographical area.
- VEBAs may provide only life, sickness, accident, or similar benefits.
- VEBAs may not provide any benefit similar to a pension or annuity payable at retirement.
- VEBAs may not provide for deferred compensation.
- Generally, VEBAs may not discriminate in favor of highly compensated employees.
- A VEBA's earnings are exempt from income tax.
- Employer contributions are deductible.
- Employees are usually not taxed on employer contributions at the time of contribution.
- Contributions are subject to income and employment taxes if they are includible in an employee's income as wages.
- IRS approval is required for a VEBA to secure tax-exempt status.

DOMESTIC PARTNERS

Nothing has changed the benefits landscape over the past 20 years as much as the evolution of domestic partner benefits. In the past, few individuals understood the term or the extent of benefits available to domestic partners. Today, nearly two-thirds of the largest U.S. companies offer domestic partner benefits, as do many nonprofit and government employers.

Defining domestic partners

The definition of domestic partner varies among employers and localities. Here are some common attributes:

♦ Two individuals, same-sex or not, in a committed and exclusive relationship;
♦ Residing in the same residence (sometimes for a prescribed length of time, such as one year);
♦ At least 18 years of age;
♦ Sharing financial obligations;
♦ Assuming mutual welfare obligations;
♦ Planning to remain each other's sole domestic partner indefinitely; and
♦ Having no relation to each other in any manner that would prohibit them marrying but for the fact they are same-sex partners (if the individuals are opposite-sex partners, they cannot be related in anyway that would bar them from legally marrying).

Observation. Domestic partners are not always same-sex couples. For example, some states and municipalities permit opposite-sex couples to register as domestic partners if one partner is age 62 or older.

STUDY QUESTION

8. A common attribute of a domestic partner relationship is:

   a. Two individuals, same-sex or not, in a committed and exclusive relationship
   b. Separate and distinct mutual welfare obligations
   c. Maintenance of separate households
   d. Plan to remain each other's domestic partner for at least one year

Tax treatment of domestic partners

Domestic partners are *not* treated as spouses for federal tax purposes. Consequently, an employee pays taxes on the fair market value of the cost of coverage for the employee's domestic partner. Employers withhold taxes on domestic partner benefits just as they do on wages.

Example. Andrea is an employee of ABC Co. She wants to add Jill, her domestic partner, to her health insurance coverage. Jill does not qualify as Andrea's dependent.

Therefore, Andrea will pay taxes on the fair market value of the cost of coverage for Jill. ABC Co.'s cost for employee-only coverage for Andrea was $566. Andrea contributes $90 on a pretax basis toward that amount. When Andrea adds one person, ABC Co.'s cost rises to $940 and Andrea would contribute $188 toward that amount. However, only Andrea's contribution toward her coverage may be made on a pretax basis. Her contribution toward Jill's coverage must be made on an after-tax basis. In addition, Andrea will have to account for imputed income due to ABC Co.'s added cost for coverage of Jill. Andrea will be liable for federal taxes on the amount of imputed income.

Observation. The IRS's determination that domestic partners are not treated as spouses was made in a 1998 private letter ruling (LTR 9717018).

The marital status of individuals was traditionally determined for IRS purposes under state law. Until recently, the most prevalent legal issue was common law marriage. If state law recognized common-law marriage, the IRS would recognize the couple as married for federal tax purposes. As domestic partnerships became more common in the 1990s, taxpayers increasingly asked whether the IRS would recognize two individuals of the same sex as spouses if a state recognized same-sex marriage or a similar arrangement.

In 2000, Vermont became the first state in the nation to recognize so-called civil unions between members of the same sex, which, in that state, bestowed on the individuals entering into the civil union many of the attributes of marriage. Nevertheless, the IRS did not change its treatment of taxpayers who entered into civil unions. The IRS is bound to follow federal law. In 1996, Congress passed, and President Bill Clinton signed, the Defense of Marriage Act which declared for federal purposes that marriage is between a man and a woman and a spouse is defined as a person of the opposite sex. Even if a state were to recognize marriage between same-sex individuals, the Defense of Marriage Act would bar the IRS from recognizing a same-sex spouse.

Observation. Since 1996, 37 states have enacted statutes similar to the federal Defense of Marriage Act.

STUDY QUESTION

9. Under federal law, domestic partners are:

   a. Treated as spouses for tax purposes
   b. Treated as spouses for tax purposes if they reside in a state that recognizes civil unions between same-sex couples
   c. Not treated as spouses for tax purposes

    d.   Treated as spouses for tax purposes if they have a dependant

Dependents

Domestic partner benefits will be tax-free if the employee's partner qualifies as a dependent. Qualifying as a dependent is not easy. Generally, a dependent is a family member who receives more than one-half of his or her support from the taxpayer. To qualify as a dependent, a nonfamily member must satisfy four tests:

1. The employee provides more than 50 percent of his or her partner's annual support;
2. The domestic partner is a member of the employee's household;
3. The domestic partner's principal abode is the employee's residence; and
4. The relationship between the employee and domestic partner does not violate local law.

> *Observation.* In *Lawrence v. Texas, 1235 S. Ct. 1512 (2003)*, the Supreme Court struck down Texas' sodomy statute. Before the ruling, 13 states had sodomy statutes on the books, which criminalized certain consensual sexual activity between adults. Although many states did not enforce these prohibitions, the laws nonetheless could defeat an employee's claim to have his or her domestic partner qualify as a dependent. The validity of these statutes is in doubt post-*Lawrence*.

> *Practice Pointer.* If an employee succeeds in qualifying a domestic partner as a dependent, flexible spending accounts (FSAs) may be a useful vehicle to fund his or her partner's medical expenses.

Court Challenges. In 2001, the Tax Court rejected a taxpayer's argument that his longtime personal and financial relationship with another man entitled him and his partner to file a joint return. The decision in *Mueller v. Comm'r, 82 TCM 764* also affirmed that the Tax Code's distinctions between married and single taxpayers are constitutional.

The taxpayer and his partner began a relationship in 1989. In 1996, the taxpayer and his partner filed a joint federal return. His partner signed the return on the line labeled "spouse's signature." However, the taxpayer and his partner crossed out the word "spouse."

They also crossed out the word "married" on the return, so it read, "filing joint return" instead of "married filing joint return." All of the income reported on the return was earned by the taxpayer.

The court turned to Code Sec. 6013. Under that provision, a husband and wife may jointly make a single return of income taxes. The court found that the taxpayer did not claim to be a husband or a wife. The taxpayer, like any unmarried person, fell into the category of "Unmarried Individuals."

The court further found that the Tax Code's distinctions between married taxpayers and unmarried domestic partners did not violate the U.S. Constitution. The classification between married and single taxpayers rests on a rational basis and is a permissible exercise of legislative power to account for the greater financial burdens of married taxpayers. The distinction also equalizes their tax treatment geographically. Whether policy considerations warrant changing the distinction is for Congress to decide, the court noted.

> **Observation.** In June, the California state assembly approved legislation authorizing domestic partners to file joint *state* income tax returns. California instituted a domestic partner registry in 1999, and more than 20,000 couples, same-sex and opposite-sex, have registered as domestic partners. Opponents have challenged the new law in court.

STUDY QUESTION

10. Domestic partner benefits provided by an employer are tax-free if the employee's partner qualifies as a:

    a. Spouse
    b. Dependant
    c. Common law spouse
    d. Partner in a civil union

CONCLUSION

Health insurance premiums rose nearly 14 percent in 2003, the biggest jump since 1990. Employers and employees are confronted with many challenges on the health care front. Employees are protective of existing benefits, while employers are increasingly aware of escalating costs. Many employers are shifting the costs of health care coverage to employees.

HRAs, VEBAs, and other arrangements may be attractive vehicles to help preserve benefits and give employees a sense of ownership and control over their health care decision making. HRAs and VEBAs also are important tools for small and struggling businesses to help curb costs. At the same time, the face of the American workplace is changing as domestic partnerships, both same-sex and opposite-sex, are increasingly common. Many traditional health care plans are not available to domestic partners. Employees may welcome participation in HRAs, VEBAs, and other arrangements that are open to domestic partners.

Learning Objectives. This chapter was prepared to provide an overview of current federal estate and gift tax rules, address the impact of recent tax cuts and low interest rates on wealth preservation, and to highlight the mechanics and transfer tax consequences of several selected estate planning techniques. Upon completion of this course, you will:

♦ Know current key federal estate and gift tax rules;
♦ Explore new capital gains, dividend, and income tax cut implications on estate planning;
♦ Understand the impact of interest rates;
♦ Become familiar with the general structure and use of several popular estate planning opportunities including the:

- Intra-family loan,
- Private annuity,
- Self-canceling installment notes (SCIN),
- Qualified personal residence trust (QPRT),
- Grantor retained annuity trust (GRAT), and
- Family limited partnership (FLP);

♦ Account for general transfer tax consequences in selected transactions; and
♦ Evaluate some of the advantages and disadvantages of specific estate planning techniques.

INTRODUCTION

Estate planning, by its nature, is usually long- term planning. Especially during the most recent years, when the stock market—and retirement and regular portfolio accounts that have been invested in the stock market—continued to languish, individuals have been returning in record numbers to more conservative, "lifetime" strategies under which wealth is preserved as well as grown. Planning that considers current circumstances, as well as future contingencies, often gets complicated rather quickly. Even the typical estate planning goals—preserving resources, making gifts, and providing a family legacy, at the same time minimizing income, gift, and estate taxes— can seem to be at odds with one another.

Estate planning has become further complicated because the federal estate tax rules are a moving target. The *Economic Growth and Tax Relief Reconciliation Act of 2001* (EGTRRA '01) gradually increases the exclusion amount for estate tax, repeals the federal estate tax altogether in 2010, and reinstates the tax in 2011. The transitory nature of the rules, coupled with the inherent uncertainty in long-range planning, can make estate planning a challenge.

Although the *Jobs and Growth Tax Relief Reconciliation Act of 2003* (JGTRRA '03) does not change any of the estate or gift tax rules, its provisions have a great impact on wealth preservation. Under JGTRRA'03, reduced tax rates for ordinary income, capital gains, and dividends not only increase wealth but could also trigger a reassessment of previous estate planning.

In addition, low interest rates and other current economic factors have become major ingredients of the wealth preservation planning mix. Despite — or perhaps because of — the twists and turns in the tax rules, and the "downs" in interest rates in 2003, various planning opportunities arose to fit these times. This chapter briefly reviews key EGTRRA '01 estate and gift tax rules, examines the effects of JGTRRA '03 on wealth preservation planning, explores several estate planning opportunities in a low-interest rate environment, and highlights two hot estate planning tools that are the outgrowth of current conditions: the grantor retained annuity trust (GRAT) and the family limited partnership (FLP).

LEGISLATIVE ISSUES

EGTRRA: Estate and gift tax

EGTRRA '01 is implementing many changes to the traditional estate tax during the next eight years. In 2003, $1 million can be excluded from federal estate tax. In 2004 and 2005, the exclusion amount increases to $1.5 million. In 2006 through 2008, the exclusion increases to $2 million, then tops off at $3.5 million in 2009. The estate tax is repealed in 2010, but returns in 2011 with an exemption of only $1 million unless Congress makes the repeal permanent.

> *Caution.* As the tax rules currently stand, the estates of people dying in 2010 will pay no transfer tax, while the estates of those dying in 2011 or beyond could pay up to a 55-percent rate on estates over $3 million.

> *Observation.* The lifetime gift tax exclusion should not be confused with the annual exclusion. An annual exclusion of $11,000 applies to exclude from the application of any gift tax the first $11,000 of all gifts given to any one individual during the calendar year. That amount doubles to $22,000 for a married couple who elect to "split" their gifts. The $1 million gift tax exclusion, on the other hand, exempts the first $1 million in value of all otherwise taxable gifts (gifts valued over the $11,000 annual gift exclusion level).

Unlike the gradual increase in the estate tax exclusion, the gift tax exclusion, which is now $1 million, will remain at $1 million. What has been commonly referred to as the "unified credit" for gift and estate tax liability will be decoupled when the estate "goes away" in 2010. In 2010 and beyond, the gift tax calculation takes on a new formula, based on a new rate schedule, minus amounts allowable as credit in preceding years. Thus, there is still a need for wealth preservation and transfer planning despite the highly anticipated federal estate tax "repeal."

STUDY QUESTION

1. The Economic Growth and Tax Relief Reconciliation Act of 2001 (EGTRRA '01):

    a. Gradually increases the federal estate tax exclusion amount
    b. Repeals the federal estate tax in 2010
    c. Reinstates the federal estate tax in 2011
    d. All of the above

JGTRRA's wealth preservation opportunities

JGTRRA '03, one of the largest tax cuts in history, reduces tax rates for capital gains, dividends, and individual marginal tax rates on income. Although JGTRRA '03 makes no changes to the federal estate and gift tax scheme set in motion by EGTRRA '01, the new cuts on capital gains rates, dividend tax rates, and individual income rates have a significant impact on gifting and wealth preservation planning overall. JGTRRA's key wealth preservation provisions are outlined here.

Capital gains. The maximum net capital gains tax rate falls from 20 to 15 percent, but only for tax years 2003-2008, after which it is scheduled to return to 20 percent. The current 10 percent capital gains rate for lower-income taxpayers falls to 5 percent for the 2003 through 2008 period, then drops to zero for one year, 2008, before returning to 10 percent in 2009. Lower tax rates for property held for five years, rather than the regular long-term capital gain holding period of one year, however, have been eliminated.

Dividends. Under JGTRRA, dividends will be taxed at a maximum rate of 15 percent for most taxpayers. The 15 percent rate is effective for dividends received in tax years beginning after 2002 and terminating on December 31, 2008. The 5 percent rate falls to zero percent for 2008.

Income tax rates. JGTRRA accelerates into 2003 EGTRRA's individual margin rate cuts that were not set to kick in until 2006 and beyond. The highest rate of 38.6 percent falls to 35 percent. The other rates are 10, 25, 28, and 33 percent. All rates are retroactive to January 1, 2003 and all are subject to EGTRRA's sunset provisions, which revive the old 15, 28, 31, 36, and 39.6 percent rate brackets after 2010.

JGTRRA in action. Lower capital gains rates and lower tax rates on dividends yield more to invest, preserve, or give to family members or charitable organizations. Capital gains rate changes, along with the new treatment of dividends, should prove to be good fortune for individuals who are heavily invested in appreciated stocks and in real estate.

> *Practice Pointer.* Taxpayers with appreciated assets should consider transferring assets to family members in lower tax brackets, including children over age 13 (who are exempt from the "kiddie tax"). If the assets produce income, relatives in lower tax brackets will pay less income tax on the asset.

> *Observation.* The annual gift exclusion is currently $11,000. A parent can only give each child $11,000 per year without filing a federal gift tax return and potentially dipping into the parent's lifetime gift exemption ($1 million).

JGTRRA offers tax savings opportunities in multiple planning instances: income tax, capital gains, and estate tax. The new, low tax rate on dividends means more money for investing or for transferring to the next generation. The family's overall income tax liability can be lowered by transferring assets to lower-bracketed relatives. Family members in lower tax brackets will have less capital gains tax exposure when the property is sold (if the individual is in the 5 percent capital gains bracket). Plus, appreciation on a gifted asset is removed from the grantor's estate and thus is not subject to potential estate tax (so long as the grantor lives for three years after the transfer).

Estate planning and JGTRRA's basis boon. JGTRRA's changes in the tax rates ease some of the tax apprehension that can arise when taxpayers sell low-basis assets. The lower tax rate on capital gains means that taxpayers can diversify the family portfolio by selling highly appreciated assets without the historically harsh capital gains tax hit.

Moreover, the frequent dilemma of whether an asset should be gifted to a child during the parent's lifetime or should transfer to the child at the parent's death may be less daunting now that the capital gains rate has taken a dip. Inherited assets get a step-up in basis to date-of-death fair market value—for now (this step-up in basis goes away in 2010). Gifted assets, on the other hand, keep the giver's basis, but with a lower capital gains tax, a low basis has less tax bite. Consequently, lifetime gifts to family members may now be more attractive.

> *Observation.* After the temporary repeal of the federal estate tax in 2010, property acquired from a decedent's estate will no longer enjoy a step-up in basis to the fair market value of that property on the date of death. Instead, carryover basis will

apply. Inherited property will have the same basis as it would have in the hands of the decedent, just as gifted property is currently treated. Carryover basis is usually lower than a basis step-up, meaning that when heirs sell the inherited property, the amount exposed to capital gains tax will be greater than before the repeal of the federal estate tax.

Practice Pointer. It's never too early to encourage and assist clients in gathering and maintaining records on each asset the client owns, from securities (confirmation statements), to real estate (recorded deeds), to household items of more than nominal value (receipts or historical appraisals). As 2010 nears, knowledge of an asset's tax basis will command even greater attention in transfer planning.

STUDY QUESTIONS

2. JGTRRA accomplished all *except:*

   a. Lowering tax on capital gains
   b. Reducing tax on dividend income
   c. Accelerating individual marginal rate cuts
   d. Increasing the gift tax annual exclusion

3. Mr. Smith dies in January 2010 and leaves a parcel of unimproved real estate to his niece, Sally. Mr. Smith originally bought the property for $15,000. On the day he died, it was worth $50,000. In November 2011, Sally sells the property for $51,000. Under the current rules, what could Sally expect the capital gains tax exposure to be as to this parcel?

   a. Tax on $1,000
   b. Tax on $36,000
   c. Tax on $51,000
   d. No capital gains consequence

4. Mary owns property valued at $100,000. In 2003, she sold the property to her daughter, Jane, for $75,000. What amount is potentially subject to gift tax?

   a. $25,000
   b. $15,000
   c. $14,000
   d. $0

ECONOMIC ISSUES: THE LOW INTEREST RATE ENVIRONMENT

When interest rates are low, as they have been recently, certain wealth preservation opportunities take the spotlight. Asset transfer tools that are "advantaged" by low interest rates include family loans, installment sales, private annuities, self-canceling installment notes, and charitable lead trusts. Techniques that may be "disadvantaged" by low interest rates are charitable remainder trusts, grantor retained annuity trusts, and the qualified personal residence trust. However, astute individuals, maximizing on the planning opportunities, can strategize for the future.

Applicable federal rate

The applicable federal rate of interest, which is used in a variety of estate planning computations, is key in creating potentially favorable tax outcomes. Released each month by the IRS, the federal interest rates typically mirror the same highs and lows reflected in commercial interest rate trends.

Imputed interest. Applicable federal rates are used as the baseline test for imputed interest. The difference between the below-market rate used and the prevailing federal rate is imputed to both the lender and the borrower. The IRS holds both parties tax-responsible for the higher, imputed rate. The applicable federal rate is often selected as the rate of interest in family loans and sales because it is the lowest possible rate that avoids the imputed interest characterization.

Three federal rates are applicable to debt instruments, depending on the duration of the debt obligation.

Duration of Debt	Applicable Federal Rate
Not over three years	Short-term rate
Between three and nine years	Mid-term rate
More than nine years	Long-term rate

Section 7520 rate

The Code Sec. 7520 rate is used to determine the present value of an annuity, an interest for life or a term of years, and a remainder or reversionary interest. The Section 7520 rate is used in series of increasingly popular estate planning tools: private annuities, self-canceling installment notes, grantor retained annuity trusts, qualified personal residence trusts, and charitable lead trusts, among others.

The Section 7520 rate is equal to 120 percent of the federal midterm rate in effect for the month in which the valuation date falls, rounded to the nearest 2/10 of 1 percent. When using the Section 7520 rate, the planner has a choice among three rates:

♦ The rate for the month in which the valuation date falls;
♦ The rate for the prior month; and
♦ The rate for two months prior to the month in which the valuation date falls.

Some recent examples: In July 2003, the Section 7520 rate fell to an all-time low of 3.0 percent. In previous months, the rate bounced up, then back down from the now-shattered record of 3.6 percent released in

November 2002, and again in both April and June 2003. In November 1999 the rate was a much higher 7.4 percent. In certain circumstances, the more than halving of the interest rate has meant a more than doubling of the possible estate planning benefits.

STUDY QUESTION

5. Imputed interest is:

    a. Minimum federal interest
    b. Foregone interest
    c. Below-market interest
    d. The difference between minimum federal interest and interest actually paid

ESTATE PLANNING VEHICLES

Are intrafamily loans still viable tools?

One strategy for making lifetime transfers to family members without taking a gift tax hit has been to gift up to the annual exclusion amount, then provide additional sums in the form of a loan. When interest rates are low, loans to family members are more attractive. Parents or grandparents may consider making loans to family members, rather than an outright gift. Low interest rates can:

♦ Preserve the annual gift tax exclusion, if the loan is a "true loan;"
♦ Avoid gift tax on additional amounts transferred, with proper planning; and
♦ Ease the loan repayment "sting."

"True Loan." The annual gift exclusion only allows the giver an $11,000 transfer, per recipient per year, without gift tax consequences. Loans do not affect the annual gift tax exclusion, if they are "true loans," because they are not considered gifts. Care should be taken that all of the rules necessary to create a legitimate loan are satisfied. To make sure that the loan is recognized as a "true loan" and not a gift, a promissory note with default provisions and penalties for late payments should be executed. The borrower should make interest payments at least annually, and the lender should report the interest payments as ordinary income on his or her tax return. In support of the "true loan," practitioners should assist clients with the proper documentation, determine that the intrafamily loan is not part of a preexisting gifting plan, and ensure that the loans are not part of a regular gifting pattern.

Impact of interest rate. The interest rate is also an important factor in making sure that the loan is not treated, in whole or in part, as a gift. Although a low interest rate can translate into a more affordable repayment arrangement for the borrower, practitioners should caution clients against setting an interest rate that is too low. In the case of intrafamily loans, the foregone interest may be imputed as taxable income to the lender and then treated as a gift to the borrower. In general, so long as the applicable federal rate is used, interest won't be imputed and the IRS won't consider the loan to be a gift loan. The foregone interest is treated as a gift. However, under Code Sec. 7872(C)(2), a *de minimis* exception applies to gift loans over $10,000, so long as the loan proceeds are not directly used to purchase income-producing assets. If the *de minimis* exception applies, the foregone interest does not result in a gift.

> *Observation.* "Foregone" interest is the difference between the amount of interest that would have been due during a given period calculated at the applicable federal rate and the amount of interest actually payable on the loan for the period. Forgone interest is imputed to both the lender and the borrower.

Gift tax consequence. If the loan is not a "true loan," the lender may incur a gift tax consequence. The timing of the lender's gift tax liability for a gift loan depends on whether the loan is a demand or a term loan. If the loan is a demand loan, the lender is deemed to have made a gift to the borrower on the last day of each year the loan is outstanding. The amount of the gift is calculated on December 31 of the year the demand loan is still outstanding. If the loan is a term loan, the lender is deemed to have made a cash gift to the borrower on the date the loan was made.

In the following example, Stella has gift tax consequences because she gave her daughter an interest-free loan that was more than $10,000 in a single year. If Stella had used the prevailing applicable federal rate as the intrafamily loan's rate of interest, she may have avoided potential gift tax.

> *Example.* Stella makes a demand loan to her daughter, Luna, in the amount of $1 million on October 2, 2002. The interest rate on the loan is 2 percent. However, the federal applicable rate for October 2002 was 4.2 percent. The amount of foregone interest on the loan, as of December 31, 2002, was $22,000 (the excess of $42,000 (4.2 percent of $1 million) over $20,000 (2 percent of $1 million, the amount of interest payable on December 31, 2002)).

> *Example.* Using the same scenario as in the previous example, the amount of the gift is calculated on December 31 and is equal to the amount of interest forgone during the year. Thus, Stella's gift to Luna is $22,000.

Have private annuities remained a good investment?

A private annuity from a family member is the transfer of property in exchange for a promise to make a series of payments. A parent can use such an annuity to move appreciated property out of his or her estate to a child while at the same time creating cash flow available to the parent.

The amount of the annuity is calculated by dividing the annuity factor into the value of the transferred property. The annuity factor is derived from the actuarial tables found in IRS Publication 1457. The factor takes into account the annuitant's age and the appropriate interest rate (the applicable Code Sec. 7520 rate).

> *Example.* A parent, age 76, transfers a parcel of real estate valued at $1,000,000 to his child in exchange for an annuity. The interest rate is 5.2 percent. The annuity factor is 7.3193 (using Table S of IRS Publication 1457). To calculate the amount of the annuity, the asset value is divided by the annuity factor ($1,000,000 ÷ 7.3193). The amount of the annuity payment over the parent's lifetime is $136,625.

> *Example.* All the facts in the previous example apply, except a lower interest rate of 3.2 percent is available. The annuity factor is 8.312 and the amount of the annuity payment over the parent's lifetime is $120,308.

> *Observation.* The IRS actuarial tables cannot be used if there is a 50 percent chance that the annuitant will die within one year after the annuity is issued. To avoid an IRS "sham trust" challenge, a written medical opinion should be obtained regarding the annuitant's chances of surviving for one year after the issuance of the annuity.

> *Practice Pointer.* The goal is to calculate the value of the annuity so that it equals the value of the transferred property. If the value of the property transferred from the parent to the child exceeds the present value of the annuity, the excess value is a gift with gift tax consequences.

STUDY QUESTION

6. Where can a practitioner find the annuity factor used in calculating the amount of a private annuity?

    a. All of those below
    b. IRS Publication 550
    c. IRS actuarial tables in Publication 1457
    d. Code Sec. 1274

Advantages of a private annuity. A low interest rate environment means that the child's annuity payment is less. A low interest rate can also benefit the parent's estate planning in another way: fewer dollars are returning to the parent's estate; thus, a lower federal estate tax burden will result in the future. The annuity payments, however, are included in the parent's estate.

During the parent's lifetime, a portion of each annuity payment represents tax-free recovery of the parent's investment in the arrangement and a portion represents gain on the transfer. The balance is ordinary income.

A private annuity is essentially a sale of property. At the end of the term (measured by the life of the parent), the asset is not subject to estate tax. Although the child does not get a step-up in basis at the parent's death, the fair market value of the asset at the time of the transfer applies as basis, rather than the parent's original (most likely lower) basis.

Disadvantages of a private annuity. Disadvantages of a private annuity include:

♦   If the parent outlives his or her life expectancy, the child ultimately overpays for the property because the annuity payments must continue throughout the parent's lifetime.
♦   No part of a private annuity payment is deductible as interest.
♦   The private annuity cannot be secured, so there is no guarantee that the annuity will be paid.
♦   If the parent "forgives" a payment, the IRS might view the arrangement as a sham.

STUDY QUESTION

7.   Optimally, the value of a private annuity should:

   a.   Exceed the value of the transferred property
   b.   Equal the value of the transferred property
   c.   Be less than the value of the transferred property
   d.   Be recalculated annually

Self-canceling installment notes: Just smoke and mirrors?

A self-canceling installment note (SCIN) is used to transfer property from one individual to another, often between family members. The SCIN's best feature is that the child's obligation to repay the note ends when the parent dies, even if amounts are still due. Self-canceling installment notes, like intrafamily loans, installment sales, and private annuities, are advantaged by low interest rates because a lower rate means the child pays less.

> *Observation.* In order for the IRS to accept a SCIN as evidence of a sale and not a gift, the note must reflect a premium, either in the form of a higher purchase price or a

higher interest rate, providing consideration for the self-canceling feature.

Advantages of a SCIN. Besides the benefits just noted, SCINs offer valuable estate planning features:

- Property transfer is characterized as a sale, rather than a gift;
- Income stream to the seller or noteholder;
- Eliminates estate tax on the transfer because the SCIN becomes worthless upon the seller's death;
- Seller holds security on the transferred property; and
- Buyer can deduct interest paid on the SCIN.

Federal tax consequences are also beneficial:

- No gift tax is incurred, if the SCIN is properly executed;
- No estate tax is due at the death of the seller because the SCIN has no value (due to the self-canceling feature). However, amounts already repaid to the seller are considered part of the seller's estate;
- Capital gains and income taxes are owed on the portion paid to the seller, but not on any portion that remains unpaid;
- Income tax deduction can be claimed by the buyer on the interest paid; and
- Cost basis for the buyer is the full purchase price (even if it is not paid due to the self-canceling feature).

When structuring a SCIN, the practitioner should ensure that:

- An accurate valuation of the transferred property is obtained;
- A reasonable selling price is set, or else the transaction will be deemed a gift;
- A reasonable interest rate is set (the note may use the federal rate);
- The terms of the SCIN are comparable to an arm's length transaction;
- A sales agreement is executed in addition to the SCIN;
- The premium factor reflects economic realities;
- The parties operate according to the terms of the note by making timely payments and enforcing penalties for any late payments;
- A reasonable expectation exists that the indebtedness will be repaid;
- The seller doesn't retain control over the property after the sale; and
- Cancellation feature is irrevocable.

SCIN caveat. Because payments must continue throughout the seller's life, the buyer might end up paying more for the property than the original selling price, just as with a private annuity. However, the

SCIN may set a payment term, which cannot be any longer than the life expectancy of the seller.

STUDY QUESTION

8. Which of the following is *not* a characteristic of a self-canceling installment note (SCIN)?

   a. The debt is canceled at the seller's death
   b. The cost of the property is known
   c. The seller holds a security interest
   d. The purchaser may deduct interest

Comparison of characteristics of installment sales, private annuities, and self-canceling installment notes

	Installment Sale	Private Annuity	SCIN
Cost of property known?	Yes	No	Yes
Duration of payments known?	Yes	No	No
Security interest?	Yes	No	Yes
Interest deductible?	Yes	No	Yes

Do qualified personal residence trusts still work?

A qualified personal residence trust (QPRT) is an irrevocable trust that enables a homeowner to make a future gift of the residence to his or her children while continuing to reside in the home for a set number of years. QPRTs are popular with many homeowners who desire to pass appreciated residential property to their children and save federal estate and gift taxes at the same time. A QPRT's tax advantages are strictly controlled by regulations under Code Sec. 2702. Despite lower interest rates and a higher capital gains exclusion on the sale of a principal residence, QPRTs have retained their usefulness. The bottom line is that real estate continues to appreciate more rapidly than most investments, and QPRTs can effectively remove that appreciation from being subject to gift and estate tax.

In a QPRT, a homeowner transfers his or her residence to a trust for a term of years, after which ownership of the residence transfers to the children. During the term of the QPRT, the homeowner continues to live in the house. At the end of the term, the property is distributed to the children without passing through the donor's estate, thereby avoiding federal estate tax on the trust's assets.

> *Observation.* Through Rev. Proc. 2003-42, the IRS issued an annotated sample declaration of trust, with alternate provisions, that meets the qualified personal residence trust (QPRT) requirements.

QPRT advantages. The primary advantage of a QPRT is that the full value of the residence ultimately can be transferred to the owner's children, but for federal gift tax purposes, the property is valued at a discount. In addition, the value of the house is "frozen" for gift tax purposes, meaning any appreciation in the value of the house after it is transferred to the trust is not subject to gift tax. Because of the necessary trust term, family members of a younger generation—grandchildren, nieces and nephews, siblings or their spouses—are generally named as QPRT beneficiaries. Although the actual transfer of the house to the QPRT is a taxable gift, the taxable value of the gift is only a fraction of the full value of the house. The actual value of the gift (and the gift tax savings) depends upon the donor's age, the duration of the QPRT, and the Code Sec. 7520 federal interest rates in effect at the time of the transfer. For example, the longer the QPRT term, the lower the gift value for gift tax purposes and the greater the gift tax savings. The value of the donor's completed gift—a contingent remainder trust interest—equals the fair market value of the transferred property minus (a) the present value of the donor's retained income interest in the property (as determined by the Section 7520 rates) and (b) the present value of the donor's retained contingent reversion in the property (also determined by Section 7520 rates).

STUDY QUESTION

9. Which would make the following statement *incorrect*? "A qualified personal residence trust (QPRT) may hold:"

   a. A mortgaged home
   b. A home jointly owned by spouses
   c. A qualified vacation home
   d. A qualified home, but no other assets

When interest rates are low, the value of the donor's right to occupy the property is also low, but the value of the gift of the residence at the end of the trust's term is higher, with higher gift tax potential. The higher the federal interest rate the higher the QPRT's potential tax savings. When interest rates are low, practitioners should consider whether the QPRT is the right estate planning technique for clients. The QPRT may still be a good planning tool for some clients for whom the personal residence is the only, or best, asset in terms of estate planning.

QPRT disadvantages. If the donor wishes to continue living in the residence after the end of the term, the donor must pay fair market rent to his or her children, the new owners of the residence. In general, the house must continue to be available to the homeowner as a personal residence during the trust term; otherwise, the trust ceases to be a QPRT. In addition, the donor must outlive the term of the trust or the trust is ineffective, and the home is included in the donor's estate.

Have low interest rates enhanced grantor retained annuity trusts?

A grantor retained annuity trust (GRAT) is an effective tool for transferring the maximum amount of wealth while minimizing gift or estate tax. A GRAT is an irrevocable trust that pays the grantor an annuity for a term of years, with the remainder going to the grantor's beneficiaries.

GRATs are authorized by Code Secs. 2702(a)(2)(B) and 2702(b). The grantor trust rules, set out in Code Sections 671 through 677 also apply to GRATS. The grantor is treated as the owner of the trust, for tax purposes, if he or she retains specific rights or powers over the trust. The grantor is taxed on trust income and receives any charitable deductions or credits.

The grantor's annuity interest in a GRAT is a specified sum or fixed percentage of the value of the assets transferred. The annuity amount is paid to the grantor regardless of the rate of return on the trust's assets. The value of the annuity payments is determined by reference to actuarial tables published by the IRS using the Code Sec. 7520 rate. The value of the remainder interest is the amount contributed to the GRAT, less the value of the annuity payments.

STUDY QUESTIONS

10. What is the effect of the "grantor trust" rule?

    a. Grantor retains certain interests in the trust
    b. Grantor is treated as the owner of the trust for income tax purposes
    c. Grantor receives any charitable deductions or credits against tax
    d. All of the above

11. A grantor retained annuity trust (GRAT) is a trust in which the grantor:

    a. Retains the right to receive a fixed amount payable not less frequently than annually
    b. Retains the right to receive a fixed percentage of the fair market value of the trust property
    c. Has an income interest, as determined by the trustee
    d. Has a remainder interest

The remainder—the amount that will eventually pass to the grantor's beneficiaries—is considered a gift at the time the GRAT is created. The IRS imposes a gift tax on the remainder at the time the trust is created, rather than when the beneficiaries actually receive the remainder. The transfer of assets to the trust does not qualify for the annual gift tax exclusion, however, because it is not a gift of a present interest.

At the end of the GRAT term, the remainder passes to the grantor's family members, free of transfer tax. If the grantor dies before the GRAT ends, however, the assets revert to the grantor's estate and are subject to estate tax. Nevertheless, the grantor's tax position is generally no worse than if he or she had not created the GRAT.

A grantor establishes a GRAT by transferring income-producing assets to a trust. Factors considered in a GRAT calculation are:

- Transfer amount;
- Annuity amount or fixed percentage;
- Timing of the payments;
- Grantor's age;
- Term of the trust; and
- Prevailing Code Sec. 7520 rate.

> *Example.* Mary, who is 65 years old, transfers $500,000 to a GRAT in June 2003 when the Section 7520 interest rate is 3.6. The trust term is 10 years. Mary retains a 10 percent interest in the trust, payable at the end of each year of the trust, and receives an annuity of $50,000 each year. The value of Mary's retained annuity is $413,740. This number is reached by multiplying $50,000 by 8.2748, the annuity factor under Table B of IRS Publication 1457.

In the preceding example, Mary made a taxable gift of $86,260 ($500,000 – $413,740) when she established the trust. However, no gift tax was due because Mary had not used her $1 million lifetime gift tax credit. At the end of the 10-year term, the trust property goes to Mary's children.

Impact of low interest rates. A low interest rate environment gives savvy individuals the opportunity to maximize tax-savings using GRATs. The interest rate applied to a GRAT is fixed at the time the GRAT is created. A lower interest rate usually translates into a lower gift tax. However, when market conditions change and interest rates increase, the rate of return on the assets increases. If the rate of return on investments exceeds the GRAT's interest rate, the assets will appreciate. The amount of the remainder interest passing to the beneficiaries becomes considerably more than was initially calculated. Any appreciation in the assets passes to the beneficiaries, free from transfer tax. No additional gift tax is imposed on the excess amounts because the gift was completed when the trust was created.

STUDY QUESTIONS

12. Which of the following techniques does *not* use the Code Sec. 7520 rate, published monthly by the IRS?

    a. Grantor retained annuity trust (GRAT)

     b.   Intrafamily loan

     c.   Self-canceling installment notes (SCIN)

     d.   Qualified personal residence trust (QPRT)

13. Any appreciation in the assets of a GRAT remainder interest passes to the grantor's beneficiaries:

     a.   With estate tax

     b.   With gift tax

     c.   Transfer tax-free

     d.   With capital gains tax

14. In a low-interest rate environment, which of the following is *false*?

     a.   Private annuity = lower payments

     b.   QPRT = increased gift tax

     c.   Intrafamily loan = no gift tax

     d.   SCIN = payor's advantage

How can family limited partnerships still transfer assets at a sizable discount?

The family limited partnership (FLP) is a popular way to transfer assets to children and grandchildren. Although FLPs are frequently used to pass on the family farm, business, or real estate interest, they can also transfer other assets that are expected to appreciate.

FLPs are created by moving assets to a partnership, according to applicable state law. In general, appreciated assets can be contributed to an FLP without triggering a tax consequence.

> *Observation.* The general rule that assets can be transferred to an FLP (or a family limited liability company, LLC), tax-free, does not apply if the FLP or LLC is an "investment partnership." If more than 80 percent of the assets comprise securities and cash, the FLP or LLC will be considered an investment partnership, in which case contributions could trigger gain recognition under Code Sec. 721(b).

In exchange for transferring assets to the FLP, the parent receives a small general partnership interest (a 1 or 2 percent interest) and a much larger limited partnership interest (the remaining 98 or 99 percent). The parent keeps the general partnership interest and transfers portions of the limited partnership interest to the children or to trusts for their benefit. The general partnership interest gives the parent control over the business.

15. In general, which of following appreciated asset combinations can be contributed to a family limited partnership (FLP) without triggering a tax consequence?

   a. 90 percent in residential property, 10 percent cash
   b. 50 percent securities, 40 percent cash, 10 percent real estate
   c. 90 percent securities, 10 percent real estate
   d. 90 percent cash, 10 percent real estate

FLP Advantages. The FLP continues to be a favored vehicle for estate planning, asset protection, and transfer of wealth from one generation to another. FLPs are an attractive estate planning tool because "more" can be transferred for "less."

Discount for lack of control. The limited partnership interests transferred to the children are worth less, for transfer tax purposes, than the fair market value of underlying assets. Court decisions have enabled taxpayers to discount the value of gifts of FLP interests by 20 to 40 percent. These discounts are allowed because a FLP minority interest cannot control how the business is run, demand distributions, or call for liquidation. In addition, the lack of control makes a FLP minority interest less marketable compared to the underlying assets held in the FLP.

> **Example.** Sandi transferred an organic berry farm, valued at $1 million, to a FLP. She retained a one percent general partnership interest and distributed 10 percent in limited partnership interests to each of her four children. By using an FLP, Sandi may transfer $400,000 in assets at a discounted value (for gift tax purposes) between and $240,000 and $320,000.

> **Example:** Sandi transferred $1 million in assets to an FLP in which she holds the general partnership interest. Sandi distributed 1 percent in limited partnership interests to each of her 10 grandchildren. A 1 percent interest in $1 million in assets would correspond to $10,000. However, for gift tax purposes, the value of the transferred limited partnership interest (discounted for lack of control) may be between $6,000 and $8,000.

Gift tax. Although the transfer of an interest in an FLP is a taxable gift, the taxable value of the gift is a fraction of the full value of assets. Moreover, FLP interests transferred to the donees are completed gifts so long as there is an immediate economic benefit. In addition, the assets transferred to the FLP are removed from the parent's estate.

Observation. In the preceding examples, Sandi can use her annual gift tax exclusion (currently $11,000) to make gifts of limited partnership interests without incurring gift tax.

Although the use of a FLP as an estate planning vehicle offers substantial federal estate and gift tax savings, there are significant nontax advantages associated with FLPs as well. Nontax benefits include the donor's retained control over transferred assets, protection of assets from creditors (limited liability feature), and the facilitation of using annual exclusion gifts.

FLP disadvantages. Family limited partnerships are not without drawbacks:

♦ *IRS attack on valuation:* The IRS may attack the FLP based on the valuation of the partnership interests. Unless it can be proven that the children have a legitimate capital interest in the partnership, the IRS can disregard their partnership interests for income tax purposes.

♦ *No basis step-up:* Even if the FLP arrangement is successful in lowering transfer taxes, it will be at the loss of the Code Sec. 1014 stepped-up basis. A FLP takes the donor's basis in the contributed assets. Although JGTRRA lowered the capital gains tax rate, there could be substantial tax consequences when the FLP assets are sold.

Recent court decisions. Features of the FLP have been issues in the case law, including:

♦ *Discount valuation:* Although the FLP continues to be a popular tax planning vehicle, the IRS and the courts have viewed many family limited partnerships discounts with skepticism. In a recent Tax Court case, *Knight v. Commr, 115 TC No. 36,* the Tax Court did not permit the valuation discounts to the extent that they were used by the taxpayers.

The Tax Court found that the fair market value of partnership interests transferred was based on a pro-rata net asset value of the partnership, less a 15 percent discount for a minority interest and lack of marketability. The court rejected the discount recommended by the taxpayers' expert, which was an aggregate 44 percent discount consisting of a 10 percent portfolio discount, a 10 percent minority interest discount, and a 30 percent lack of marketability discount. The court rejected the expert's conclusions as contrary to the evidence presented.

♦ *Economic benefit and the annual gift tax exclusion:* In *Hackl v. Commr,* CA-7, July 11, 2003, the Seventh Circuit recently affirmed the Tax Court's ruling that gifts of shares in a family limited liability company were without immediate economic benefit. The transferred family LLC shares amounted to future interests and were ineligible for the Code Sec. 2503 annual gift exclusion.

Observation. Family LLCs are comparable to FLPs in the estate planning context. Although all the members of an LLC can participate in management (in contrast to a FLP, which is managed by a general partner), LLC management is often assigned to a manager, typically a family member of an older generation.

Under the LLC operating agreement in *Hackl*, the donor/husband was manager-for-life. During his tenure, the company operated at a loss and did not make any distributions to its shareholders. The shareholders needed the manager's approval to withdraw from the company or sell shares. If a member transferred his or her shares without consent, the transferee would receive the shares' economic rights, but not any membership or voting rights. The Seventh Circuit agreed with the Tax Court and the IRS that the restrictions on the transferability of the shares meant that the shares were essentially without immediate value to the donees. The Court held that although the gifts of family LLC shares were outright gifts, they were future interest gifts that did not qualify for the annual gift tax exclusion.

FLP planning tips. Proper structuring can ensure that FLPs withstand IRS challenges. The following rules apply:

♦ The FLP buy-sell agreement must avoid terms that would diminish the economic value of the donee's interest. However, a right of first refusal generally would not be objectionable.

♦ The donor is permitted to retain ordinary controls; however, the donor cannot retain undue control over the distribution of income.

♦ The donor may not retain control over assets that are required to conduct the business and lease them to the partnership.

CONCLUSION

Multiple factors are considerations in wealth preservation planning. Thought must be given to changing tax rules, fluctuating economic conditions, and most certainly the client's personal and family circumstances.

JGTRRA'03 adds an extra layer of complexity—at the same time as it creates new opportunities—to estate planning and wealth preservation. Clients know that JGTRRA'03 was a huge tax cut, but most do not know the nuts and bolts of the new law and how it can maximize their tax savings. If clients don't respond to JGTRRA'03, they risk losing ground rapidly in the estate planning and wealth preservation areas.

As a rule of thumb in this changing environment, estate planning measures should be reviewed and updated at least once every two or three years. What was a good estate plan as late as 2000 most likely is ready to be revised. New income tax rates, gradual repeal then reinstatement of the estate tax, and the impact of lower interest rates are all reasons for ongoing reevaluation of wealth preservation and estate planning techniques.

CHAPTER 7: THE AUDIT PROCESS

Learning Objectives. This chapter was prepared to provide a description of the current state of the IRS audit program, the audit and appeals process, and the general direction of the program in the future. Upon completion of this chapter you will:

♦ Gain a general understanding of IRS's major enforcement programs;
♦ Comprehend the purpose of the audit;
♦ Explain where the tax outlays are applied;
♦ Become familiar with the types of audits and the new audit priorities;
♦ Be able to describe the administrative process (audits and Appeals options);
♦ Correctly use the tax payments options;
♦ Identify the various forums to litigate disputes; and
♦ Understand the challenges faced by the compliance and collections process.

INTRODUCTION

In recent years, there has been a growing belief among practitioners and the general public that the IRS is falling behind in audits and more taxpayers are playing the audit lottery. Widely reported substantial declines in the rate at which the IRS audits income tax returns have triggered concern that the declines could reduce taxpayers' motivation to voluntarily pay taxes. Many view the IRS's enforcement programs as critical support to our voluntary system. That is, the programs help provide taxpayers with confidence that their friends, neighbors, and business competitors are paying their share of taxes.

> *Observation.* The audit rate is calculated by dividing the number of returns examined by the total number of returns filed the previous calendar year.

> *Obseravtion.* The IRS switched from using the term "audit" to using "examination" several years ago, in part to project a less threatening public image. Tax professionals use "audits"

and "examinations" interchangeably to refer to the same process.

This chapter was created for anyone who wishes to better comprehend the subject of tax auditing. The course will review such areas as the basics of the major enforcement programs, the purpose of the audit, the new audit priorities, the administrative process, and the various forums to litigate tax disputes.

The General Accounting Office (GAO) has been reporting since the mid-nineties that audit rates had been steadily dropping for individuals, with only slight improvement seen during the past several years. For example, from 1996 to 2000 rates declined to 0.49 percent (with a slight increase in the following years). The audit rates for corporations have also generally declined. See the following table.

Year	1996	1997	1998	1999	2000	2001	2002
Total Individuals	1.67%	1.28%	0.99%	0.90%	0.49%	0.58%	0.57%
Corps < $10m	1.88%	2.22%	1.67%	1.16%	0.77%	0.60%	N/A
Corps > $10 m	25.33%	24.29%	21.43%	19.05%	16.30%	15.08%	N/A

Caution. "Audit rate" statistics portray only a portion of the IRS's efforts to enforce tax laws, and not all of those efforts have been declining. According to a recent GAO report entitled "IRS Should Continue to Expand Reporting on Its Enforcement Efforts," the IRS uses a variety of enforcement programs to check the accuracy of tax returns and contacts the taxpayer when problems are found. The IRS makes the contacts through four major enforcement programs that have existed for many years: (1) the math error program; (2) the document matching program; (3) the nonfiler program; and (4) the audit program.

Other enforcement programs

This chapter focuses on the audit program. The other three enforcement programs include:

♦   *Math error program.* While tax returns are being processed, this program uses IRS computers to identify and generate notices to contact taxpayers about obvious errors such as mathematical errors, omitted or inconsistent data, or other inconsistencies on the basis of other data reported on the return or to the IRS. These errors must be corrected to process a tax return.

♦ *Document matching program.* This program matches information on selected tax issues (usually income) reported on tax returns by individual taxpayers and reported on information returns by employers, banks, and other payers of income. Document matching also matches information returns (Schedule K-1) filed by pass-through entities—such as partnerships, trusts and S-corps—to individual tax returns. The IRS may contact taxpayers about any reporting discrepancies.

♦ *Nonfiler program.* This program identifies and contacts potential nonfilers of tax returns by using the date from information returns and previously filed income tax returns. IRS contacts can ask for the missing return or offer an IRS-generated return to substitute for the missing return.

STUDY QUESTIONS

1. The audit rate:

    a. Has been increasing over the past decade
    b. Has increased for corporations over the past decade
    c. Has increased for individuals over the past decade
    d. Is calculated by dividing the number of returns examined by the total number of returns filed the previous calendar year

2. The math error program:

    a. Is not a part of the enforcement program
    b. Matches information on selected tax issues (usually income) reported on tax returns by individual taxpayers reported on information returns by employers and banks
    c. Uses IRS computers to identify and generate notices to contact taxpayers about obvious errors, omitted or inconsistent data, or other inconsistencies on the basis of other data reported on the return or to the IRS
    d. Identifies and contacts potential nonfilers of tax returns by using the date from information returns and previously filed income tax returns

IRS'S BROAD POWERS TO AUDIT

Audits carry the broadest scope of all IRS enforcement mechanisms. They allow the IRS significant powers to obtain information, albeit defining those powers with detailed restrictions. Many of the restrictions are quite recent.

The Taxpayer Bill of Rights, for example, requires the IRS to provide a written statement detailing the taxpayer's rights and the IRS's obligations during the audit process, as well as including a general explanation of the audit and collection process. It also allows the taxpayer to make an audio recording of any in-person interview upon 10 days' advance notice.

The Internal Revenue Code does not explicitly limit the tax issues covered by an audit, unlike the limits imposed on the other enforcement programs (noted above).

Under Code Sec. 7602, audits can cover any issue on a tax return, including those that the other programs cover. The Code also establishes more rules governing the IRS's contacts with individual taxpayers under the audit program than it does for the other programs. These rules give the IRS significant powers to obtain information needed to determine an individual's tax liabilities when doing an audit, but also places restrictions on the use of those powers.

IRS auditing powers include the authority to examine books and records and take testimony for the purposes of determining the tax liability of a tax return. The IRS also has the power to use a summons to compel taxpayers and third-party recordkeepers (attorneys, enrolled agents, banks, brokers, accountants) to provide books and records, and to enter premises to examine objects subject to taxation, or relevant to the amount of tax that should be imposed. The taxpayer is to be notified of these summonses within three days of service of the summons (but in no case later than the 23rd day before the day fixed in the summons for production of records).

> *Observation.* Notice is not required for a "John Doe" summons (a summons issued to determine the identity of a person having a numbered bank account or similar arrangement). However, such a summons may be issued only after the IRS has shown adequate grounds for serving the summons.

EXAMINATIONS (AUDITS)

The IRS accepts most taxpayers' returns as filed. However, from time-to-time, the IRS may inquire about a taxpayer's return. The inquiry or examination may or may not result in more tax. The IRS may close the taxpayer's case without change or issue a refund.

The process of selecting a return for examination usually begins in one of two ways. First the IRS uses computer programs to identify returns that may have incorrect amounts. These programs may be based on information returns, such as Forms 1099 and W-2, on studies of past examinations, or on projects.

Second, the IRS uses information from outside sources that indicate that a return may have incorrect amounts. These sources may include newspapers, public records, and individuals. If the IRS determines that the information is accurate and reliable, then it may use it to select a return for examination. Audits may be handled by mail or by personal interview.

> *Observation.* In increasing numbers, the IRS's information gathering is performed in connection with the specific "enforcement" programs that it has undertaken. See "New Audit Priorities," below, for details.

Types of audits

Audits may be handled through the mail, office, or field. Audits handled through the mail are conducted by IRS Service Centers and are know as "correspondence examinations." Typically they involve a written request from the IRS service center to substantiate such items as charitable contributions.

Less complex cases are handled as office audits by tax auditors. Typically the scope of the audit is restricted to specific "significant items" identified during the screening process. If a tax auditor uncovers significant items that were not previously detected, the scope of the audit can be expanded.

More complex cases are handled as field audits by revenue agents, who are not restricted in the scope of the audit to identify significant items. Revenue agents are generally more highly educated and experienced than tax auditors; thus, they handle the more complex cases.

In a field audit, the revenue agent examines the taxpayer's books and records, usually at the taxpayer's business premises. The revenue agent's first task is to identify items that may require adjustment. Next, the agent verifies the accuracy of amounts reported by examining the taxpayer's books and records. Finally, the revenue agent analyzes the transaction underlying the return to determine whether the applicable law has been complied with by the taxpayer.

Results of an audit

Normally, when a taxpayer receives a letter from the IRS stating that it has satisfied all of the IRS's requests for additional information in an examination and that no further tax will be imposed (referred to as a "no change letter") the taxpayer's response is usually a huge sigh of relief. Based upon several recent government reports, however, the odds of receiving a no-change letter are not good.

The percent of no change on audit returns continues to be relatively low, currently ranging between 10% and 20%. This statistic means that if a taxpayer is audited, the chances are that the IRS examiner will find at least one taxpayer error for which a tax deficiency will be assessed. Prior to the DIF computerized system of selection, and the targeted programs to remedy specific non-compliance issues, 45% no-change rates were not uncommon. Statistics also indicated that the lowest no-change rate occurs in the group of taxpayers with the lowest income and the highest no-change rate occurs in audits of taxpayers with the highest income.

Our voluntary compliance system

The dreaded IRS audit performs a vital function in our tax system. It is the method by which our system of voluntary compliance is enforced. The possibility that an individual's return may be selected for audit brings about more accurate returns. However, there are those who do not file a return at all or are dishonest on their returns in hopes of never being audited.

Voluntary compliance means that each of us is responsible for filing a tax return when required and for determining and paying the correct amount of tax. While our tax system is based on self-assessment and reporting, compliance with tax laws is mandatory. Failing to file these required returns and failing to pay taxes may result in criminal prosecution and/or civil penalties.

For the vast majority of returns, the simple checking of computation (and other minor issues) is the only examination ever performed, and the taxpayer's determination of his or her tax liability is accepted by the IRS and cannot be challenged after the statute of limitations has run.

STUDY QUESTIONS

3. Audits:

    a. Are not broad in scope
    b. Are limited in scope by the Code
    c. Provide the government significant powers to obtain information
    d. Will continue to decline in the future

4. Audits are performed:

    a. To get after the taxpayer
    b. But are not vital to our tax system
    c. As the method by which our system of voluntary compliance is enforced
    d. By only checking the computations (and other minor issues)

5. If a taxpayer's return is selected for audit, what are the odds, based upon the general population, that the IRS will find nothing wrong and issue a "no-change" letter:

    a. 80 percent

> *b.* 60 percent
> *c.* 40 percent
> *d.* 20 percent

NEW AUDIT PRIORITIES

Since 2002, the IRS has spent time realigning its audit resources to focus on key areas of noncompliance. The strategy represents a new direction for the agency's compliance effort. The new approach will focus on high-risk areas of noncompliance. The IRS effort will generally focus first on promoters and then on participants in these organized schemes. The initiative will focus specifically on the following priority areas:

♦ Offshore credit card users;
♦ High-risk, high-income taxpayers;
♦ Abusive schemes and promoter investigations;
♦ High-income nonfilers;
♦ Unreported income; and
♦ The National Research Program.

In addition to refocusing its audit priorities, the IRS has also increased its resources for audits. The IRS Small Business/Self-Employed Division (SB/SE) will handle the new effort in these key areas affecting individuals and businesses. Compliance efforts will continue in other parts of the agency, such as the tax shelter initiatives in the Large and Mid-Sized Business Division (LMSB).

This strategy places a top priority on pursuing promoters of abusive schemes, shelters, and trusts and then identifying participants in these evasion efforts. The IRS has and will continue to use a full scope of tools and techniques ranging from summons enforcement, injunctions and criminal investigation of promoters to civil audits of participants. Although the IRS stated that it will continue to conduct traditional audits among the traditional cross-sections of the general taxpaying population, IRS officials have privately admitted that, with limited resources, focus on its special examination programs will necessarily lessen the number of audits conducted in other areas.

Offshore credit card project

It is not illegal to have an offshore credit card. However, there is a reasonable basis for believing that some people are using offshore credit cards to evade paying U.S. taxes. Credit cards provide easy access to offshore funds and accounts in tax haven countries that hide income. U.S. citizens must pay tax on their worldwide income. The IRS must use an extensive process to identify the taxpayer associated with each card.

Spending patterns, unusual expenses, proximity of spending, and repetitive expenses are all considered in the process. Once taxpayers are identified from credit cards, case building begins. The IRS already has developed hundreds of cases for civil audits or potential criminal investigations.

High-risk, high-income taxpayers

These taxpayers are generally upper-income taxpayers who have resources to engage in pass-through entities such as partnerships, trusts, and corporations.

The returns selected for examination will be those most likely to have unreported income or structured transactions.

> *Observation.* A structured transaction is one with limited economic benefit and whose primary purpose is to reduce or eliminate a tax liability. Structured transactions are generally done through one or more pass-through returns, such as Forms 1065 or 1120-S. The pass-through returns create paper losses that flow back to individual income tax returns, offsetting income from other sources.

Abusive schemes and promoter investigations. IRS efforts to combat abusive schemes and scams include:

♦ Schemes, reducing a person's tax liability by claiming inflated expenses, false deductions, unallowable credits, or excessive exemptions;

♦ Frivolous return arguments, telling taxpayers compliance is voluntary or the U.S. Constitution does not provide for tax collection;

♦ Promotion of slavery reparation claims, scams that claim compensation for people who have ancestors who were slaves;

♦ Abusive shelters and trusts, investments established for the purpose of hiding income from taxation;

♦ Employment tax schemes, employee leasing, paying in cash, and filing false payroll tax returns

High-income nonfilers

The IRS is focusing on the most egregious and high-risk segments of the population. Although "underworld figures" will be investigated under the program, its main focus will be on "main street." The target of this program includes physicians, lawyers, engineers and other professionals who for one reason or another have stopped filing income tax returns (and have been "encouraged" to continue to do so in the past for lack of getting caught).

Unreported income

Unreported income represents the largest component of the tax gap. The IRS has developed a new tool for identifying returns with a high probability of unreported income. The new tool is known as the Unreported Income Discriminant Index Formula (UI DIF).

All individual returns have traditionally been assigned a DIF score rating the probability of income being omitted from the return. The IRS has customarily used indirect examination methods to identify unreported income but until now has had no systemic method for selecting the returns at highest risk for unreported income.

UI DIF gives the IRS the ability to systemically identify returns at high risk for unreported income and all returns will now receive a UI DIF score in addition to the traditional DIF score.

National Research Program (NRP) examinations

These examinations will measure reporting compliance and identify compliance issues. NRP will enable the IRS to improve the examination selection. Each of these audits will be thorough. The taxpayers selected will be at random within each category of taxpayer and tax data subject to statistical sampling. However, the IRS has promised to make NRP examinations as quick as possible, in contrast to its predecessor, the Taxpayer Compliance Measurement Program (TCMP), which in the late nineteen nineties were being called "the audit from hell" by many taxpayers and tax practitioners.

Success of the National Research Program is crucial if the IRS is to target audits effectively, former Commissioner Charles Rossotti stated immediately before his departure in early 2003. Without new data, the IRS cannot formulate audit strategies that guarantee positive results. Every year, thousands of audits ultimately prove unnecessary because IRS personnel conclude that no-change is required to the taxpayer's return. These "no change" audits waste the limited resources of the IRS, Rossotti observed.

RESOLUTION OF THE AUDIT

Agreed cases

When the revenue agent or auditor has completed his or her examination of a return, he or she must explain any proposed adjustments to the taxpayer. If the taxpayer agrees with the proposed adjustments, he or she is asked to sign an appropriate form, which will usually have the effect of preventing the taxpayer from challenging any deficiency in Tax Court.

Unagreed cases

If a taxpayer does not agree with the examiner's proposed changes, the examiner's determination may be appealed to the Appeals Office (see discussion below). On the other hand, if a taxpayer does not wish to use the Appeals Office or disagrees with its findings, the case may be taken to the U.S. Tax Court, U.S. Court of Federal Claims, or the U.S. District Court where the taxpayer resides (for an individual) or where the taxpayer's principal place of business is located.

> *Caution.* Administrative and litigation costs may not be recovered unless the taxpayer first tries to resolve the case administratively, including going through the Appeals system, and provides the IRS with the information necessary to resolve the case.

Still no agreement; what now?

If a taxpayer does not agree with any or all of an IRS agent's findings, a telephone conference or meeting may be requested with the supervisor of the person who issued the findings. If a taxpayer still does not agree, the case may be appealed to the Appeals Office.

For those cases involving an examination of income, estate, gift, and certain excise taxes or penalties, the taxpayer will receive a formal Notice of Deficiency. The Notice of Deficiency allows the taxpayer to go to the Tax Court and provides the procedure to follow. If a taxpayer decides not to go to Tax Court, the IRS bills the amount due.

For cases involving a trust fund recovery penalty, or certain employment tax liabilities, the IRS bills the taxpayer a bill for the penalty. If the taxpayer does not appeal a denial of an offer in compromise or a denial of a penalty abatement, the IRS will continue its collection action.

"Fast track" programs

The IRS issued guidance to make permanent two "fast track" programs that enable taxpayers and the IRS to reach agreement on tax disputes more quickly. It also announced a pilot program to expedite the resolution of tax exempt bond disputes. If any issues remain unresolved, or the taxpayer decides not to use this process, then the taxpayer still has the right to use the normal Appeals process.

> *Observation.* So far, the fast-track programs have worked well and promise to be models for expanded future programs.

Fast track mediation program (FTM). This program gives small businesses, self-employed taxpayers, and the IRS the opportunity to mediate disputes through an IRS Appeals Officer, who acts as a neutral party. In this program, most tax disputes are resolved within

40 days compared to several months through the regular Appeals process.

FTM is optional for the taxpayer. FTM does not eliminate or replace existing dispute resolution options, including the taxpayer's opportunity to request a hearing before Appeals or a conference with a manager. The FTM Appeals Officer, serving as a neutral participant, will assist SB/SE and the taxpayer to understand the nature of the dispute and to reach a mutually satisfactory resolution consistent with applicable law. The FTM Appeals Officer may also recommend to the parties a resolution on the merits based on the FTM Appeals Officer's analysis of the issues. Either party may withdraw from the mediation process at any time by notifying the other party and the FTM Appeals Officer in writing of the withdrawal.

FTM is generally available for all nondocketed cases and collection source work over which SB/SE has jurisdiction, including offer in compromise (OIC), trust fund recovery penalty (TFRP), and collection due process (CDP) cases.

No FTM. The following issues and cases are **not** eligible for inclusion in the FTM:

♦ Issues in a taxpayer's case designated for litigation;
♦ Issues in a taxpayer's case under consideration for designation for litigation;
♦ Issues for which there is an absence of legal precedent;
♦ Issues for which there are conflicts between circuit courts of appeal;
♦ "Whipsaw" issues, for example, issues for which resolution with respect to one party might result in inconsistent treatment in the absence of the participation of another party;
♦ Collection appeals program cases;
♦ Automated collection system cases; and
♦ Cases in which the taxpayer has failed to respond to IRS communications and no documentation has been previously submitted for consideration by the examiner.

Fast track settlement program (FTS). This program enables the IRS to resolve tax disputes with large and mid-size businesses at an earlier stage, often within a much shorter time than through the normal audit and Appeal process. The FTS pilot program became available for large and mid-size businesses on November 14, 2001, with the goal of reaching settlement with taxpayers within 120 days. By May 31, 2003, the IRS and 104 LMSB taxpayers had successfully settled through the pilot program, in an average time of 69 days, just over half of the expected time.

LMSB and the Office of Appeals offer a joint process that uses Appeals personnel as mediators in LMSB cases. Based on the Appeals Officer's analysis of the issues, Appeals may also recommend a settlement. Under certain circumstances, other IRS divisions and taxpayers may also participate in the FTS program.

FTS does not eliminate or replace existing dispute resolution options, including the taxpayer's opportunity to request a conference with a manager or a hearing before Appeals. In the FTS process, Appeals' role is to provide a neutral party, someone who will help the taxpayer and LMSB understand the nature of the dispute and reach a mutually satisfactory resolution. The Appeals Officer may also recommend a settlement.

The taxpayer may withdraw from the FTS process at any time. The LMSB team manager of the Appeals Officer may stop the fast track process as well, if either determines that they are not progressing toward resolution of the issues. If there are any issues at the end of the FTS process, the taxpayer retains all applicable appeal rights.

No FTS. The following issues are not eligible for inclusion into the FTS program:

♦ Issues in a taxpayer's case designated for litigation;
♦ Issues in a taxpayer's case under consideration for designation for litigation;
♦ Issues for which the taxpayer has submitted a request for competent authority assistance;
♦ Issues generally outside LMSB jurisdiction;
♦ "Whipsaw" issues (issues for which resolution with respect to one party might result in inconsistent treatment in the absence of the participation of another party);
♦ Issues for which mediation would be consistent with sound tax administration; and
♦ Issues that have been identified in a Chief Counsel Notice, or equivalent publication, as excluded from the FTS process.

STUDY QUESTION

6. FTS:

    a. Enables the IRS to resolve tax disputes with large and mid-size businesses at an earlier stage, often within a much shorter time than through the normal audit and Appeals process

    b. Gives small businesses, self-employed taxpayers, and the IRS the opportunity to mediate disputes through an IRS Appeals Officer

    c. Is required for the taxpayer

    d. Is not a permanent program, but merely a pilot program

Fast track mediation program for tax-exempt bonds (TEB Mediation). This program will allow the IRS and issuers of tax-exempt bonds to expedite the resolution of cases more quickly than through the standard appeals process.

The tax-exempt bond mediation dispute resolution pilot program (TEB Mediation) will use the services of trained mediator from the IRS Appeals Office to resolve cases. TEB Mediation takes place after the IRS analyzes the issues under examination and advises the bond issuer of its preliminary adverse finding, but before the IRS sends out the proposed adverse determination letter. The mediation should be completed in fewer than 60 days.

TEB Mediation is generally available in bond cases under examination where a limited number of unagreed issues exist. It is optional and both parties must agree to use mediation. An Appeals Officer with tax-exempt bond experience will serve as mediator, but bond issuers may also elect to use a non-IRS co-mediator at the issuer's expense.

TEB Mediation is generally available for all TEB cases within the jurisdiction of TEB in which:

♦ The factual issues are fully developed;
♦ There are a limited number of unresolved issues;
♦ The preliminary adverse determination letter has been issued; and
♦ A written response to the preliminary adverse determination letter has been provided by the issuer.

APPEALS

"Appeals" is the shorthand name used for the administrative appeals office for the IRS. A taxpayer may appeal most IRS decisions with the local Appeals Office. The Appeals Office is separate from, and independent of, the IRS office taking the action the taxpayer contests. The Appeals Office is the only level of administrative appeal within the IRS. A conference with Appeals may be held by correspondence, by telephone or in person.

If a personal conference is requested, the taxpayer should follow the instruction in the IRS's communication to the taxpayer. In most cases, the taxpayer may be eligible to take cases to court if the taxpayer does not reach agreement at the Appeals conference or does not want to appeal the case to the Appeals Office.

PAYMENT OF ASSESSMENT AFTER AUDIT

After the IRS is done with its examination and after appeals within the IRS are exhausted, the IRS generally issues a notice of deficiency if a taxpayer still owes taxes. The taxpayer should pay the entire amount (assuming the case would not be appealed to the Tax Court) or inform the IRS that he or she cannot pay the entire amount.

If taxes are owed and a taxpayer does not pay them, the IRS can request that the taxpayer take action to pay his or her taxes, such as selling or mortgaging any assets or obtaining a loan.

If a taxpayer still makes no effort to pay or work out a payment plan, the IRS may take more serious action, such as seizing the taxpayer's bank account, levying his or her wages, or taking other income or assets.

STUDY QUESTION

7. Which of the following collection tools have *not* declined sharply after the enactment of the *IRS Restructuring and Reform Act of 1998* (RRA '98)?

    a. Levies
    b. Audits
    c. Liens
    d. Seizure

Alternatives to enforcement actions

The use of the major collection enforcement tools--levies, liens, and seizures--declined sharply after the enactment of the *IRS Restructuring and Reform Act of 1998* (RRA '98). This resulted from both the continuing decline in IRS staff and from the need to develop and implement procedures to comply with the new taxpayer rights provisions. This drop has been reversed, although collection activities have not returned to pre-1998 levels.

Levies	2,721,823	3,108,926	3,659,417	2,503, 09	504,403	219,778	447,201
Liens	798,677	750,225	543,613	382,755	167,867	287,517	428,376
Seizures	10,707	10,449	10,090	2,307	161	174	255

Contact the IRS. The taxpayer should inform the IRS that he or she cannot pay the total amount due. The IRS may ask the taxpayer to complete a Collection Information Statement to assist in comparing the taxpayer's monthly income with his or her expenses and to determine the amount that the taxpayer can afford to pay. Taxpayers have several options:

♦ Making monthly payments through an installment agreement;
♦ Using an offer in compromise; or
♦ Qualifying for a temporary delay due to hardship.

The IRS has the authority to collect federal taxes for 10 years from the date of assessment. If a taxpayer enters into an installment agreement, the IRS may request you to sign a waiver to extend the collection period.

Installment agreements. Installment agreements allow the full payment of the taxpayer's debt in smaller, more manageable amounts. They generally require equal monthly payments. The amount of a taxpayer's installment payment will be based on the amount he or she owes and the ability to pay that amount within the time available to the IRS to collect the tax debt. However, it is more costly than borrowing funds to pay the amount owed. The IRS charges interest and penalties on the tax owed and charges interest on the unpaid penalties and interest that has been charged to the taxpayer's tax account. Failure to make timely payments could terminate the agreement.

> *Practice Pointer.* The U.S. House of Representatives approved the *Taxpayer Protection and IRS Accountability Act of 2003* (HR 1528). HR 1528 would allow taxpayers to make partial payment of tax liability in an installment agreement. The companion bill to the House bill in the Senate is the *Tax Administration Good Government Act of 2003* (S 882).

Moreover, the IRS cannot levy against a taxpayer's property while his or her request for an installment agreement is being considered, for 30 days after the taxpayer's request for an agreement has been rejected, or for any period while an appeal of the rejection is being evaluated.

Offer in compromise. The IRS may accept an offer in compromise to settle unpaid tax accounts for less than the full amount of the balance. This applies to all taxes, including any interest, penalties, or additional amounts under the laws. The IRS may legally compromise a tax liability for one of the following reasons: (1) doubt as to liability; (2) doubt as to collectibility; or (3) promotion of effective tax administration.

Temporary delay. A tax debt may be delayed until the taxpayer's financial condition improves. However, any delay will increase the debt because penalties and interest are charged until the full amount is paid. A *Notice of Federal Tax Lien* may be filed to protect the government's interest in the taxpayer's assets.

STUDY QUESTION

8.   A temporary delay:

   a.   Enables the IRS to settle unpaid tax accounts for less than the full amount of the balance
   b.   Postpones the tax debt until the taxpayer's financial condition improves
   c.   Allows the full payment of the taxpayer's debt in small, more manageable amounts

d. Will not increase the debt because penalties and interest are charged until the full amount is paid

APPEALS TO THE COURTS

Tax Court

A taxpayer can go to the Tax Court for controversies involving whether a taxpayer owes additional income tax, estate tax, gift tax, certain excise taxes or penalties related to these proposed liabilities. (Certain types of tax controversies, such as those involving some employment tax issues or manufacturers' excise taxes, cannot be heard by the Tax Court.) A taxpayer can file a petition in Tax Court after the IRS issues a formal letter, stating the amounts that it believes the taxpayer owes (the notice of deficiency).

A taxpayer has 90 days from the date the notice is mailed to file a petition (or 150 days if the notice is addressed to the taxpayer outside the U.S.). The last date to file will be provided on the notice. If a petition is not filed, the IRS will assess the proposed liability and send the taxpayer a bill.

> *Observation.* If the dispute involves no more than $50,000 for any one tax year, there are simplified procedures.

> *Practice Pointer.* In March 2003, the IRS announced that 38 persons who attempted to delay tax collections by pursuing frivolous court cases ended up with $126,000 in penalties during the last two years. The IRS warned that the Tax Court may impose sanctions of up to $25,000 on those who misuse their right to a court review of IRS collection procedures merely to stall their tax payments.

> The *IRS Restructuring and Reform Act* (RRA '98) set forth various taxpayer rights related to tax liens or levies, including the right to seek judicial review. While an appeal is pending, the IRS usually may not enforce collection. In December 2000, the Tax Court warned taxpayers that it would impose penalties against those who "institute or maintain a lien or levy action primarily for delay or whose position in such a proceeding is frivolous or groundless" (*Pierson, 115 T.C. 581*). The Tax Court has repeatedly stated that frivolous cases waste its limited resources and delay the resolution of other taxpayers' genuine controversies. Using its authority under Code Sec. 6673, the Tax Court is levying increasingly severe penalties on those pursuing such cases.

STUDY QUESTION

9. The Tax Court can adjudicate controversies involving:

    a. Some employment tax issues

    b.   Manufacturers' excise taxes

    c.   Refunds for tax liabilities paid

    d.   Whether a taxpayer owes additional income tax, estate tax, or gift tax

District Court and Court of Federal Claims

If a taxpayer claims a refund for tax liabilities paid, a taxpayer has a choice of the refund forums—a U.S. District Court or the Court of Federal Claims. Certain types of cases, such as those involving some employment tax issues or manufacturers' excise taxes, can be heard only by these courts.

> *Practice Pointer.* If a taxpayer files a formal refund claim with the IRS and the IRS has not responded, a taxpayer may file suit for a refund immediately in either of these courts. If, however, the IRS sends a letter disallowing the taxpayer's claim, the taxpayer may either request an Appeals review or file suit no later than two years from the date of notice. An Appeals review of a disallowed claim does not extend the two-year period for filing suit. However, it may be extended by mutual agreement.

Recovering administrative and litigation costs

In certain instances, a taxpayer may be able to recover reasonable litigation and administrative costs if he or she is the prevailing party and if other requirements are met. The taxpayer must exhaust his or her administrative remedies within the IRS and must not unreasonably delay the administrative or court proceedings. Administrative costs include costs incurred on or after the date the taxpayer receives the Appeals decision letter, the date of the first letter of proposed deficiency, or the date of the notice of deficiency, whichever is earliest.

Recoverable litigation or administrative costs may include:

- Attorney's fees that generally do not exceed $125 per hour;
- Reasonable amounts for court costs or any administrative fees or similar charges by the IRS;
- Reasonable expenses of expert witnesses; and
- Reasonable costs of studies, analyses, tests, or engineering reports that are necessary to prepare the case.

STUDY QUESTION

10.   Administrative costs:

    a.   Are not recoverable

    b.   Include costs incurred on or after the date of the notice of deficiency

c. Include costs incurred on or after the date the taxpayer receives the Appeals decision letter

d. Include reasonable amounts for court costs or any administrative fees or similar charges by the IRS

COLLECTIONS

IRS payment actions begin with the audit (examination), then issuance of the notice of deficiency, then assessment and demand for payment. If payment is not forthcoming, the IRS process shifts to "collections," which takes the appropriate legal steps to obtain payment from the taxpayer or from the taxpayer's property. The General Accounting Office (GAO) reported in May 2002 that between 1996 and 2001, trends in the collection of delinquent taxes showed declines in the program's performance, in terms of coverage of workload, cases closed, direct staff time used, productivity, and amount of unpaid taxes collected.

Collection staffing

Since 2001, the IRS's budget requests have made increasing its compliance and collection staff one of several key priorities. However, staffing in two key compliance and collection occupations was lower in 2002 than in 2000. The commissioner attributed the decline in compliance staffing to increases in workload in other essential operations. Also, the IRS during 2002 faced unbudgeted cost increases, such as rent and pay increases of about $106 million. As a result, the IRS had to delay hiring revenue agents and officers.

FY	1995	1996	1997	1998	1999	2000	2001
Revenue Officers	5,908	5,537	5,439	4,989	4,354	3,601	3,792

Field professionals

The IRS has provided that the major reason for the drop in examination coverage is that the examination staff has declined while workload has increased.

	1995	1996	1997	1998	1999	2000	2001
Staff							
Revenue Agents	15,772	15,083	14,399	13,647	13,061	12,550	11,598
Tax Auditors	2,632	2,485	2,318	2,113	1,930	1,702	1,420
Total	18,404	17,568	16,717	15,760	14,991	14,252	13,018
Change		-4.54%	-4.84%	-5.72%	-4.88%	4.93%	-8.66%

Since peaking at 116,673 full time equivalents (FTEs) in 1992, the IRS's workforce has dropped 15 percent to just over 99,500 FTEs in 2001, while the number of returns filed increased 13 percent to 230 million. In addition to the normal growth in returns, the *IRS Restructuring and Reform Act of 1998* (RRA '98) created significant resource demands on the exam staff.

For example, RRA '98's innocent spouse provisions required additional staff for administration, while the requirements for notification of third parties added to the completion time for an exam.

STUDY QUESTIONS

11. The General Accounting Office (GAO) reported in May 2002 that between 1996 and 2001, trends in the collection of delinquent taxes showed _____ in the program's performance, in terms of coverage of workload, cases closed, direct staff time used, and productivity.

    a. Dramatic increases
    b. No changes
    c. Declines
    d. Slight improvement

12. What factor is *not* true about the decline in examination coverage?

    a. The examination staff declined while the workload increased.
    b. The *IRS Restructuring and Reform Act of 1998* (RRA '98) created significant resource demands on the exam staff.
    c. The number of revenue officers declined between 1995 and 2001.
    d. Innocent spouse provisions did not require additional staff for administration.

Proposal for IRS collections to use private collection agencies

Under the current law, federal tax liabilities must be collected by the IRS and cannot be referred to a private collection agency (PCA) for collection.

Between 1990 and 2002, unpaid assessments grew from $100 billion to $280 billion. The problem is so enormous and continuing to grow at such a fast pace, the IRS believed that it needed to do something dramatically different. Many of these accounts represent taxpayers who have filed returns showing tax due but have subsequently failed to pay the tax.

These individuals are aware of their outstanding liabilities, but the IRS is hampered by a lack of personnel and funds to pursue every taxpayer having an outstanding liability.

It is believed that many taxpayers with outstanding tax liabilities would make payment if contacted by telephone and, if necessary, offered the chance to pay in full in installments. If PCAs could perform such tasks for this group of taxpayers, without affecting any taxpayer protection, the IRS would be able to focus its resources on more complex cases and issues.

Terms proposed. As part of his fiscal year 2004 budget, President Bush urged Congress to open tax collection to private collection agencies.

Legislation (H.R. 1169) has been introduced in Congress that would enable the IRS to use PCAs to support IRS collection efforts by having the PCAs locate and contact taxpayers with outstanding tax liabilities. The PCAs would be permitted to request payment of the liability, either in full or in installments, but would not be able to take enforcement action against a taxpayer. Taxpayer rights would be safeguarded with the use of PCAs.

Under the proposal, PCAs:

♦ Could contact each taxpayer by a letter meeting the requirements of the Fair Debt Collection Practices Act (FDCPA) as well as the requirements for comparable notices issued by the IRS;

   Observation. For address checks, PCAs could resort to on-line or electronic "white pages" or directory assistance. However, they would not be permitted to contact relatives and neighbors or employers to locate the taxpayer.

♦ Would be able to contact a taxpayer by telephone to request payment;

♦ Would be given specific, limited information regarding an outstanding tax liability (type of tax, amount of the outstanding liability, tax years affected, and prior payments);

♦ Would be subject to careful monitoring by the IRS (live monitoring of telephonic communications, review of recorded conversations, taxpayer-satisfaction surveys, audits of PCA records, and periodic reviews of PCA performance);

♦ Would not be able to communicate with taxpayers at unusual or inconvenient times or places;

♦ Would be required to provide annual reports outlining the safeguards that protect taxpayer confidentiality; and

♦ Would be required to inform taxpayers of their right to obtain assistance from the Office of the National Taxpayer Advocate and to immediately refer any case in which such assistance is requested to the local Taxpayer Advocate's office.

The proposal would create a revolving fund from the tax revenue collected under the program, and the amounts in this fund would be used to compensate the PCAs. The proposal would be effective after the date of enactment.

The IRS provided the following estimates of revenue collected under this program:

Revenue Estimate
Fiscal Years
$'s in millions

2004–2008	2004–2013
476	1,008

Mixed reviews. The IRS's plans to use private agencies to collect federal tax debts received a less-than-enthusiastic response from NTEU (National Treasury Employees Union) President Colleen M. Kelly and private practitioners. (NTEU is the largest independent federal union, representing approximately 150,000 employees in 29 agencies and departments, including some 98,000 in the IRS.)

At an American Bar Association (ABA) conference in May 2003 Nina Olson, the National Taxpayer Advocate, sympathized with many practitioners who expressed reservations about engaging private contractors in tax collection. She was initially distressed because of her experiences at the state level. She expressed concerns about abuses among private collection agencies before the House of Representatives in 2002. However, Olson indicated that her initial concerns have been mitigated. Some of her concerns included:

♦ Collection agents' skills that differ greatly within and between contractors;
♦ Contractors that convinced unrepresented low-income taxpayers to enter into unreasonable collection arrangements; and
♦ Success being dependent on the statutory tax collection authority, the taxpayer rights protections, the guidance, and training and oversight of contractors

Kelly recently indicated that the bill, which at press time is being marked-up by the Senate, is unwise and misguided. "Turning the inherently governmental function of tax collection over to private companies not only would cost more than having IRS employees perform the work," she said in a recent statement, "it would make available to contractors private taxpayer information and it would subject taxpayer to the most aggressive collection techniques."

Kelly asserted that privatizing tax collections flies in the face of congressional intent expressed in the passage of the *IRS Restructuring and Reform Act* (RRA '98). One key provision of that law was to prevent the IRS from evaluating its employees, including its managers, by using collection statistics.

In a letter to every member of the Senate, Kelly wrote "Instead of rushing to privatize tax collection functions and putting taxpayer information in the hands of private collectors, the IRS should increase compliance staffing levels so that the compliance gap can be closed without compromising taxpayer rights."

STUDY QUESTIONS

13. Under current law, federal tax liabilities:

    a. Must be collected by the IRS and cannot be referred to a private collection agency for collection
    b. May be referred to a private collection agency for collection
    c. Are fully collected
    d. Have decreased

14. As part of his fiscal year 2004 budget, President Bush urged Congress to open tax collection to private collection agencies (PCAs). Under the proposal, PCAs:

    a. Could contact each taxpayer using a letter meeting the requirements of the Fair Debt Collection Practices Act (FDCPA)
    b. Would not be able to contact a taxpayer by telephone
    c. Would be permitted to subcontract their work for the IRS
    d. Would not be subject to careful monitoring by the IRS

15. The taxpayer, when audited:

    a. Will not receive a statement detailing his or her rights
    b. Will not receive an explanation of the audit and collection process
    c. Has the right to make an audio recording of any in-person interview conducted by the IRS
    d. Cannot be represented at an interview

CONCLUSION

The IRS deals directly with more Americans than any other institution, public or private. It also is one of the world's most efficient tax administrators. In 2002, the IRS collected more than $2 trillion in revenue and processed nearly 227 million tax returns.

Although the IRS audit process is dreaded by all Americans, it does perform a vital function in our tax laws. Given the possibility that their returns may be selected for audit, many taxpayers are coerced by the audit process to submit complete and truthful returns.

Especially over the past several years, newspapers and other media have reported on the widespread use of questionable tax shelters by corporations and individuals, and on the lower audit rates among all taxpayer segments. In reaction, the IRS has felt great pressure to step up its audit coverage.

The audit process itself is continuously changing. In fact, the IRS is realigning its audit resources to focus on key areas of noncompliance with the tax laws. The strategy represents a new direction for the agency's compliance effort.

In addition, the IRS is modifying its administrative process to assist the taxpayer with any outstanding issues without going to court—the system of last resort. More specifically, the IRS has made permanent two "fast track" programs that enable taxpayers and the IRS to reach agreement on disputes more quickly and efficiently. These programs offer a great number of options to the taxpayer—beyond the regular appeals process. In the future, taxpayers should expect to see even more methods to resolve their tax disputes in an efficient and effective manner.

ANSWERS TO STUDY QUESTIONS

CHAPTER 1

1.   **The correct answer is B**. JGTRRA reduces the maximum tax rate applied to long-term capital gains from 20 to 15 percent from 2003 through 2009.

A is incorrect. The 18-percent rate was to be the lowest tax rate available on capital gains for taxpayers in income tax brackets higher than 15 percent. To the detriment of some five-year property holders, however, Congress decided to lower the general rate to 15 percent without recognizing any economic disadvantage that may have befallen holders of "five-year" property who had elected prior to JGTRRA to recognize "built-in gain" to be, thereafter, entitled to an 18-percent rate (instead of a then 20-percent rate) on the sale of five-year property after 2005.

C is incorrect. No actual, or proposed, provision had adopted a 12 percent rate for net capital gains.

D is incorrect. The 8-percent rate was allowed for net capital gain property held for more than 5 years and sold by a taxpayer in the 15 percent (or lower) general tax bracket.   The 8-percent rate was available for 5-year property sold on or before May 5, 2003. Ironically, "5-year" property sold after that date is taxed at 10 percent rather than 8 percent.

2.   **The correct answer is A**. JGTRRA creates a new 5 percent tax rate for individuals in the 10 and 15 percent rate brackets. This replaces the old 10 percent rate for these taxpayers.

B is incorrect. The rule before JGTRRA was that property held for at least five years was entitled to an 8 percent rate. After transactions post May-6, 2003, however, the 8-percent rate no longer applies.

C is incorrect. The 10-percent rate for capital gain was applicable to pre-May 6, 2003 transactions by 10- or 15-percent tax bracket taxpayers. After that date, that rate disappeared.

D is incorrect. JGTRRA continued the preferential capital gain treatment for individuals in the general 10 or 15 percent income tax bracket. It created a new 5 percent rate for individuals in the 10 and 15 percent rate brackets.

3. **The correct answer is C.** JGTRRA is a temporary tax cut. The lower tax rates on capital gains expire on December 31, 2008. Of course, between now and then, Congress may decide to extend the rate cuts beyond December 31, 2008.

A is incorrect. JGTRRA's lower bonus depreciation ends after 2006. The enhanced capital gains rate, however, continues past that date, to 2009.

B is incorrect. JGTRRA's lower capital gains tax rates run through 2008, not up to be beginning of that year.

D is incorrect. JGTRRA's lower capital gains tax rates are set to expire after December 31, 2008. The general tax bracket rates for ordinary income are set to revert to pre-2001 Act levels only after 2010. Capital gains rate reductions revert earlier, back to the 20 percent level.

4. **The correct answer is B.** Because Congress did not make the lower rates retroactive to January 1, 2003, many taxpayers will have to compute their capital gains tax under a transitional rule that applies to assets sold or exchanged on or after May 6, 2003.

A is incorrect. Congress did not make the lower rates retroactive to January 1, 2003, but instead imposed a start date of May 6, 2003.

C is incorrect. JGTRRA's lower tax rates on capital gains take effect on May 6, 2003. They expire on December 31, 2008.

D is incorrect. JGTRRA's lower tax rates on capital gains expire on December 31, 2008.

5. **The correct answer is D.** JGTRRA made no changes to these special rates for collectibles, such as gold coins, and unrecaptured Section 1250 gain, such as gain from the installment sale of real depreciable property.

A is incorrect. JGTRRA made no changes to the 28 percent rate on long-term gain from collectibles and the 25 percent rate for unrecaptured Section 1250 gain. Long-term gain from real estate is subject to the reduced maximum rate of 15 percent.

B is incorrect. The tax rate on corporate capital gains remained the same (no difference from regular corporate income). Net capital gain on collectibles, however, remained at 28 percent, both before and after JGTRRA.

C is incorrect. After JGTRRA, qualified dividends are taxed as net capital gains (i.e., at 15 percent) rather than at the maximum income tax bracket (now 35 percent). Gain on collectibles remains taxed at 28 percent.

6.   **The correct answer is A.** Along with reducing the maximum rate on capital gain to 15 percent, JGTRRA allowed qualified dividends to be subject to the same rate.

B is incorrect. JGTRRA allowed those in the 10- and 15-percent ordinary income tax brackets to be taxed on dividend income (within those tax brackets) at 10 percent.

C is incorrect. The 8-percent rate applied only to five-year gain property sold before May 6, 2003. After that date, the 8-percent disappeared. It was never applicable to dividend income, even though the lowered rate on dividends applies generally to tax years beginning after 2002.

D is incorrect. The zero percent bracket applied in 2008 only and then only for qualified dividends received by individuals, estates, and trusts is 15 percent.

7.   **The correct answer is A.** JGTRRA lowers the tax rate for qualified dividends to zero percent for individuals in the 10 and 15 percent tax brackets for one year only: 2008. Before 2008, the rate is 5 percent.

B is incorrect. The estate tax disappears in 2011, not the preferred dividend rate that ends earlier, for tax years after 2008.

C is incorrect. These dates encompass dividends and capital gains subject to the 15 percent rate (that reverts to 20 percent after 2007).

D is incorrect. JGTRRA lowers the tax rate for qualified dividends to 5 percent for those in the 10 or 15 percent general income tax brackets within these dates. Only for 2008 is the net capital gains rate for these taxpayers zero.

8.   **The correct answer is B.** JGTRRA's lower dividend tax rates apply to dividends paid by domestic corporations and dividends paid by some foreign corporations. The foreign corporation's stock must be traded on a U.S. securities market or satisfy other criteria.

A is incorrect. In addition to dividends paid by domestic corporations, dividends paid by some foreign corporations qualify for the lower tax rates in JGTRRA. The foreign corporation's stock must be traded on a U.S. securities market or satisfy other criteria.

C is incorrect. Ownership of a foreign corporation by a US taxpayer is not reason to allow dividends from that corporation to be "qualified."

D is incorrect. JGTRRA does not limit the lower tax rates to first-time dividends. Dividends qualify for the lower rates if they are paid by domestic corporations and by some foreign corporations. The foreign corporation's stock must be traded on a U.S. securities market or satisfy other criteria.

9.   **The correct answer is D.** JGTRRA imposes restrictions on taxpayers purchasing stock relatively close to the ex-dividend date. A taxpayer must hold a stock for more than 60 days in the 120-day period beginning 60 days before the ex-dividend date for the lower rates to apply.

A is incorrect. The JGTRRA time restriction is double these amounts, on both sides of the ex-dividend date.

B is incorrect. The preferred rate on dividends is not given unless there is a long-term commitment by the taxpayer to the value of the underlying stock. The 60-day period after the ex-dividend date helps prevent the stock from being artificially inflated for a limited period of time by its dividend.

C is incorrect. JGTRRA drafters reasoned that not only does a relatively long period of time before a dividend is declared needed to prevent short-term holdings for dividends-rate purposes, but also the taxpayer's investment in the underlying stock must be similarly lengthy after the dividend is declared to reward investment in the underlying stock rather than speculation on the strength of the lower dividend rate.

10.   **The correct answer is B.** JGTRRA's lower tax rates on dividends expire on December 31, 2008, unless a future Congress decides to extend them.

A is incorrect. May 6, 2003, is the date beginning on which sales of capital assets are entitled to the 15 percent rate. Dividends, on the other hand, are entitled to the 15 percent rate for any tax year beginning on and after January 1, 2003.

C is incorrect. December 31, 2010, is the date after which the general tax rate reductions revert to their previous levels. Regular capital gains tax rates, on the other hand, will continue at their maximum 20 percent level.

D is incorrect. JGTRRA's lower regular tax rates on income tax expire on January 1, 2011. The 15 percent net capital gains rate is scheduled to end a full two years earlier, after December 31, 2008, unless Congress decides to extend them.

11.   **The correct answer is B.** The "kiddie tax" under which a child's 2003 unearned income is taxed at his or her parents' marginal tax rate is unaffected by JGTRRA. Transfers of assets to children under who have not reached age 14 generally do not produce significant tax savings.

A is incorrect. JGTRRA makes no changes to the kiddie tax under which a child's 2003 unearned income is taxed at his or her parents' marginal tax rate.

C is incorrect. The amount of the kiddie tax is already adjusted for inflation each year. The amount tax at the child's regular tax bracket remains the same.

D is incorrect. The $500 level (times 2) was the original amount exemption from the kiddie tax. That amount has risen over the years to $1,500 due to inflation adjustments.

12. **The correct answer is A.** JGTRRA lowered the tax rate on dividends. Lowered dividend rates reduce the tax impact of taxation at the C-corporation shareholder level. The lower the tax on dividends, the lower the tax paid by shareholders upon the distribution of dividends.
B is incorrect. Lowered dividend rates decrease, rather than increase, the impact of double taxation.
C is incorrect. Although JGTRRA lowered the dividend tax rate, it did not eliminate the tax, nor did it eliminate double taxation
D is incorrect. JGTRRA did not eliminate, nor distribute the tax liability to any other taxpayer. Shareholders remain liable for tax on dividends.

13. **The correct answer is B.** The C corporation's earnings are "double-taxed" at both the corporate and shareholder levels. Under JGTRRA, dividend income is taxed at a reduced rate. A reduced tax on dividend income lowers the tax responsibility at the shareholder level, thereby easing the double tax.
A is incorrect. Reduced tax rates on dividend income stand to decrease shareholder tax liability.
C is incorrect. Lower dividend tax rates may favor the C corporation as a choice of entity.
D is incorrect. Partnerships do not distribute dividends. Dividends are not directly related to partnerships.

CHAPTER 2

1. **The correct answer is D.** All costs to get a business started or reorganize a business are treated as capital expenses. The costs are added to the basis of the asset and recovered through depreciation or amortization. These costs may include expenses for advertising, travel, or wages for training employees.
A is incorrect. Current business expenses are ordinary and necessary expenses of carrying on a trade or business, which are paid or incurred under the taxpayer's method of accounting.
B is incorrect. If they are completed to keep the property in normal, efficient operating condition, the costs are treated as business expenses, subject to an immediate deduction. If, however, replacements are considered to be improvements to an asset, their costs are capitalized.
C is incorrect. Personal expenses are usually neither deductible nor capitalized. A personal, living, or family expense is not deductible unless the Code specifically provides otherwise.

2. **The correct answer is D.** Installing a new roof is a capital expense, which is one that adds to the value or useful life of property.

A is incorrect. Replacing a part of property would keep it in normal, efficient operating condition. It is similar to a repair; it is not an improvement.

B is incorrect. Maintenance checks would keep the property in normal, efficient operating condition. They are not considered improvements, which would be capital expenses.

C is incorrect. Repairs would keep the property in normal, efficient operating condition. They are not improvements.

3. **The correct answer is B.** The costs of making improvements to a business asset are capital expenses if the improvements add to the value of the asset, appreciably lengthen the time a taxpayer can use it, or adapt it to a different use. Repairs that keep property in normal, efficient operating condition are treated as business expenses. Repairs include repainting, mending leaks, and plastering.

A is incorrect. A capital expense does not occur if an item is currently deducted.

C is incorrect. An improvement is a capital expense, assuming it adds to the value of the asset or appreciably lengthens the time the taxpayer can use it.

D is incorrect. Startup expenses are generally capitalized.

4. **The correct answer is C.** Taxpayers may elect to currently expense capital expenditures to abate or control hazardous substances at designated contaminated sties under Code Sec. 198. As in the case of other trade or business expenses, a cleanup expense is not deductible prior to the tax year for which it is paid or incurred.

A is incorrect. Code Sec. 263 addresses the capitalization of costs.

B is incorrect. Code Sec. 162 addresses trade or business expenses.

D is incorrect. Code Sec. 197 addresses the acquisition of intangibles.

5. **The correct answer is B.** The two "upfront" business deductions that have been enhanced are the Section 179 expensing deduction and the first-year bonus depreciation deduction. Both are intended to encourage capital spending. For smaller businesses, the Section 179 expense limit is increasing from $25,000 to $100,000. For all businesses, the first-year bonus depreciation is expanded from 30 percent to 50 percent

A is incorrect. Both are intended to encourage capital spending. A taxpayer already had the option of current deductions; however, under JGTRRA, the deductions became larger.

C is incorrect. The tax benefits attributed to these deductions are temporary.

D is incorrect. Both are intended to encourage capital spending. Capitalized expenditures are added to the basis of the property and recovered through depreciation, amortization, or when the property is sold or otherwise transferred. Therefore, depreciation is merely a recovery method; JGTRRA was intended to encourage spending.

6.   **The correct answer is C.** Married taxpayers filing a joint return are treated as one taxpayer for purposes of the annual dollar limit and the phaseout reduction.

A is incorrect. Even though each taxpayer may have his and her own separate business, they are treaded as a unit for purposes of divvying up on $100,000 expensing limit and one $400,000 phase-out level annually.   However, they treat each business that they may own separately for purposes of determining whether the income generated from each of their businesses is sufficient to cover the maximum amount of the deduction. Here, if the couple file separate returns, the taxable income limitation applies as if they are two separate taxpayers.

B is incorrect. The phaseout reduction amount presently starts at $400,000, not $200,000.

D is incorrect. The phaseout reduction amounts apply to all taxpayers, whether married, single, divorced, or as a corporation or partnership.

7.   **The correct answer is D.** Partnerships and S corps may carry forward the disallowed portion (because of the taxable income limit) at the entity level.

A is incorrect. A partnership or S corporation is limited to the annual direct expense deduction limitation, which must be allocated among the partners or shareholders.   Each partner or shareholder must include the amount passed through to him for purposes of computing his own separate direct expense deduction limitation.

B is incorrect. Each partner must add up all items that partner wishes to expense, from that partnership and any other business, in computing the $100,000 limit, not only items received from that particular partnership.

C is incorrect. The partnership is first treated as a unit to determine the amount of the section 179 deduction that it will pass through to each partner, based on each partner's partnership interest. Whether each particular partner then can use all that is passed through to that partner is then separately determined at the partner level.

8.   **The correct answer is D.** The *Jobs and Growth Tax Relief Reconciliation Act of 2003* (JGTRRA) has one quirk that is not detailed in Code Sec. 179. Taxpayers who purchase "large" SUVs in 2003 for business purposes can have the government pay as much as $100,000 of the costs of the first year the SUV is placed in service. To qualify for this break, the SUV must be placed in service after December 31, 2002, and have a loaded gross vehicle weight rating of more than 6,000 pounds.

A is incorrect. Off-the-shelf computer software is not included as qualifying property that may be expensed under Code Sec. 179.

B is incorrect. Section 179 qualifying property is "tangible Code Sec. 1245 property, depreciable under Code Sec. 168, and acquired by purchase for use in the active conduct of a trade or business." This includes personal property.

C is incorrect. This includes other tangible property used as an integral part of manufacturing, production, or extraction, or of furnishing electricity, gas, water, or sewage disposal services or used in a research facility for these activities.

9. **The correct answer is A.** Because all asset purchases of Section 179-type property cannot exceed $499,000 for any one property to qualify, Section 179 expensing is limited to small businesses.

B is incorrect. Estates are business taxpayers that are officially excluded from using Section 179.

C is incorrect. Noncorporate lessors are business taxpayers that are officially excluded from using Section 179.

D is incorrect. Trusts are business taxpayers that are officially excluded from using Section 179.

10. **The correct answer is A.** The bonus depreciation deductions under the *Jobs and Growth Tax Relief Reconciliation Act of 2003* (JGTRRA) encourage capital investment, which should stimulate the economy.

B is incorrect. A bonus depreciation is a tax brake that all business owners should carefully consider, especially under the *Jobs and Growth Tax Relief Reconciliation Act of 2003* (JGTRRA).

C is incorrect. The bonus depreciation has become so generous under this new law that it has become incumbent on any business tax advisor to suggest that capital purchases that are being planned for some date in the future be made now or at least before 2006.

D is incorrect. Under the *Jobs and Growth Tax Relief Reconciliation Act of 2003* (JGTRRA), the additional first-year depreciation allowance percentage was increased to 50 percent. Generally, to qualify for the higher percentage, the qualifying property must be acquired after May 5, 2003, and placed in service before January 1, 2005.

11. **The correct answer is A.** For purposes of bonus depreciation deductions, qualified property includes computer software that is depreciable under another code section, as opposed to software subject to a 15-year amortization under Code Sec. 197.

B is incorrect. For purposes of bonus depreciation deductions, qualified property includes new MACRS property with a recovery period of 20 years or less (MACRS) is the cost recovery system used to determine the amount of the depreciation deduction for tangible personal property.

C is incorrect. For purposes of bonus depreciation deductions, qualified property includes computer software that is depreciable under Code Sec. 167, as opposed to software subject to a 15-year amortization under Code Sec. 197.

D is incorrect. For purposes of bonus depreciation deductions, qualified property includes qualified leasehold improvement property.

12. **The correct answer is A.** The bonus depreciation is $500 (($1,500 – $500) x 50 percent).

B is incorrect. This answer is reached by multiplying (($1,500 – $500) x (30 percent)). The 30 percent figure was the original percentage for the additional first-year depreciation allowance under the *Job Creation and Worker Assistance Act of 2002* (JCWAA).

C is incorrect. This is the amount of the regular first-year MACRS allowance. It is calculated at ($500 x 20 percent).

D is incorrect. This is a fictitious figure and has no significance to the problem.

13. **The correct answer is D.** The bonus depreciation must be claimed unless a taxpayer makes an election out.

A is incorrect. The bonus depreciation must be claimed unless a taxpayer makes an election out.

B is incorrect. The bonus depreciation, which encourages capital investment and stimulates the economy, should be carefully considered by all business owners.

C is incorrect. The bonus depreciation encourages capital investment and stimulates the economy.

14. **The correct answer is A.** A corporation (other than an S corp) claiming depreciation or amortization on any asset, regardless of when it was placed in service, must file Form 4562.

B is incorrect. Generally they are not required to file Form 4562, given certain exceptions.

C is incorrect. Corporate taxpayers must file, but not individuals, so the entire answer is incorrect.

D is incorrect. Partnerships are not taxed as corporations (they are noncorporate entitles) and are generally not required to file Form 4562 unless certain deductions are claimed.

CHAPTER 3

1. **The correct answer is A.** A corporation (other than an S corp) claiming depreciation or amortization on any asset, regardless of when it was placed in service, must file Form 4562.

B is incorrect. Usually they are not required to file Form 4562 unless any of the following deductions are claimed: (1) a depreciation or amortization deduction on an asset placed in service in the current year; (2) a Code Sec. 179 expense deduction; or (3) a deduction based on the standard mileage rate.

C is incorrect. Corporate taxpayers must file, but not individuals, so the entire answer is incorrect.

D is incorrect. Partnerships are not taxed as corporations (they are noncorporate entities) and are generally not required to file Form 4562 unless they claim any of the following deductions: (1) a depreciation or amortization deduction on an asset placed in service in the current year; (2) a Code Sec. 179 expense deduction; or (3) a deduction based on the standard mileage rate.

2.   **The correct answer is C.** An ordinary expense is one that is common and accepted in a taxpayer's trade or business.

A is incorrect. It is defined as a necessary expense.

B is incorrect. It is not an ordinary expense. An ordinary expense usually brings about an immediate deduction.

D is incorrect. This is defined as depreciation. Depreciation is the annual deduction allowed to recover the cost or other basis of business or investment property having useful life substantially beyond the tax year. Depreciation starts when a taxpayer first uses the property in a business or for the production of income. It ends when a taxpayer takes the property out of service, deducts all depreciable costs or other basis, or no longer uses the property in the business or for the production of income.

3. **The correct answer is A.** A taxpayer cannot deduct more for a business expense than the amount it actually spends. There is usually no other limit on how much you can deduct if the amount is reasonable. However, if a taxpayer's deductions are large enough to produce a net business loss for the year, the tax loss may be limited.

B is incorrect. This answer implies that it is in the taxpayer's discretion as to how much to deduct for a business expense.

C is incorrect. This would enable the taxpayer to always deduct more for a business expense that the amount the taxpayer actually spent. A taxpayer cannot deduct more for a business expense than the amount it actually spends.

D is incorrect. A taxpayer cannot deduct more for a business expense than the amount it actually spends. It is not discretionary for the taxpayer to deduct more.

4.   **The correct answer is A.** All costs to get the business started are treated as capital expenses. The costs can be recovered through depreciation. These costs may include expenses for advertising, travel, or wages for training employees. If a corporation attempts to go into a new trade or business and is not successful, it may be possible to deduct all investigatory costs as a loss.

B is incorrect. These expenses are ordinary and necessary expenses (such as computer equipment) of carrying on a trade or business, which are paid or incurred in the tax year.

C is incorrect. If replacements are completed to keep the property in normal efficient operating condition, then the cost is treated as a business expense, subject to an immediate deduction. If, however, the replacement is considered an improvement to an asset, then the cost is capitalized.

D is incorrect. Personal expenses are usually neither deductible nor capitalized. A personal, living or family expense is not deductible unless the Code specifically provides otherwise. Nondeductible expenses include rent and insurance premiums, paid for the taxpayer's own dwelling, and payments for food.

5.   **The correct answer is B.** The costs of making improvements to a business asset are capital expenses if the improvements add to the value of the asset, appreciably lengthen the time a taxpayer can use it, or adapt it to a different use. Repairs that keep property in a normal, efficient operating condition are treated as business expenses. Repairs include repainting, mending leaks, plastering, and conditioning gutters on buildings.

A is incorrect. A capital expense does not occur if an item is currently deducted.

C is incorrect. It is a capital expense, assuming it adds to the value of the asset or appreciably lengthens the time the taxpayer can use it.

D is incorrect. Startup expenses are generally capitalized.

6.   **The correct answer is C.** If a taxpayer goes into business, all costs to get the business started would be treated as capital expenses. A taxpayer can amortize these expenses over a period of not less than 60 months, starting with the month in which the business begins. The election must be made no later than the date (including extensions) for filing the return for the tax year in which the business begins or is acquired. The election is made on Part VI of Form 4562.

A is incorrect. Only if a corporation that attempts to go into a new trade or business is *not* successful, then it may be possible to deduct all costs at a loss.

B is incorrect. Expenses that are capitalized may be amortized over a period of not less than 60 months, starting with the month in which the business begins.

D is incorrect. Costs incurred to get a business started are not ignored. They must be accounted for, that is, generally capitalized.

7.   **The correct answer is A.** Capital expenditures are those with useful lives of more than one year. They add value or useful life to the property. Generally, capital expenses must be deducted by means of depreciation and amortization.

B is incorrect. Capital expenditures are those assets of a more permanent nature—those with useful lives of more than one year.

C is incorrect. If a taxpayer goes into business, all costs to get the business started would be treated as capital expenses. A taxpayer can amortize these expenses over a period of no fewer than 60 months, starting with the month in which the business begins.

D is incorrect. Repairs keep the property in normal, efficient operating condition. Repairs are not improvements and should therefore not be capitalized.

8. **The correct answer is B.** The cost of any business asset is a capital expense. Business assets include machinery, furniture, trucks, and franchise rights. These are assets with useful lives of more than one year.

A is incorrect. The cost of any business asset may or may not be a depreciable expense.

C is incorrect. A business asset may or may not be immediately expensed.

D is incorrect. Business assets may or may not be amortized, depending on the type of asset. Amortization is an accounting procedure that gradually reduces the cost value of an intangible asset, such as goodwill, through periodic charges to income.

9. **The correct answer is D.** This is a capital expense, one that adds to the value or useful life of property.

A is incorrect. Replacing a part of property would keep it in normal, efficient operating condition. It is similar to a repair; it is not an improvement.

B is incorrect. Maintenance checks would keep the property in normal, efficient operating condition. They are not considered an improvement, which would be a capital expense.

C is incorrect. Repairs would keep the property in normal, efficient operating condition. They are not an improvement.

10. **The correct answer is A.** This is one of the components that define depreciable property.

B is incorrect. It must have a determinable useful life exceeding one year.

C is incorrect. It must wear out, decay, become obsolete, etc. in order to depreciate the property.

D is incorrect. If property is currently deducted as an expense for the year in which the costs are incurred, then the property is not depreciated.

11. **The correct answer is C.** Capital expenditures may be subject to depreciation because they are expenses associated with permanence. That is, those with useful lives of more than one year. Generally, capital expenses may be deducted by means of depreciation or amortization. If the expense is not subject to depreciation or amortization, it is added to the cost basis of the property.

A is incorrect. By definition, capital expenditures are not currently deducted. They may be subject to depreciation.

B is incorrect because capital expenditures may be subject to depreciation.

D is incorrect. Repairs keep the property in normal, efficient operating condition. Repairs are not improvements and should therefore not be capitalized.

12. **The correct answer is C.** Code Sec. 162 addresses trade or business expenses. A taxpayer—whether a corporation, an individual, a partnership, a trust, or an estate—generally may deduct from gross income the ordinary and necessary expenses of carrying on a trade or business that are paid or incurred in the tax year.

A is incorrect. Code Sec. 174 addresses these issues.

> *Note.* Costs of research, whether carried on by the taxpayer or on behalf of the taxpayer by a third party, are deductible. Once made, the election is applicable to all research costs incurred in the project for the current and all subsequent years. As an alternative, the taxpayer can elect to capitalize the costs and amortize them ratably over a period of at least 60 months beginning with the month when benefits are first realized from them, assuming that the property created does not have a determinable useful life at that time.

B is incorrect. Code Sec. 263 addresses these issues.

D is incorrect. Rev. Proc. 2000-50 addresses these issues. Rev. Proc 2000-50 provides that the costs of developing software (for a taxpayer's own use or for sale or lease to others) may be deducted currently or amortized over a five-year period (or shorter if established as appropriate), so long as such costs are treated consistently.

13. **The correct answer is C.** Payments to rent a computer should be currently deductible if they constitute ordinary and necessary expenses.

A is incorrect. Payments cannot be capitalized if they are currently deductible.

B is incorrect. Payments cannot be depreciated if they are currently deductible as ordinary and necessary expenses.

D is incorrect. In a few cases if payments to rent a computer **do not** constitute ordinary and necessary expenses, the payments may be capitalized.

14. **The correct answer is B.** For costs associated with developing software, which are not treated as current expenses, the amortization period can be 60 months from the date of completion of the development or 36 months from the date the software is placed in service.

A is incorrect. For costs associated with developing software, which are not treated as current expenses, the amortization period can be 60 months from the date of completion of the development.

C is incorrect. For costs associated with software that is developed, which are not treated as current expenses, the amortization period can be 60 months from the date of completion of the development or 36 months from the date the software is placed in service.

D is incorrect. For costs associated with software that is developed, which are not treated as current expenses, the amortization period can be 60 months from the date of completion of the development or 36 months from the date the software is placed in service. The number 15 is fictitious.

CHAPTER 4

1.   **The correct answer is D.** The new regulations state that listed transactions must be reported. Listed transactions include those that are not only identical to those described in published guidance, but those that are similar to such transactions.

A is incorrect. The guidance plan outlines issues on which the IRS plans to offer published guidance during its fiscal year. The topics covered may include listed transactions. However, merely placing an item on the guidance plan does not definitively mean that the item will be issued.

B is incorrect. A taxpayer confessing to participating in an abusive tax shelter does not, by itself, render the transaction listed/reportable. A transaction would likely need to have been listed first through published guidance.

C is incorrect. Neither the dollar amount nor the substantiation factors bear on whether a transaction is or will be listed. The listed transaction requirement means that the transaction is either identical to or substantially similar to an existing transaction. Additional transactions become listed through published guidance, not through either of the elements indicated in this answer.

2.   **The correct answer is A.** The new regulations require that loss transactions meet certain thresholds. For corporations, the threshold for a loss transaction in a single year is $10 million.

B is incorrect. The threshold for individuals regarding losses spread over a combination of taxable years is $4 million.

C is incorrect. The threshold for pass-through entities, such as partnerships and limited partnerships, is a transaction that generated a loss of $5 million in a single year.

D is incorrect. The threshold for Code Sec 988 loss transactions is $50,000 in a single year.

3.   **The correct answer is C.** Rev. Proc. 2003-24 states that losses from the sale or exchange of assets with a "qualifying basis" will not be

taken into account in determining whether the transaction is a loss transaction.

A is incorrect. Rev. Proc. 2003-24 specifically references that basis increases as a loss item will not be taken into account because such a loss is not likely to be planned as a tax shelter.

B is incorrect. Since involuntary conversions are by definition unplanned events, they are not viable tax shelters.

D is incorrect. Mark-to-market treatment is automatically required by the Internal Revenue Code for certain securities and commodities dealers and traders and therefore is a "forced" transaction not susceptible to being arranged to benefit other taxpayers.

4. **The correct answer is C.** Concurrent with the new regulations, the IRS issued two revenue procedures outlining details for loss (Rev. Proc. 2003-24) and book–tax (Rev. Proc. 2003-25) transactions. Losses from hedging transactions are specifically referenced in the loss revenue procedure.

A is incorrect. Adjustments required by changes in accounting are generally made to prevent the taxpayer from enjoying benefits due only to an accounting change. Since the accounting change, rather than the adjustment, is capable of advance planning, it is excepted from consideration.

B is incorrect. Capitalization and amortization differences are frequently mandated by differing tax and accounting rules. Since book-tax differences here are a normal occurrence, taxpayers will not be penalized indirectly for having them.

D is incorrect. There was no intention of the book-tax difference rules being applied to penalize charitable contributions.

5. **The correct answer is D.** Although loss transactions are reportable under the new regulations, each type of loss must exceed specified amounts. The threshold loss amount for a trust in a single year is $2 million.

A is incorrect. The new regulations specifically require transactions with contractual protections to be disclosed since they tend to remove the downside of the transaction or investment.

B is incorrect. The new regulations specifically require transactions marketed under conditions of confidentiality to be disclosed since the cloak of confidentiality has been used frequently in the recent past to prevent a tax-shelter deal from being known to others, including the IRS.

C is incorrect. Reportable transactions include "listed transactions." These are transactions similar to those the IRS has identified as abusive under published guidance. This type of reinsurance arrangement is identified as a listed transaction in Notice 2002-70.

6. **The correct answer is B.** The new regulations specifically state that certain transactions that generate a tax credit are reportable if

certain criteria are met. The amount of tax credits generated must exceed $250,000 and the underlying asset giving rise to the credit must have been held for 45 days or less.

A is incorrect. The holding period is 45 or fewer days. The "shelter" aspect depends on the taxpayer being locked into the investment value of the asset for only a short period of time.

C is incorrect. The dollar value of tax credits must exceed $250,000 and the holding period is 45 or fewer days. The IRS is primarily after transactions creating a substantial credit. It also believed that setting the limit too low might occasionally capture regular business or investment transactions.

D is incorrect. The holding period is 45 or fewer days. If the taxpayer holds the underlying investment for six months, it would be clear that the taxpayer is betting on the overall investment value of the arrangement as well as benefiting from any subsidiary tax benefits.

7. **The correct answer is A.** The IRS website provides detailed instructions explaining the background, law and examples of each type of abuse, as well as instructions on how best to come back into compliance. At this point, the Service is only offering these toolkits to abusive trusts and offshore arrangements.

B is incorrect. Although it is certain that corporations and individuals participate in abusive trusts and offshore arrangements, they are not the subject of the toolkits.

C is incorrect. This answer gives possible examples of how a taxpayer might shelter income, or at least defer recognition, but neither is the subject of the toolkits.

D is incorrect. Although the toolkits provide that abusive trusts can be subcategorized into foreign and domestic, the subject matter of "trusts" represents only one type of toolkit.

8. **The correct answer is B.** The new regulations state that the minimum fee is $250,000 if every party who benefits from the tax statement regarding a transaction is a corporation.

A is incorrect. The new regulations lower the minimum fee to $50,000 for tax statements provided in connection with a transaction, but the benefiting parties must be a partnership or trust.

C is incorrect. Tax shelters in the corporate world usually involve significant sums. To justify the list-maintenance burdens required of material advisors, the regulations chose to include only advisors who are otherwise making a substantial fee. $100,000 was thought to be too low.

D is incorrect. The new regulations state that the minimum fee is $250,000 if every party who benefits from the tax statement regarding a transaction is a corporation. However, if the advisor receives five separate payments of $25,000 from different parties for the same transaction, the material advisor rules would apply.

9.   **The correct answer is C.** In a recent line of cases, the federal district and circuit courts have, in light of the issuance of John Doe summonses, revisited the application and scope of the taxpayer-practitioner privilege. These cases, bolstered by Code Sec. 7525, have said that the privilege applies where: (1) tax advice of any kind is sought; (2) from a federally authorized tax practitioner in his or her capacity as such; (3) and a communication is made in confidence; (4) that relates to that purpose; and (5) is made or received by the client. Although receipt of payment may aid in proving the existence of a relationship to which the privilege applies, it is not a necessary element.

A is incorrect. Tax advice is an element required to establish the privilege under case law and Code Sec. 7525.

B is incorrect. Involvement of a federally authorized tax practitioner is an element required to establish the privilege under case law and Code Sec. 7525.

D is incorrect. The expectation of confidentiality is an element required to establish the privilege under case law and Code Sec. 7525.

10.   **The correct answer is B.** A line of cases has emerged recently concerning the application of the Code Sec. 7525 taxpayer–practitioner privilege as it relates to requests from the IRS to obtain information regarding the identities of tax shelter participants. The cases all recognize that the privilege does not apply where the taxpayer has sought the aid of a tax practitioner to prepare his or her tax return because returns are not confidential documents. Thus, information exchanged between taxpayer and practitioner for that purpose is not confidential. However, courts have recognized that tax advice that is beyond mere return preparation would likely fall within the scope of the privilege.

A is incorrect. Because the likely purpose of such a transmission is to provide a tax practitioner information for purposes of return preparation and the form itself was likely prepared by a third-party employer, there is no expectation of confidentiality.

C is incorrect. The purpose of the correspondence was to confer regarding documents to which the privilege does not apply, namely, tax returns. This might warrant some further analysis, but answer A is the best response.

D is incorrect. The preponderance of case law holds that this type of information is generally submitted for the purpose of return preparation and so is not privileged. However, in cases where the information was submitted for the purpose of obtaining tax advice, courts have struggled and one has found that such information might be privileged if its mere disclosure would expose confidential communications between the taxpayer and the practitioner.

11. **The correct answer is A.** Notice 2003-55 states that a general lease-stripping transaction occurs when one party claims the income from the rental property and another party claims the deductions related to the income. Essentially, the income and related deductions are stripped from each other when they should match.

B is incorrect. Lease-stripping transactions typically do not involve gift and quid pro quo arrangements in the manner contemplated in the answer. In this case, there is no "stripping" of the tax benefits. This is likely a type of sham transaction.

C is incorrect. This scenario is not really a shelter at all. It does not involve any kind of "stripping" but presents a better case for fraudulently underreporting income.

D is incorrect. In this case, the taxpayer properly matched income and related deductions. Thus, there is no "stripping." Because the taxpayer fails to report the income, it is likely tax fraud.

12. **The correct answer is C.** Notice 2002-70 sets forth the details concerning producer owned reinsurance companies (PORCs). In these arrangements, a taxpayer sells a product (a car), and in addition, sells insurance to the customer as an agent for an actual insurance company. The taxpayer then sets up an offshore subsidiary to reinsure the policies it sold. The offshore company usually receives preferential tax treatment.

A is incorrect. There is nothing illegal, from a tax perspective or otherwise, with a producer who buys insurance for the goods it produces.

B is incorrect. Such arrangements trigger a number of other code sections of which taxpayers should be aware, but which are well beyond the scope of this chapter.

D is incorrect. This is a type of listed transaction under Notice 2003-54 called a "common trust fund straddle tax shelter."

13. **The correct answer is A.** Announcement 2002-63, as modified by Chief Counsel Notice 2003-012, set forth the IRS's position regarding its right to request tax accrual workpapers where taxpayers are claiming the benefits of a listed transaction. However, neither of these documents applies to tax reconciliation workpapers.

B is incorrect. As the notice makes clear, the IRS reserves the right to request tax accrual workpapers that pertain only to a disclosed listed transaction.

C is incorrect. The IRS has also indicated that it has the right to request all tax accrual workpapers if the transaction had not been disclosed.

D is incorrect. If the Service determines that tax benefits claimed on a return flow from multiple investments in listed transactions, the IRS will request all tax accrual workpapers.

14. **The correct answer is B.** Section 3001 of the American Jobs Creation Act of 2003 creates new Code Sec. 6707A, under which failures to provide required information regarding a listed transaction may be met with a $100,000 penalty imposed on natural persons and $200,000 on all other parties.

A is incorrect. The $10,000 to $50,000 penalty applies to information reporting failures that relate to reportable transaction. Section 3001 of the Jobs Act creates a special category for listed transactions and imposes higher penalties for violations (see the discussion for answer B).

C is incorrect. Although Section 3001 does impose penalties for information reporting failures that fall within the $100,000 to $200,000 range, those penalties pertain to failures related to listed transactions.

D is incorrect. The $50,000 to $250,000 figures do not relate to information reporting failures. These figures represent the minimum fee that a material advisor must collect with regard to providing tax shelter advice before a material advisor is required to comply with the list maintenance requirements.

CHAPTER 5

1. **The correct answer is C.** Unused funds in an HRA at the end of the year may be rolled over to the next coverage period. Any unused portion of the maximum dollar amount at the end of the coverage period is carried forward to increase the maximum reimbursement amount in subsequent coverage periods.

A is incorrect. Unused HRA funds at the end of the coverage period may be rolled over to the next coverage period.

B is incorrect. Federal tax law does not impose a penalty on unused HRA funds at the end of the coverage period.

D is incorrect. There is no "use it or lose it" feature in HRAs resulting in forfeiture of unused funds at the end of the coverage period.

2. **The correct answer is D.** HRA distributions must be for medical expenses and/or health insurance premiums. Nonqualifying distributions taint all distributions, even ones for qualifying purposes. Consequently, all distributions would then be included in the employee's gross income.

A is incorrect. Age is not a determinative factor.

B is incorrect. Although HRAs are not portable, they may be part of COBRA health plan coverage, and this does not cause distributions to be included in an employee's gross income.

C is incorrect. Unused funds at the end of the coverage period may be rolled over to the next coverage period. They are not included in an employee's gross income.

3. **The correct answer is C.** To qualify as an eligible participant in an HRA, an individual must be a current or retired employee, the

spouse or dependant of a current or retired employee, or the spouse or dependant of a deceased employee.

A is incorrect. It does not include dependants of current employees, retired employees and their spouses and dependants, and spouses and dependants of deceased employees.

B is incorrect. It does not include retired employees and their spouses and dependants, and spouses and dependants of deceased employees. **D is incorrect.** It does not include current employees, their spouses, and their dependants.

4.   **The correct answer is A.** The IRS has expressly identified this as an attribute of a permissible debit-credit card arrangement in an HRA. **B is incorrect.** Duplicate verification by service providers and third parties is not necessary. The IRS requires that service providers *or* third parties verify a charge is for a medical expense; not both. **C is incorrect.** The IRS has not identified this as an attribute of a permissible debit-credit card arrangement in an HRA. **D is incorrect.** While many plans have a $20 copayment, the IRS has not identified this as an attribute of a permissible debit-credit card arrangement in an HRA.

5.   **The correct answer is A.** A VEBA must be independent of an employer. The employer cannot exercise any control over the actions of the VEBA. **B is incorrect.** If it is under the employer's control, even as a subsidiary, it is not independent of the employer. **C is incorrect.** If the employer controls the operations of the VEBA, including the selection or election of trustees and officers, the VEBA will not be recognized as an independent entity. **D is incorrect.** If it is quasi-independent or the employer exercises any control over it, the VEBA will not be recognized as an independent entity.

6.   **The correct answer is D.** Members direct the activities of a VEBA through trustees or officers selected by them. Members may elect or appoint the trustees or officers. **A is incorrect.** If trustees or officers are selected by the employer, the VEBA will be deemed to be under employer control and will not be recognized as an independent entity. **B is incorrect.** If trustees or officers are selected by a joint labor-management committee, the VEBA will not be recognized as an independent entity. Additionally, there is no requirement that a VEBA be created or operated jointly by labor and management. **C is incorrect.** If trustees or officers are elected or selected by an international union, the VEBA will not be recognized as an independent entity. In addition, VEBAs exist outside of unionized

workplaces so it is not necessary to have union involvement in the creation or operation of a VEBA.

7.   **The correct answer is D.** Permissible VEBA benefits include life, sickness, accident, and similar benefits.
A is incorrect. Impermissible VEBA benefits include any benefit similar to a pension.
B is incorrect. Malpractice insurance is not a permissible VEBA benefit.
C is incorrect. Permissible VEBA benefits do not include loans to members in times of hardship.

8.   **The correct answer is A.** The definition of domestic partner varies among employers and localities but one component—two individuals, same-sex or not, in a committed and exclusive relationship—is practically universal.
B is incorrect. Domestic partners generally assume mutual welfare obligations.
C is incorrect. The definition of domestic partners varies among employers and localities but generally requires that domestic partners live in the same residence, sometimes for a prescribed length of time.
D is incorrect. Generally, domestic partners intend to remain in their relationship indefinitely.

9.   **The correct answer is C.** The federal Defense of Marriage Act of 1996 declared that marriage is between a man and a woman and a spouse is defined as a person of the opposite sex. Therefore, under federal law, same-sex domestic partners are not treated as spouses for tax purposes.
A is incorrect. Same-sex partners are not spouses of opposite sexes and therefore cannot be treated as spouses for tax purposes.
B is incorrect. State recognition is irrelevant for IRS purposes. The agency is bound to follow federal law.
D is incorrect. The law makes no exception for same-sex domestic partners with dependants.

10.   **The correct answer is B.** Employer-provided domestic partner benefits are tax-free if the employee's partner qualifies as a dependant. The employee must provide more than 50 percent of his or her partner's support and satisfy three other dependency tests.
A is incorrect. A domestic partner is not recognized as a spouse under federal law; therefore, employer-provided benefits can only be tax-free if the employee's partner qualifies as a dependent.
C is incorrect. Same-sex domestic partners cannot be considered common law spouses because the federal Defense of Marriage Act defines marriage as occurring between a man and a woman.

D is incorrect. Domestic partners may have participated in a civil union ceremony but their civil union is not recognized for federal tax purposes.

CHAPTER 6

1.   **The correct answer is D.** EGTRRA '01 gradually increases the federal estate tax exclusion amount from $1 million in 2003 to $3.5 million in 2009. Also, the federal estate tax is repealed in 2010, but because of EGTRRA's sunset provision, the federal estate tax is reinstated in 2011 unless Congress makes the repeal permanent.
A is incorrect. EGTRRA '01 also repeals the federal estate tax in 2010, reinstating it in 2011 unless Congress makes the repeal permanent. Answer A , alone, is not the best answer.
B is incorrect. The estate tax exclusion amount is increasing until 2010. Not only is the estate tax repealed in 2010, but it will be reinstated in 2011 unless Congress makes the repeal permanent. Answer B, alone, is not the best answer.
C is incorrect. EGTRRA '01 gradually increases the federal estate tax exclusion amount through 2009 and repeals the estate tax in 2010. The tax will be reinstated in 2011 unless Congress makes the repeal permanent. Answer C, alone, is not the best answer.

2.   **The correct answer is D.** JGTRRA did not address further reduction in estate and gift taxation, or an acceleration of those reductions scheduled over the next several years. The gift tax annual exclusion remains the same, adjusted each year by inflation. For 2003 and 2004 that exclusion amount is $11,000.
A is incorrect. JGTRRA lowered capital gains from 20 to 15 percent.
B is incorrect. Dividends will be taxed at a maximum of 15 percent.
C is incorrect. The EGTRRA's individual marginal rates cuts, not set to kick in until 2006, were knocked down to 10, 25, 28, 33, and 35 percent levels by JGTRRA in 2003.

3.   **The correct answer is B.** In 2010, step-up in basis is repealed and replaced by the modified carryover basis at death rules (Code Sec. 1014, as amended by EGTRRA '01). Heirs will take the less of (a) the decedent's basis in inherited property or (b) the current fair market value. (Code Sec. 1022, added by EGTRRA '01). Thus, Sally's basis in the parcel will be $15,000. When she sells the property for $51,000, the difference between the basis and the sale price--$36,000--will be subject to capital gains tax.
A is incorrect. This answer contemplates that Sally has a step-up basis of $50,000, making her gain only $1,000 at the time the asset is sold. In 2010, however, Sally will not have the advantage of a step-up basis, as per EGTRRA '01.

C is incorrect. It assumes that Sally has no basis at all. In 2010, Sally's basis will be the lesser of the decedent's basis or the current fair market.

D is incorrect. When Sally sells the property the property, she will have a capital gains consequence rather than ordinary income (subject to income tax rates), so long as she held the property for more than one year.

4.   **The correct answer is C.** Jane paid $25,000 less than the property is worth. However, so long as Mary didn't give Jane any other gifts that year, Mary can use her annual exclusion to give Jane the first $11,000 without incurring gift tax. The amount potentially subject to gift tax is $14,000.

A is incorrect. Mary can use her annual exclusion to defray the potential gift tax consequence by $11,000.

B is incorrect. The annual exclusion amount is $11,000, not $10,000. As per Code Sec. 2503(b)(2), the $10,000 limit is adjusted for inflation, rounded to the lowest multiple of $1,000.

D is incorrect. Although Mary sold the property to her daughter, she did not do so for full value. The difference, which exceeds Mary's annual gift exclusion, is subject to gift tax. However, Mary may not have to actually pay a gift tax if she has enough of her $1 million lifetime gift exemption (unified credit) still available to her.

5.   **The correct answer is D.** The IRS charges the difference between the interest rate actually used and the prevailing federal rate to both the lender and the borrower. The IRS holds the parties responsible for the higher rate.

A is incorrect. Minimum federal interest refers to the applicable federal rate published each month by the IRS.

B is incorrect. Foregone interest, as well as minimum federal interest and below-market interest, are part of an imputed interest analysis. However, imputed interest is the difference between the tax actually paid and the minimum federal interest.

C is incorrect. Below-market interest, as well as foregone interest and minimum federal interest, as part of an imputed interest analysis. However, imputed interest is the difference between the tax actually paid and the minimum federal interest.

6.   **The correct answer is C.** The annuity factor is found in the IRS actuarial tables found in IRS Publication 1457.

A is incorrect. Of the potential answers listed, the annuity factor is included only in the IRS actuarial tables.

B is incorrect. Rules for private or "below market" loans may be found in IRS Publication 550.

D is incorrect. Code Section 1274 addresses the applicable federal rate for debt instruments.

7.   **The correct answer is B.** The planning goal is to calculate the value of the annuity so that it equals the value of the transferred property. If the value of the property transferred from the parent to the child exceeds the present value of the annuity, the excess is a gift with gift tax consequences.

A is incorrect. The child "overpays" the parent's annuity compared to the value of the asset originally transferred to the child. The "extra" payments are also included in the parent's estate and are subject to estate tax.

C is incorrect. The difference between the annuity and the transferred property is a gift, with accompanying gift tax.

D is incorrect. The value of a private annuity is calculated at the time the annuity is established.

8.   **The correct answer is B.** Because payments must continue throughout the seller's life, the buyer might end up paying more for the property than the original "selling" price.

A is incorrect. By definition, canceling debt at the seller's death is a basic feature of a SCIN.

C is incorrect. The security interest is an element of the SCIN. Unlike a private annuity, in the case of a SCIN, the individual who transfers the property in exchange for payment can require security to ensure that the note will be paid. In fact, the presence of adequate security helps to defeat an IRS argument that the SCIN is a gift.

D is incorrect. It also describes an element of the SCIN. The buyer can deduct interest payments (unlike in the case of a private annuity). Under Code Sec. 163(h) an interest deduction is allowed for interest on the purchase of a qualified residence, investment interest, and for purchases allocable to a trade or business.

9.   **The correct answer is D.** It would make the statement incorrect. A QPRT may hold property other than a personal residence, with limitations. Cash may be added to the trust for limited purposes, such as to pay expenses (including mortgage payments), pay for improvements to the residence, or purchase or replace the residence. Reg. §25. 2702-5(c)(2)).

A is incorrect. Reg. § 25.2702-5(c)(2) (ii) provides that a mortgage on the residential property would not disqualify it as a personal residence.

B is incorrect. A QPRT may hold a home jointly owned by spouses. Reg.§25.2702-5(c)(2)(iv) provides that if spouses hold interests in the same residence, they may transfer those interests (or a fractional part of those interests) to the same QPRT, provided that the governing instrument of the trust prohibits any person other than one of the spouses from holding a term interest in the trust concurrently with the other spouse.

C is incorrect. A vacation home qualifies for transfer to a QPRT so long as the donor personally occupies it for at least 18 days per year Reg. 25.2702-5(d), example 2. (See also IRS Letter Ruling 200117021.)

10. **The correct answer is D.** For income tax purposes, the grantor is treated as the owner of the trust. Code Secs. 671–677 set out the grantor trust rules.
A is incorrect. This is only one of the effects of the grantor trust rule.
B is incorrect. Ownership in the view of the IRS is only one facet of the grantor trust rule.
C is incorrect. Deductions and credits are just one feature of the grantor trust rule.

11. **The correct answer is A.** A grantor retained annuity trust (GRAT) is an irrevocable trust that pays the grantor an annuity for a term of years, with the remainder of funds going to the grantor's beneficiaries. The grantor retains the right to receive a fixed amount payable not less frequently than annually. GRATs are specifically authorized by Code Secs. 2702(a)(2)(B) and 2702(b).
B is incorrect. Such a feature is found in a grantor retained unitrust (GRUT) rather than a GRAT. How the annuity amount is determined is a major difference between a GRAT and a GRUT. A GRUT is a trust in which the grantor retains the right to receive amounts that are payable not less frequently than annually and are a fixed percentage of the fair market value of the property in the trust (determined annually).
C is incorrect. Although the grantor does have an income interest in the form of an annuity, the annuity amount is fixed. The trustee does not have discretion as to the annuity amount and payment.
D is incorrect. The grantor's family members, not the grantor, have a remainder interest in the GRAT.

12. **The correct answer is B.** Intrafamily loans may use the applicable federal rate (AFR) as "adequate" interest to avoid being characterized as a below-market loan. The Code Sec. 7520 rate is derived from the AFR. Under Code Sec. 7520, annuities, term interests, remainders, and reversions are valued by applying a rate equal to 120 percent of the federal midterm rate, rounded to the nearest two-tenths of 1 percent.
A is incorrect. Code Sec. 7520 rates are used in GRATS. GRATs involve remainder interests.
C is incorrect. SCINs involve an interest for life. Code Sec. 7520 rates are used in SCINs.
D is incorrect. QPRTs involve reversionary interests. Sec. 7520 rates are used in QPRTs.

13. **The correct answer is C.** Any appreciation passes to the GRAT beneficiaries, transfer tax-free. No additional gift tax is imposed on the

additional amounts because the gift was completed when the trust was created.

A is incorrect. Neither the GRAT remainder, nor its appreciation, is part of the grantor's estate, so long as the grantor survives three years after the establishment of the GRAT

B is incorrect. The gift tax is imposed at the time the trust is created on the original amount. Any future appreciation escapes gift tax.

D is incorrect. T the capital gains tax does not apply until the asset is sold.

14. **The correct answer is C.** C is false. A no-interest or low-interest loan may be subject to gift tax consequences. Any foregone interest may be imputed as taxable income to the lender and then treated as a gift to the borrower. So long as the applicable federal rate is used as the minimum rate of interest, imputed interest can be avoided.

A is incorrect. A is true. The present value of the income stream of the private annuity is calculated using the Section 7520 rates. When interest rates are low, the annuity payments are "low." Although the parent who is receiving the annuity receives less if the interest rate is low, the children have lower payments to make.

B is incorrect. B is true. With a qualified personal residence trust (QPRT), a lower interest means the homeowner's retained interest is lower; therefore, the larger the gift to the homeowner's beneficiaries. The larger the gift, the greater the potential gift tax.

D is incorrect. D is true. Self-canceling installment notes, like intrafamily loans, installment sales, and private annuities, are advantaged by low interest rates because a lower rate means a lower payment for the family-member purchaser. In addition, raising the interest rate as the SCIN premium may be a more attractive option (rather than raising the principle) in a low interest rate environment.

15. **The correct answer is A.** Less than 80 percent of the assets is securities and cash. The general rule that assets can be transferred to an FLP or LLC tax-free does not apply if the FLP or LLC is an "investment partnership." If more than 80 percent of the assets comprise securities and cash, the FLP or LLC will be considered an investment partnership, in which case contributions could trigger gain recognition under Code Sec. 721(b).

B is incorrect. This mix could trigger gain recognition under Code Sec. 721(b).

C is incorrect. This combination could cause gain recognition under Code Sec. 721(b).

D is incorrect. This mix could trigger gain recognition under Code Sec. 721 (b).

CHAPTER 7

1. **The correct answer is D.** The audit rate is calculated by dividing the number of returns examined by the total number of returns filed the previous calendar year.

A is incorrect. The General Accounting Office (GAO) reported that the audit rates have steadily dropped for individuals, corporations with less than $10 million in assets, and corporations with more than $10 million in assets.

B is incorrect. The audit rates for corporations have declined. For corporations with assets of less than $10 million, the audit rate dropped from 1.88 percent to .77 percent from 1996 to 2000, respectively. For corporations having assets exceeding $10 million, the audit rates dropped from 25.33 percent to 16.30 percent from 1996 to 2000, respectively.

C is incorrect. The GAO reported that audit rates have steadily dropped for individuals, for example, from 1996 to 2000, declining to 0.49 percent.

2. **The correct answer is C.** The math error program uses IRS computers to identify and generate notices to contact taxpayers about obvious errors, omitted or inconsistent data, or other inconsistencies on the basis of other data reported on the return or to the IRS. These errors must be corrected in order to process a tax return.

A is incorrect. There are four major enforcement programs. They include the: (1) math error program; (2) document matching program; (3) nonfiler program; and (4) audit program.

B is incorrect. This describes the document matching program. Document matching also matches information returns (Schedule K-1) filed by pass-through entitles--such as partnerships, trusts and S-corps--to individual tax returns.

D is incorrect. This describes the nonfiler program. The contacts can ask for the missing return or offer an IRS-generated return to substitute for the missing return.

3. **The correct answer is C.** These powers include the authority to examine books and records and take testimony for the purposes of determining the tax liability of a tax return. The IRS also has the power to use a summons to compel taxpayers and third parties to provide books and records, and to enter premises to examine objects subject to taxation.

A is incorrect. Audits have the broadest scope. Under Code Sec. 7602, audits can cover an issue on a tax return.

B is incorrect. The Code does not explicitly limit the tax issues covered by an audit. Under Code Sec. 7602, audits can cover an issue on a tax return.

D is incorrect. The General Accounting Office (GAO) has reported a slight increase in the following years (currently and in the future).

However, the IRS enforcement program will become more of a critical support to our voluntary system, that is, for filing a tax return when required and for determining and paying the correct amount of tax.

4. **The correct answer is C.** The possibility that an individual's return may be selected for audit brings about more accurate returns. Voluntary compliance means that each taxpayer is responsible for filing a tax return when required and for determining and paying the correct amount of tax.

A is incorrect. Audits perform a vital function in our tax system. It is the method by which our system of voluntary compliance is enforced.

B is incorrect. Audits perform a vital function in our tax system. It is the method by which our system of voluntary compliance is enforced. Voluntary compliance means that each taxpayer is responsible for filing a tax return when required and for determining and paying the correct amount of tax.

D is incorrect. For a vast majority of returns, the simple checking of computation (and other minor issues) is the only examination ever performed.

5. **The correct answer is D.** With IRS resources continuing to be stretched because of federal budget concerns, the focus of IRS's examination activities is to squeeze more from less through surgically refining the audit selection process to guarantee fewer no-change letters.

A is incorrect. According to various reports and statements by the GAO, the IRS Data Book, and former IRS Commissioners the general audit rate may have remained relatively low but the IRS has about an 80 percent track record on finding additional taxes due as the result of those audits.

B is incorrect. Although statistically lower-income groups have a higher "no-change" rate than higher income taxpayers, no group escapes will a 60 percent no-change rate.

C is incorrect. Prior to computerized selection of audits, a 40 percent no-change rate was common. However, with DIF computer selection and targeted audit programs, that no-change rate has been cut in half.

6. **The correct answer is A.** The fast track settlement program (FTS) enables the IRS to resolve tax disputes with large and mid-size businesses at an earlier stage, often within a much shorter time period than through the normal audit and Appeals process. By May 31, 2003, the IRS and 104 LMSB taxpayers had successfully settled through the program, in an average time of 69 days, just over half of the expected time. FTS does not eliminate or replace existing dispute resolution options, including the taxpayer's opportunity to request a conference with a manager or a hearing before Appeals.

B is incorrect. This process describes the fast track mediation program (FTM).

C is incorrect. FTS does not eliminate or replace existing dispute resolution options, including the taxpayer's opportunity to request a conference with a manager or a hearing before Appeals. In the FTS process, Appeals' role is to provide a neutral party, someone who will help the taxpayer and LMSB understand the nature of the dispute and reach a mutually satisfactory resolution. Either party may stop the process at any time.

D is incorrect. This program has been formally established in Rev. Proc. 2003-40.

7. **The correct answer is B**. Audits (examinations) are not enforcement tools.

A is incorrect. Levies are considered one of the major collection enforcement tools. The use of this tool has declined sharply after the enactment of the *IRS Restructuring and Reform Act of 1998* (RRA '98). This resulted from both the continuing decline in IRS staff and from the need to develop and implement procedures to comply with the new taxpayers' rights provisions.

C is incorrect. Liens are considered one of the major collection enforcement tools. The use of this tool has declined sharply after the enactment of the *IRS Restructuring and Reform Act of 1998* (RRA '98). This resulted from both the continuing decline in IRS staff and from the need to develop and implement procedures to comply with the new taxpayers' rights provisions.

D is incorrect. Seizures are considered one of the major collection enforcement tools. The use of this tool has declined sharply after the enactment of the *IRS Restructuring and Reform Act* (RRA '98). This resulted from both the continuing decline in staff and from the need to develop and implement procedures to comply with the new taxpayer rights provisions.

8. **The correct answer is B**. However, any delay will increase the debt because penalties and interest are charged until the full amount is paid.

A is incorrect. This program is referred to as the offer in compromise. This program applies to all taxes, including any interest, penalties, or additional amounts under the laws. The IRS may legally compromise a tax liability for one of the following reasons: (1) doubt as to liability; (2) doubt as to collectibility; and (3) promotion of effective tax administration.

C is incorrect. This program refers to installment agreements. The agreement generally requires equal monthly payments. The amount of a taxpayer's installment payment will be based on the amount he or she owes and the ability to pay that amount within the time available to the IRS to collect the tax debt. However, it is more costly than borrowing funds to pay the amount owed.

D is incorrect. Any delay will increase the debt because penalties and interest are charged until the full amount is paid.

9. **The correct answer is D**. For controversies involving whether a taxpayer owes additional income tax, estate tax, or gift tax, certain excise taxes or penalties related to these proposed liabilities, a taxpayer can go to the Tax Court.
A is incorrect. Certain types of tax controversies, such as those involving some employment tax issues, cannot be heard by the Tax Court.
B is incorrect. Certain types of tax controversies, such as those involving manufacturers' excise taxes, cannot be heard by the Tax Court.
C is incorrect. If a taxpayer claims a refund for tax liabilities paid, the taxpayer has a choice of the refund forums--a U.S. District Court or the Court of Federal Claims. Once the liability has been paid, the Tax Court does not have jurisdiction over the dispute.

10. **The correct answer is D**. Administrative costs include costs incurred on or after the date the taxpayer receives the Appeals decision letter, the date of the first letter of proposed deficiency, or the date of the notice of deficiency, whichever is **earliest**. These costs may include reasonable amounts for court costs or any administrative fees or similar charges by the IRS.
A is incorrect. In certain instances, a taxpayer may be able to recover reasonable litigation and administrative costs if he or she is the prevailing party and if other requirements are met. The taxpayer must exhaust his or her administrative remedies within the IRS and must not unreasonably delay the administrative or court proceedings.
B is incorrect. Administrative costs include costs incurred on or after the date the taxpayer receives the Appeals decision letter, the date of the first letter of proposed deficiency, or the date of the notice of deficiency, whichever is **earliest**. Here, only one component of the puzzle is provided to determine what costs should be covered.
C is incorrect. Administrative costs include costs incurred on or after the date the taxpayer receives the Appeals decision letter, the date of the first letter of proposed deficiency, or the date of the notice of deficiency, whichever is **earliest**. Here, only one component of the puzzle is provided to determine what costs should be covered.

11. **The correct answer is C**. The General Accounting Office (GAO) reported in May 2002 that between 1996 and 2001, trends in the collection of delinquent taxes showed **declines** in the program's performance, in terms of coverage of workload, cases closed, direct staff time used, productivity, and amount of unpaid taxes collected.
A is incorrect. The GAO reported in May 2002 that between 1996 and 2001, trends in the collection of delinquent taxes showed **declines** in the program's performance, in terms of coverage of workload, cases

closed, direct staff time used, productivity, and amount of unpaid taxes collected.

B is incorrect. The GAO reported in May 2002 that between 1996 and 2001, trends in the collection of delinquent taxes showed **declines** in the program's performance, in terms of coverage of workload, cases closed, direct staff time used, productivity, and amount of unpaid taxes collected.

D is incorrect. The GAO reported in May 2002 that between 1996 and 2001, trends in the collection of delinquent taxes showed **declines** in the program's performance, in terms of coverage of workload, cases closed, direct staff time used, productivity, and amount of unpaid taxes collected.

12. **The correct answer is D.** The *IRS Restructuring and Reform Act of 1998* (RRA '98) created significant resource demands on the exam staff. For example, the innocent spouse provisions **required** additional staff for administration.

A is incorrect. The statement is true about the decline in examination coverage. The IRS has indicated that the major reason for the drop in examination coverage is that the examination staff has declined while the workload has increased.

B is incorrect. RRA '98 created significant resource demands on the exam staff. For example, the innocent spouse provisions required additional staff for administration, while the requirements for notification of third parties added to the completion time for an exam.

C is incorrect. Revenue officers declined from 5,908 in 1995 to 3,601 in 2000. The commissioner attributed the decline in compliance staffing to increases in workload in other essential operations.

13. **The correct answer is A.** Under the current law, federal tax liabilities must be collected by the IRS and cannot be referred to a private collection agency (PCA) for collection.

B is incorrect. Under the current law, federal tax liabilities must be collected by the IRS and cannot be referred to a private collection agency (PCA) for collection. However, a proposal for the use of PCAs was introduced in Congress.

C is incorrect. As of July 2002, the IRS designated more than $13 billion in delinquent tax liabilities as uncollectible due to IRS collection and resource priorities, and these amounts continue to increase. Many of these accounts represent taxpayers who have filed a tax return showing an amount of tax due, but who have failed to pay the tax. Other accounts are from taxpayers who have been assessed additional tax by the IRS and have made three or more payments, but for some reason have stopped making payments. In both situations, the IRS is unable to continuously pursue each taxpayer.

D is incorrect. As of July 2002, the IRS designated more than $13 billion in delinquent tax liabilities as uncollectible due to IRS collection and resource priorities, and these amounts continue to **increase**.

14. **The correct answer is A.** Under H.R. 1169, private collection agencies (PCAs) could contact each taxpayer using a letter meeting the requirements of the Fair Debt Collection Practices Act (FDCPA).
B is incorrect. Under the legislative proposal, PCAs would be able to contact a taxpayer by telephone to request payment.
C is incorrect. Under the legislative proposal, PCAs would not be permitted to subcontract any of their work for the IRS.
D is incorrect. Under the legislative proposal, PCAs would be subject to careful monitoring by the IRS (live monitoring or telephonic communication, review of recorded conversations, taxpayer-satisfaction surveys, audits of PCAs' records, and periodic reviews of PCAs' performance).

15. **The correct answer is C.** The taxpayer has the right to make an audio recording of any in-person interview, conducted by the IRS, upon 10 days' advance notice.
A is incorrect. The Taxpayer Bill of Rights requires the IRS to provide a written statement detailing the taxpayer's rights and the IRS's obligations during the audit process.
B is incorrect. The IRS must explain the audit and collection process to the taxpayer.
D is incorrect. A taxpayer is guaranteed the right to be represented by any individual currently permitted to practice before the IRS.

CPE Quizzer Instructions

The CPE Quizzer for this course is divided into two modules. There is a $70.00 processing fee **per Quizzer module** that is submitted for grading. Successful completion of Module 1 is worth **9 hours** of credit. Successful completion of Module 2 is worth **8 hours** of credit. You can complete and submit one module at a time, or both modules at once for a total of **17 hours** of credit.

To obtain CPE credit, return your completed answer sheet for each Quizzer module to **CCH INCORPORATED, Continuing Education Department, 4025 W. Peterson Ave., Chicago, IL 60646**, or fax it to (773) 866-3084. Each Quizzer answer sheet will be graded and a CPE Certificate of Completion awarded for achieving a grade of 70 percent or greater. Successful completion of **Quizzer Module 1** should qualify you to receive **9 hours** of Continuing Education credit in conjunction with your CPE governing body's qualifications. Successful completion of **Quizzer Module 2** should qualify you to receive **8 hours** of Continuing Education credit in conjunction with your CPE governing body's qualifications. A Quizzer answer sheet is located after each module's Quizzer questions for this course.

Evaluation: To help us provide you with the best possible products, please take a moment to fill out the course evaluation located at the back of this course and return it with your Quizzer answer sheet(s).

Express Grading: Processing time for your answer sheet is generally 8-12 business days. If you are trying to meet a reporting deadline, our Express Grading Service is available for an additional $19 per module. To use this service, please check the "Express Grading" box on your answer sheet, and provide your CCH account or credit card number and your fax number. CCH will fax your results and a certificate of completion (upon achieving a passing grade) to you by 5:00 p.m. the business day following our receipt of your answer sheet. **If you mail your answer sheet for express grading, please write "ATTN: CPE OVERNIGHT" on the envelope.** *NOTE:* CCH will not Federal Express Quizzer results under any circumstances.

Date of Completion: The date of completion on your certificate will be the date that you put on your answer sheet. However, you must submit your answer sheet to CCH for grading within two weeks of completing it.

Expiration Date: December 31, 2004

Recommended CPE:	9 hours for module 1
	8 hours for module 2
	17 hours for both modules
Processing Fee:	$ 70.00 per module
	$ 140.00 for both modules

1. The *Jobs and Growth Tax Relief Reconciliation Act of 2003* (JGTRRA) accelerates the endpoint of the 10 percent bracket created by EGTRRA, by adding an additional:

   a. $1,000 for married couples filing jointly
   b. $2,000 for married couples filing jointly
   c. $2,000 for married taxpayers filing separately
   d. $500 for head-of-household filers

2. Under JGTRRA, marriage penalty relief is:

   a. Delayed
   b. Repealed
   c. Accelerated
   d. Cut in half

3. Under JGTRRA, the tax rate for accumulated earnings tax and personal holding company tax is reduced to ____ percent for 2002 and 2009.

   a. 10
   b. 15
   c. 20
   d. 22

4. JGTRRA:

   a. Delays scheduled cuts in the individual marginal tax rates
   b. Follows scheduled cuts in the individual marginal tax rates
   c. Repeals the Economic Growth and Tax Relief Reconciliation Act of 2001
   d. Decreases the top individual marginal rate to 35 percent

5. Under JGTRRA the five-year holding period for capital assets is:

   a. Eliminated
   b. Accelerated
   c. Expanded
   d. Delayed

6. Regarding capital gains, JGTRRA:

   a. Lowered all capital gains rates
   b. Reduced the holding period to 10 months
   c. Increased the capital loss limit to $5,000 per year
   d. Requires a transitional computation in 2003

7. JGTRRA temporarily reduces the maximum tax rate generally applied to long-term capital gains from 20 percent to _____ percent through _____.

   a. 18 percent; December 31, 2005
   b. 18 percent; December 31, 2008
   c. 15 percent; December 31, 2005
   d. 15 percent; December 31, 2008

8. Under JGTRRA, dividend income is taxed at:

   a. Individual marginal tax rates
   b. Modified individual marginal tax rates
   c. Capital gains rates
   d. Corporate rates

9. Lower dividends rates sunset at the end of:

   a. 2005
   b. 2008
   c. 2009
   d. 2010

10. For individuals in the 10 and 15 percent brackets in 2008, qualified dividends will be:

    a. Zero
    b. 5 percent
    c. 8 percent
    d. 10 percent

11. Distributions from qualified plans, such as 401(k) plans and IRAs, will be taxed as:

    a. Capital gains
    b. Ordinary income
    c. Dividends
    d. Accumulated earnings

12. An ordinary and necessary business expense is:

   a. An expense that is common, accepted, helpful, and appropriate in a taxpayer's trade or business
   b. A capital expenditure
   c. A reasonable allowance of the exhaustion, wear and tear, and obsolescence on certain types of property used in a trade or business
   d. Can be deducted in the following year that it is paid for or incurred

13. Code Sec. 162 addresses which of the following?

   a. Capitalization of costs
   b. Trade or business expenses
   c. Cleanup expenses
   d. Acquisition of intangibles

14. A taxpayer may take a current deduction for:

   a. A repair to maintain the operating condition of the property
   b. Expenses to get a business started
   c. An improvement
   d. A capital expense

15. Costs of repairs or improvements may be capitalized if they:

   a. Prolong the useful life of the asset
   b. Maintain the operating condition of the property
   c. Do not have a determinable useful life exceeding one year
   d. Are currently deducted as expenses for the year in which the costs associated with repairs or improvements are incurred

16. Environmental cleanup costs:

   a. May be classified as ordinary and necessary business expenses
   b. Are always capitalized
   c. May be currently expensed under Code Sec. 162
   d. Are considered improvements

17. Environmental remediation expenses:

   a. Are the same as abatement activities
   b. Were at issue in *Cinergy Corp.*
   c. Are always expensed
   d. Must be frequently capitalized

18. Which of the following is *not* a safe harbor/administrative assumption under the proposed regs for the capitalization of intangibles?

    a. 12-month rule
    b. De minimis rule
    c. Employee compensation rule
    d. 20-year safe harbor

19. Under the proposed regs for the capitalization of intangibles, which of following is **not** considered one of the categories within "self-created intangibles"?

    a. Costs that facilitate an acquisition
    b. Certain types of membership rights
    c. Expenses incurred in connection with the perfection of titled
    d. Rights obtained from the government

20. Transaction costs, as described under the proposed regs for the capitalization of intangibles:

    a. May be broken down into four categories
    b. Do not include fees paid to attorneys or brokers who aid in negotiating deals
    c. Are determined by using a fact and circumstances test
    d. Should be expensed

21. Under the *Jobs and Growth Tax Relief Reconciliation Act of 2003* (JGTRRA), for smaller business, the Section 179 expense limit:

    a. Remained the same
    b. Increased from $25,000 to $50,000
    c. Increased from $25,000 to $100,00
    d. Temporarily decreased from $25,000 to $15,000

22. Under the *Jobs and Growth Tax Relief Reconciliation Act of 2003* (JGTRRA), the level at which the phaseout limitation for Section 179 expensing starts:

    a. Was raised to $100,000
    b. Was raised to $400,000
    c. Was raised to $200,000
    d. Remained the same

23. To stimulate the economy, the *Jobs and Growth Tax Relief Reconciliation Act of 2003* (JGTRRA) increased the additional first-year depreciation allowance percentage from ____ percent to ____ percent.

    a.   15; 30
    b.   15; 50
    c.   30; 50
    d.   30; 60

24. For purposes of the bonus depreciation, as a general rule qualified property must be placed in service by:

    a.   September 11, 2003
    b.   May 6, 2003
    c.   May 6, 2005
    d.   January 1, 2005

25. The original use of qualified property must commence with the taxpayer on or after September 11, 2001, for the ____ percent bonus depreciation; and on or after May 6, 2003, but before January 1, 2006 for the ____ percent bonus depreciation.

    a.   15; 30
    b.   15; 50
    c.   30; 50
    d.   30; 60

26. What is the purpose of Form 4562?

    a.   To claim a deduction for depreciation and amortization
    b.   To avoid reporting the election under Code Sec. 179 to expense certain tangible property
    c.   To claim only a portion of your depreciation for property placed in service during the tax year
    d.   To claim only a portion for depreciation on a corporate income tax return

27. What is the rationale for the increase in expensing for a new investment?

    a.   To encourage small business owners to purchase technology, machinery, and other equipment they need in order to expand
    b.   To satisfy the small business constituency
    c.   To create more jobs
    d.   There was no specific rationale provided by Congress

28. Which of the following costs are *not* involved with going into business?

   a. Expenses for advertising
   b. Travel
   c. Wages for training employees
   d. Investigatory costs as a loss

29. Rev. Proc. 2000-50 is significant because it addresses which of the following?

   a. Research and experimentation expenditures
   b. Capitalization of costs
   c. Trade or business expenses
   d. Treatment of costs of computer software

30. Code Sec. 263 addresses which of the following?

   a. Research and experimentation expenditures
   b. Capitalization of costs
   c. Trade or business expenses
   d. Treatment of costs of computer software

31. Real property, personal property, and intangible property are:

   a. Subject to a 15-year amortization
   b. Depreciable if the property is not inventory or stock in trade
   c. Depreciable if the property is not used in a trade or business or is not held for the production of income
   d. Never depreciable

32. When is computer software considered a Code Sec. 197 intangible?

   a. Never
   b. When it is readily available for purchase by the general public, is subject to a nonexclusive license, and has not been substantially modified
   c. When it is acquired, developed, or leased in general
   d. When it is acquired, developed, or leased in connection with the acquisition of assets that constitute a trade or business

33. If a depreciation deduction is allowable under Code Sec. 167 for computer software, the deduction is computed by using the straight-line method and a useful life of:

   a. 24 months
   b. 48 months
   c. 36 months
   d. 46 months

34. Under the *Jobs and Growth Tax Relief Reconciliation Act of 2003* (JGTRRA '03), the new bonus depreciation _____ to _____ percent for property acquired after May 5, 2003 and before January 1, 2005.

   a. Decreases; 30
   b. Decreases; 50
   c. Increases; 30
   d. Increases; 50

35. How are payments for leased software treated?

   a. Payments are capitalized
   b. Payments are deductible
   c. Payments are never deducted
   d. Payments are neither capitalized nor deducted

36. Which of the following would *not* be a deductible home office expense?

   a. Transportation expense
   b. Computer and related equipment expense
   c. Employment-related business telephone calls
   d. Basic local telephone service provided for the taxpayer's residence

37. Improvements may include:

   a. Repairs
   b. Expenses that keep property in an ordinary, efficient operating condition
   c. Expenses that do not add value to the property
   d. New plumbing

38. Code Sec. 174 addresses which of the following?

   a. Trade or business expenses
   b. Depreciation
   c. Research and experimentation expenditures
   d. Capitalization of costs

39. Code Sec. 195 addresses which of the following?

    a. Trade or business expenses
    b. Depreciation
    c. Research and experimentation expenditures
    d. Amortization of goodwill and certain other intangibles

40. Which of the following is a reportable tax shelter transaction:

    a. A securities offering that contains confidentiality provisions in an agreement under which tax aspects of the transaction are discussed
    b. A transaction under which a book-tax loss of $1 million is generated
    c. A tax free acquisition under which the taxpayer is allowed to discuss the tax benefits when the acquisition is made public
    d. A transaction under which IBM generates a Code Sec. 165 tax loss of $15 million in 2003

41. Participants in reportable transactions are generally required to retain all tax shelter related documents for a period of _____.

    a. 6 years
    b. 3 years
    c. 3 years where income has been grossly understated
    d. 6 years if the amount reported falls within a de minimus exception

42. Listed transactions are those that are the same or substantially similar to those identified in _____.

    a. Notices, regulations or other forms of published guidance
    b. The Treasury's Annual Tax Shelter Registration Publication
    c. The Taxpayer Advocate's Annual Report
    d. Case law only

43. Which of the following is *not* a Code Sec 165 loss transaction subject to the reporting requirements:

    a. A transaction in which Warren Buffett generated a series of Code Sec 165 losses from 2003 to 2004 in excess of $5.25 million
    b. A transaction in which the Buffet Family Trust generated a series of Code Sec. 165 losses from 2003 to 2004 of $3.75 million
    c. A transaction in which Intel generated a Code Sec. 165 loss of $13,125,000 in 2002
    d. A transaction in which ABC, L.P. generated a Code Sec. 165 loss of $7.5 million in 2002

44. Under Rev. Proc. 2003-25, certain book-tax differences are not to be taken into account, *except* differences arising from:

   a. Cancellation of indebtedness
   b. Federal taxes
   c. Involuntary conversions
   d. Amortization

45. Under which of the following forms is a promoter required to register a tax shelter:

   a. 8264
   b. 8886
   c. 8885
   d. 8396

46. Which of the following programs are aimed at obtaining information about tax shelter participation:

   a. Fast Track Settlement and Mediation
   b. Offshore Voluntary Compliance Initiative and John Doe Summonses
   c. Abusive Trust and Offshore Tool Kits
   d. Workpaper requests

47. The tax practitioner privilege would most likely apply to:

   a. Information used to amend a taxpayers return from the previous year
   b. Information prepared to file employee withholding taxes
   c. Advice sought by a taxpayer in connection with a tax shelter
   d. Advice sought by a taxpayer in connection with return preparation and planning for the current taxable year

48. Which of the following is *not* a list transaction under published guidance:

   a. A contingent installment sale of securities by a partnership used to accelerate and allocate income to a partner
   b. Trusts purporting to qualify for a special foreign income-exclusion
   c. Transactions where the profit is overshadowed by the foreign tax credits generated
   d. A transaction in which a partner contributes appreciated property to a partnership

49. A transaction in which one participant claims to realize rental or other income from property and another participant claims the deductions related to that income is known as a:

    a. Lease Strip
    b. Common Straddle
    c. A basis shifting shelter
    d. A PORC

50. The IRS has identified a number of tax shelter transactions that target individuals which include all of the following, *except:*

    a. A series of shelters targeted for those in the medical profession
    b. Home-based business shelters
    c. Offshore financial transactions
    a. The Frequent Flier program shelter

51. An HRA cannot be provided under a:

    a. Salary reduction plan
    b. Retiree health plan
    c. Multiemployer plan
    d. New hire plan

52. At the end of the coverage period, unused funds in an HRA:

    a. May not be rolled over to the next coverage period
    b. May be rolled over to the next coverage period
    c. Are forfeited to the employer
    d. Are subject to an excise tax for nonuse during the coverage period

53. Eligible participants in an HRA include:

    a. Current employees only
    b. Retired employees only
    c. Current and retired employees and their spouses and dependants
    d. Current and retired employees but not spouses and dependants

54. The IRS recently authorized HRA reimbursements to be made by debit or credit cards. Debit and credit card arrangements must have specific attributes, including:

    a. Transaction dollar limit equals copayment, recurring expenses match previously approved expenses, and service providers and independent third parties verify the charge is for a medical expense
    b. Transaction dollar limit equals copayment, recurring expenses match previously approved expenses, and employee's parties verify the charge is for a medical expense
    c. Transaction dollar limit is less than copayment, recurring expenses match previously approved expenses, and service providers or independent third parties verify the charge is for a medical expense
    d. Transaction dollar limit equals copayment, recurring expenses match previously approved expenses, and service providers or independent third parties verify the charge is for a medical expense

55. A VEBA may operate as a nonprofit corporation or a trust and it must be:

    a. Organized as a subsidiary of the employer
    b. Spun off from the employer in a tax-free reorganization
    c. Independent of the employer
    d. Controlled by the employer

56. Membership in a VEBA is limited to individuals who qualify based on their status as:

    a. Active employees
    b. Spouses and dependants of active and retired employees
    c. Retired employees
    d. Active and retired employees

57. A VEBA may include nonmembers but they may compose no more than _____ percent of the total membership.

    a. 5
    b. 10
    c. 20
    d. 25

58. A VEBA may provide benefits in cash or noncash form. However, it cannot provide _____ benefits

    a. Current
    b. Future
    c. Disability
    d. Child care

59. Permissible VEBA benefits include:

    a. Pension benefits
    b. Pension and sickness benefits
    c. Life, sickness, and pension benefits
    d. Life, sickness, accident, and similar benefits

60. Common attributes of a domestic partner relationship include:

    a. Two same-sex individuals age 18 or over in a committed and exclusive relationship
    b. Two individuals, same-sex or not, over age 18, in a committed and exclusive relationship, and residing in the same residence
    c. Two individuals, one of whom may be claimed as the other's dependant, same-sex or not, over age 21, and in a committed and exclusive relationship
    d. Two same-sex individuals, residing in the same residence, and filing joint income tax returns

61. Under federal law, domestic partners are:

    a.   Treated as spouses

    b.   Treated as spouses if the partners are united in a civil union or registered in a state or local domestic partner registry

    c.   Treated as codependants

    d.   Not treated as spouses

62. For federal tax purposes:

    a.   A spouse is a person of the opposite sex or a member of the same sex so long as the couple is united in marriage or a civil union equivalent to marriage

    b.   A spouse is a person of the opposite sex

    c.   A spouse is a member of the opposite sex or same sex if the couple are married in a foreign jurisdiction and one spouse is a U.S. citizen

    d.   The definition of spouse is determined by reference to state law

63. An employee generally pays taxes on the fair market value of the cost of employer-provided coverage for his or her domestic partner. However, benefits are tax-free if the employee's partner qualifies as a:

    a.   Dependant

    b.   Spouse

    c.   Common law spouse

    d.   Beneficiary

64. The Jobs and Growth Tax Relief Reconciliation Act of 2003 (JGTRRA '03):

    a.   Accelerates EGTRRA's estate and gift tax rules

    b.   Supercedes EGTRRA's estate and gift tax provisions

    c.   Does not affect estate planning

    d.   None of the above

65. In 2003, the following amount can be excluded from federal estate tax:

    a. $675,000

    b. $1 million

    c. $1.5 million

    d.   Unlimited

66. In an estate planning context, Section 7520 rates are used to determine:

    a. Imputed interest
    b. Fair market value
    c. Present value of an annuity
    d. None of above

67. Sarah (the annuitant) transfers property to her son, Herman (the payor), in exchange for a private annuity. At the end of the private annuity term, what is Herman's basis in the property?

    a. Step-up basis
    b. Step-down basis
    c. Fair market value at the end of the term
    d. Fair market value upon the transfer

68. Charlie wants to pass the family business to his son, Dan, but keep control for at least a "few more years." Which planning technique offers Charlie both control and transfer tax advantages?

    a. A gift
    b. A QPRT
    c. A will
    d. An FLP

69. Susan establishes a grantor retained annuity trust (GRAT). When does the potential gift tax apply?

    a. No gift tax consequence
    b. At the time the GRAT is created
    c. When Susan's beneficiaries receive the remaining assets (the remainder interest)
    d. When Susan receives her first annuity payment

70. If the grantor dies before the GRAT term ends, the trust assets:

    a. Pass directly to the grantor's beneficiaries
    b. Pass to the grantor's beneficiaries, estate tax-free
    c. Convert to a QPRT
    d. Revert to the grantor's estate and the assets are subject to estate tax

71. A qualified personal residence trust (QPRT):

    a. Is an irrevocable trust
    b. Allows a homeowner to make a future gift of the residential property to his or her children
    c. Allows a homeowner to retain the right to continue residing in the home for a defined number of years.
    d. All of the above

72. In 2003, the annual gift tax exclusion is:

    a. $10,000
    b. $11,000
    c. $1 million
    d. Unlimited

73. Limited partnership interests in an FLP may enjoy a discount in value for transfer tax purposes due to:

    a. Minority interest status
    b. Lack of control of the business
    c. Impaired marketability
    d. All of the above

74. What tax basis does a family limited partnership take in transferred assets?

    a. Carryover
    b. Step-up
    c. Discounted
    d. None of the above

75. Which of the following techniques may be disadvantaged in a low interest rate environment?

    a. Intrafamily loans
    b. Private annuities
    c. Qualified personal residence trusts
    d. Self-canceling installment notes

76. The audit rates for individuals declined to ____ percent in 2000 (with a slight increase in the following years).

    a. 1.67
    b. 1.88
    c. 25.33
    d. .49

77. Which of the following docs *not* constitute a component within the IRS's enforcement programs?

    a. The math error program
    b. The nonfiler program
    c. The document matching program
    d. The FTS program

78. The IRS:

    a.   Does not have the authority to examine books and records

    b.   Does not have the authority to take testimony for purposes of determining the tax liability of a tax return

    c.   Has the power to use a summons to compel taxpayers and third parties to provide books and records

    d.   Does not have the authority to enter premises to examine objects subject to taxation

79. Revenue agents:

    a.   Handle office audits

    b.   Are restricted in the scope of the audit to identify significant items

    c.   Are more educated and experienced than tax auditors

    d.   Do not handle field audits

80. New audit priorities include (select all that apply):

    a.   Offshore credit card users, and high-risk and high-income taxpayers

    b.   Abusive schemes and promoter investigations

    c.   High-income nonfilers and unreported income

    d.   All of the above

81. FTM:

    a.   Gives small businesses, self-employed taxpayers and the IRS the opportunity to mediate disputes through an IRS Appeals Officer

    b.   Is required for the taxpayer

    c.   Is not a permanent program, but is merely a pilot program

    d.   Enables the IRS to resolve tax disputes with large and mid-size businesses at an earlier stage, often within a much shorter time than through the normal audit and Appeals process

82. Which of the following is *not* an optimal option for the taxpayer to pay his or her taxes?

    a.   Making monthly payments through an installment agreement

    b.   Avoiding payment until the taxpayer can afford to pay

    c.   Using an offer in compromise

    d.   Qualifying for a temporary delay due to hardship

83. Installment agreements:

    a.   Enable the IRS to settle an unpaid tax account for less than the full amount of the balance

    b.   Delay the tax debt until the taxpayer's financial condition improves

    c.   Allows the full payment of the taxpayer's debt in small, more manageable amounts

    d.   Would enable the IRS to levy against a taxpayer's property while his or her request for an agreement is being considered

84. An offer in compromise:

    a.   Enables the IRS to settle unpaid tax accounts for less than the full amount of the balance

    b.   Delays the tax debt until the taxpayer's financial condition improves

    c.   Allows the full payment of the taxpayer's debt in small, more manageable amounts

    d.   Does not apply to all taxes, including any interest, penalties, or additional amounts

85. If a taxpayer claims a refund for tax liabilities paid, he or she has the initial choice of which of the following courts?

    a.   The Tax Court
    b.   The U.S. District Court
    c.   The U.S. Bankruptcy Court
    d.   A federal circuit court

86. Recoverable litigation or administrative costs do **not** include:

    a.   Attorney's fees that generally do not exceed $175 per hour

    b.   Reasonable amounts for court costs or any administrative fees or similar charges by the IRS

    c.   Reasonable expenses of expert witnesses

    d.   Reasonable costs of studies, analyses, or tests that are necessary to prepare the case

87. The major reason provided by the IRS for the drop in examination coverage is:

    a.   That examination is not a priority

    b.   That the *IRS Restructuring and Reform Act of 1998* (RRA '98) created more demands on the workforce.

    c.   That the examination staff has declined while the workload has increased

    d.   No reason has been provided because there has been no drop in examination

88. As part of his fiscal year 2004 budget, President Bush urged Congress to open tax collection to private collection agencies (PCA). Under the proposal, PCAs:

   a. Would be able to communicate with taxpayers at unusual times
   b. Would not be required to provide annual reports
   c. Would not be required to inform the taxpayers of their rights to obtain assistance from the National Taxpayer Advocate
   d. Would work with a PCA oversight team

89. Private collection agencies (PCAs) would be compensated:

   a. By the IRS
   b. By Congress
   c. From the tax revenue collected
   d. By the PCA oversight team

90. The IRS:

   a. Does not have the authority to issue summonses to third-party recordkeepers
   b. Must notify the taxpayer of the summons within 10 days of service of the summons
   c. Must give notice for a "John Doe" summons
   d. May issue summonses to attorneys, enrolled agents, banks, brokers, or accountants

Module 1—Answer Sheet

NAME _____

COMPANY NAME _____

STREET _____

CITY, STATE, & ZIP CODE _____

BUSINESS PHONE NUMBER _____

DATE OF COMPLETION _____

SOCIAL SECURITY NUMBER _____

On the next page, please answer the Multiple Choice questions by indicating the appropriate letter next to the corresponding number.

For each Module submitted a $70.00 processing fee will be billed to your CCH account, designated charge card or you may enclose a check payable to CCH INCORPORATED.

Please remove this Answer Sheet from this booklet and return it with your completed Evaluation Form to CCH at the address below. You may also fax your answer sheet to CCH at 773-866-3084.

METHOD OF PAYMENT:

☐ Check Enclosed   ☐ Visa   ☐ Master Card   ☐ AmEx

      ☐ Discover   ☐ CCH Account _____

Card No._____ Exp. Date_____

Fax No._____ Signature _____

EXPRESS GRADING: Please fax my Course results to me by 5:00 p.m. the business day following your receipt of this answer sheet. By checking this box I authorize CCH to charge an additional $19.00 for this service.

☐ Express Grading $19.00

SEND TO:

CCH INCORPORATED
Continuing Education Department
4025 W. Peterson Ave.
® Chicago, IL 60646-6085
1-800-248-3248

(Over)

Module 1—Answer Sheet

Please answer theMultiple Choice questions by indicating the appropriate letter next to the corresponding number.

1. ____	14. ____	27. ____	39. ____
2. ____	15. ____	28. ____	40. ____
3. ____	16. ____	29. ____	41. ____
4. ____	17. ____	30. ____	42. ____
5. ____	18. ____	31. ____	43. ____
6. ____	19. ____	32. ____	44. ____
7. ____	20. ____	33. ____	45. ____
8. ____	21. ____	34. ____	46. ____
9. ____	22. ____	35. ____	47. ____
10. ____	23. ____	36. ____	48. ____
11. ____	24. ____	37. ____	49. ____
12. ____	25. ____	38. ____	50. ____
13. ____	26. ____		

Please complete the Evaluation Form (located after the Module 2 answer sheet) and return it with this Quizzer Answer Sheet to CCH at the address on the previous page. Thank you.

Module 2—Answer Sheet

NAME _____

COMPANY NAME _____

STREET _____

CITY, STATE, & ZIP CODE _____

BUSINESS PHONE NUMBER _____

DATE OF COMPLETION _____

SOCIAL SECURITY NUMBER _____

On the next page, please answer the Multiple Choice questions by indicating the appropriate letter next to the corresponding number.

For each Module submitted a $70.00 processing fee will be billed to your CCH account, designated charge card or you may enclose a check payable to CCH INCORPORATED.

Please remove this Answer Sheet from this booklet and return it with your completed Evaluation Form to CCH at the address below. You may also fax your answer sheet to CCH at 773-866-3084.

METHOD OF PAYMENT:

☐ Check Enclosed ☐ Visa ☐ Master Card ☐ AmEx

☐ Discover ☐ CCH Account _____

Card No._____ Exp. Date_____

Fax No._____ Signature _____

EXPRESS GRADING: Please fax my Course results to me by 5:00 p.m. the business day following your receipt of this answer sheet. By checking this box I authorize CCH to charge an additional $19.00 for this service.

☐ Express Grading $19.00

SEND TO: **CCH** INCORPORATED
Continuing Education Department
4025 W. Peterson Ave.
® Chicago, IL 60646-6085
1-800-248-3248

(Over)

Module 2—Answer Sheet

Please answer the Multiple Choice questions by indicating the appropriate letter next to the corresponding number.

51. ____	61. ____	71. ____	81. ____
52. ____	62. ____	72. ____	82. ____
53. ____	63. ____	73. ____	83. ____
54. ____	64. ____	74. ____	84. ____
55. ____	65. ____	75. ____	85. ____
56. ____	66. ____	76. ____	86. ____
57. ____	67. ____	77. ____	87. ____
58. ____	68. ____	78. ____	88. ____
59. ____	69. ____	79. ____	89. ____
60. ____	70. ____	80. ____	90. ____

Please complete the following Evaluation Form and return with this Quizzer Answer Sheet to CCH at the address on the previous page. Thank you.

Please take a few moments to fill out and mail or fax this evaluation to CCH so that we can better provide you with the type of self-study programs you want and need. Thank you.

About This Program

1.Please circle the number that best reflects the extent of your agreement with the following statements:

		Strongly Agree				Strongly Disagree
a.	The course objectives were met.	5	4	3	2	1
b.	This course was comprehensive and organized.	5	4	3	2	1
c.	The content was current and technically accurate.	5	4	3	2	1
d.	This course was timely and relevant.	5	4	3	2	1
e.	The prerequisite requirements were appropriate.	5	4	3	2	1
f.	This course was a valuable learning experience.	5	4	3	2	1
g.	The course completion time was appropriate.	5	4	3	2	1

2.This course was most valuable to me because of:

____ Continuing Education credit
____ Relevance to my practice/ employment
____ Other (please specify)

____ Convenience of format
____ Timeliness of subject matter
____ Reputation of author
____ Price

3.How long did it take to complete this course? (Please include the total time spent reading or studying reference materials, and completing CPE quizzer).

Module 1 _____
Module 2 _____

4.What do you consider to be the strong points of this course?

5.What improvements can we make to this program?

1. Preferred method of self-study instruction:

____ Text   _____ Audio   _____ Computer-based/Multimedia   ___ Video

2. What specific topics would you like CCH to develop as self-study programs? (Select more than one if appropriate.)

____ Income Tax Preparation   ____ Small Business Tax Issues
____ Financial Planning   ____ Tax Planning
____ Estates and Trusts   ____ Tax News/Legislation
____ Retirement Planning   ____ Business Entities
____ Compensation   ____ Dealing with the IRS
____ Depreciation

3. Please list other topics of interest to you _____

_____

_____

About You

1. Your profession:

CPA   _____   Enrolled Agent   _____
Attorney   _____   Tax Preparer   _____
Financial Planner _____   Other (please specify) _____

_____

2. Your employment:

____ Self-employed   ____ Public Accounting Firm
____ Service Industry   ____ Non-Service Industry
____ Banking/Finance   ____ Government
____ Education   ____ Other

_____

3. Size of firm/corporation:

1 ___   2-5 ___   6-10 ___   11-20 ___   21-50 ___   51+

4. Your Name _____

Firm/Company Name _____

Address _____

City, State, Zip Code _____

5. I would like to be informed of new CCH Continuing Education products by electronic message. My e-mail address is: _____.
If you prefer, send your e-mail address to CCH.CPE@cch.com.

THANK YOU FOR TAKING THE TIME TO COMPLETE THIS SURVEY!